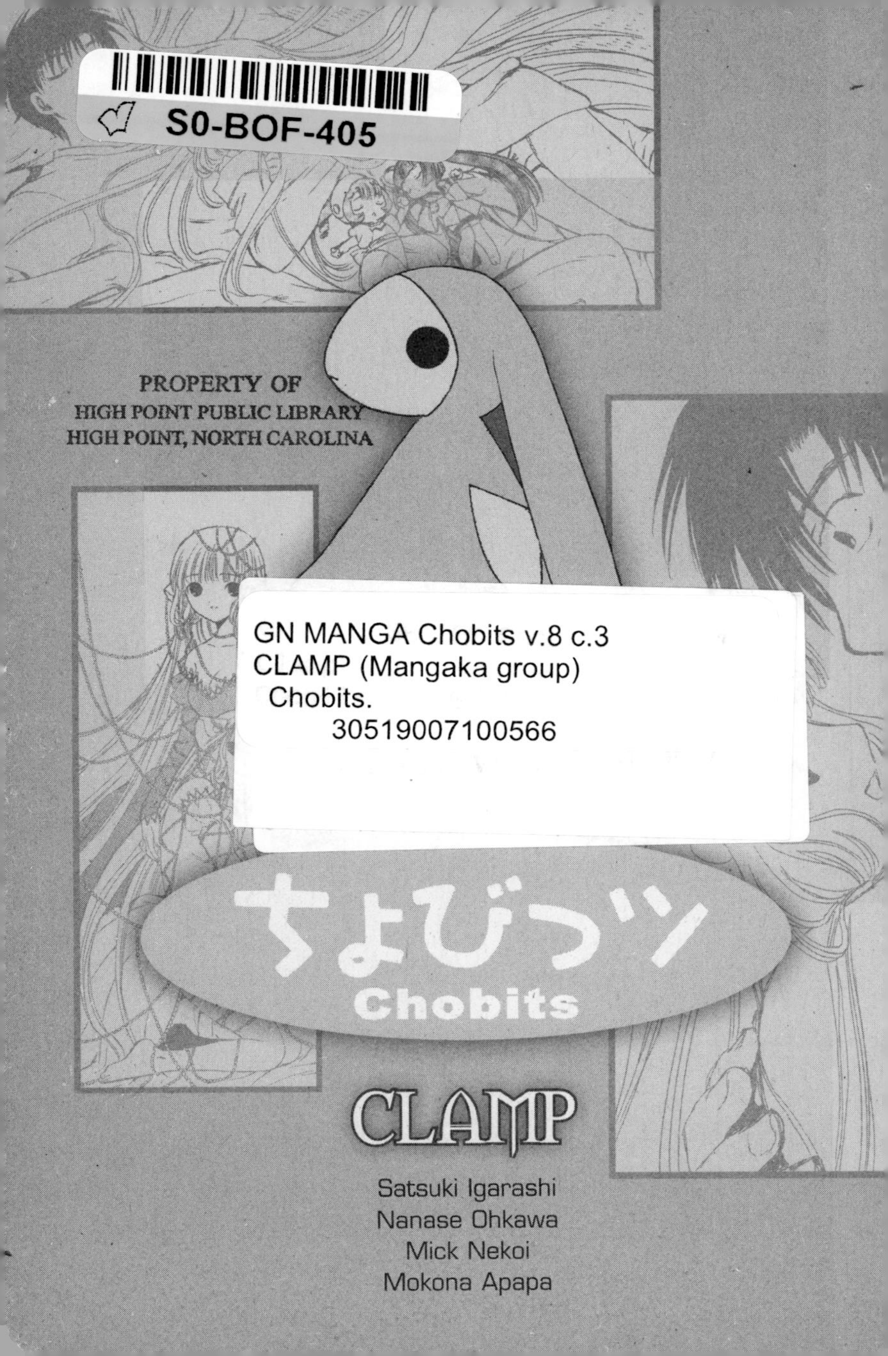





# ちょびっツ
# Chobits

CLAMP

Satsuki Igarashi
Nanase Ohkawa
Mick Nekoi
Mokona Apapa

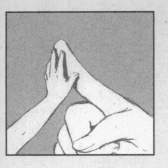

### Chobits Vol. 8
#### Created by CLAMP

Translator - Shirley Kubo
English Adaptation - Jake Forbes
Copy Editor - Paul Morrissey
Retouch and Design - Monalisa J. de Asis
Layout and Lettering - Jake Forbes
Cover Layout - Anna Kernbaum

Editor - Jake Forbes
Digital Imaging Manager - Chris Buford
Pre-Press Manager - Antonio DePietro
Production Manager - Jennifer Miller and Mutsumi Miyazaki
Art Director - Matt Alford
Managing Editor - Jill Freshney
VP of Production - Ron Klamert
President & C.O.O. - John Parker
Publisher & C.E.O. - Stuart Levy

Email: info@TOKYOPOP.com
Come visit us online at www.TOKYOPOP.com

A  Manga

TOKYOPOP Inc.
5900 Wilshire Blvd. Suite 2000, Los Angeles, CA 90036

ISBN: 1-59182-409-5
First TOKYOPOP printing: October 2003
10 9 8
Printed in the USA

## Volume 8 of 8

### Story and Art By
# CLAMP

HAMBURG // LONDON // LOS ANGELES // TOKYO

# www.Contents.com

Once upon a time, a brilliant inventor married a lovely scientist and they were truly happy. The scientist was unable to bear children, so the inventor made for her two beautiful "children" using the latest technology, and again, the family was as happy as could be. But then one of the "children" did something forbidden—she fell in love with the father who created her. In time, the child broke from the strain on her circuits, but before she "died," she transferred her memories into her sister in order to protect her. The other child, not wanting to befall the same fate as her sister, had her own memories erased and had her parents leave her to the world so that she could find someone who could love her back in the way she was programmed to love. Now the second daughter has found the one she loves, but can he love her back even though she isn't human?

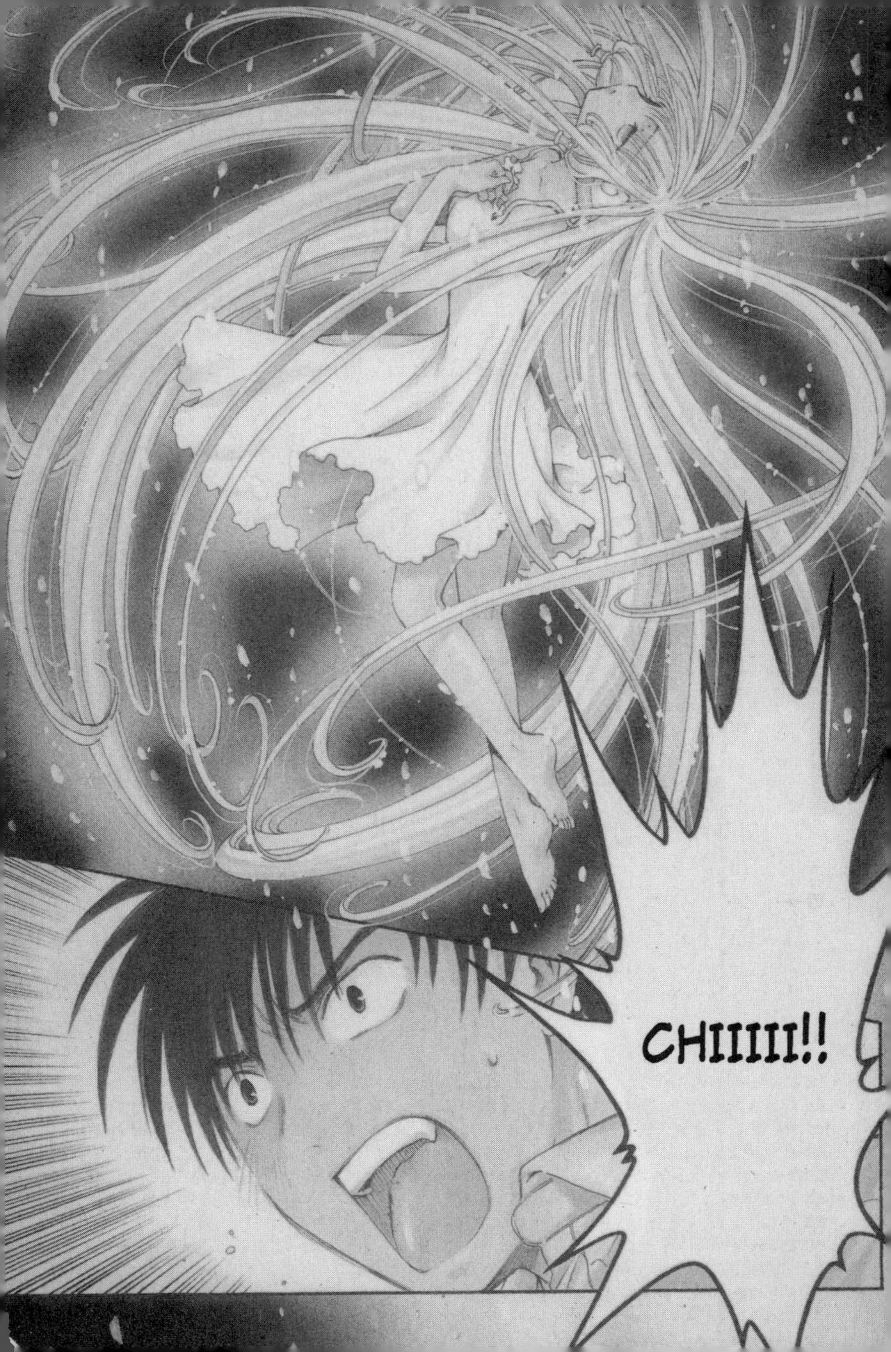
CHIIIII!!

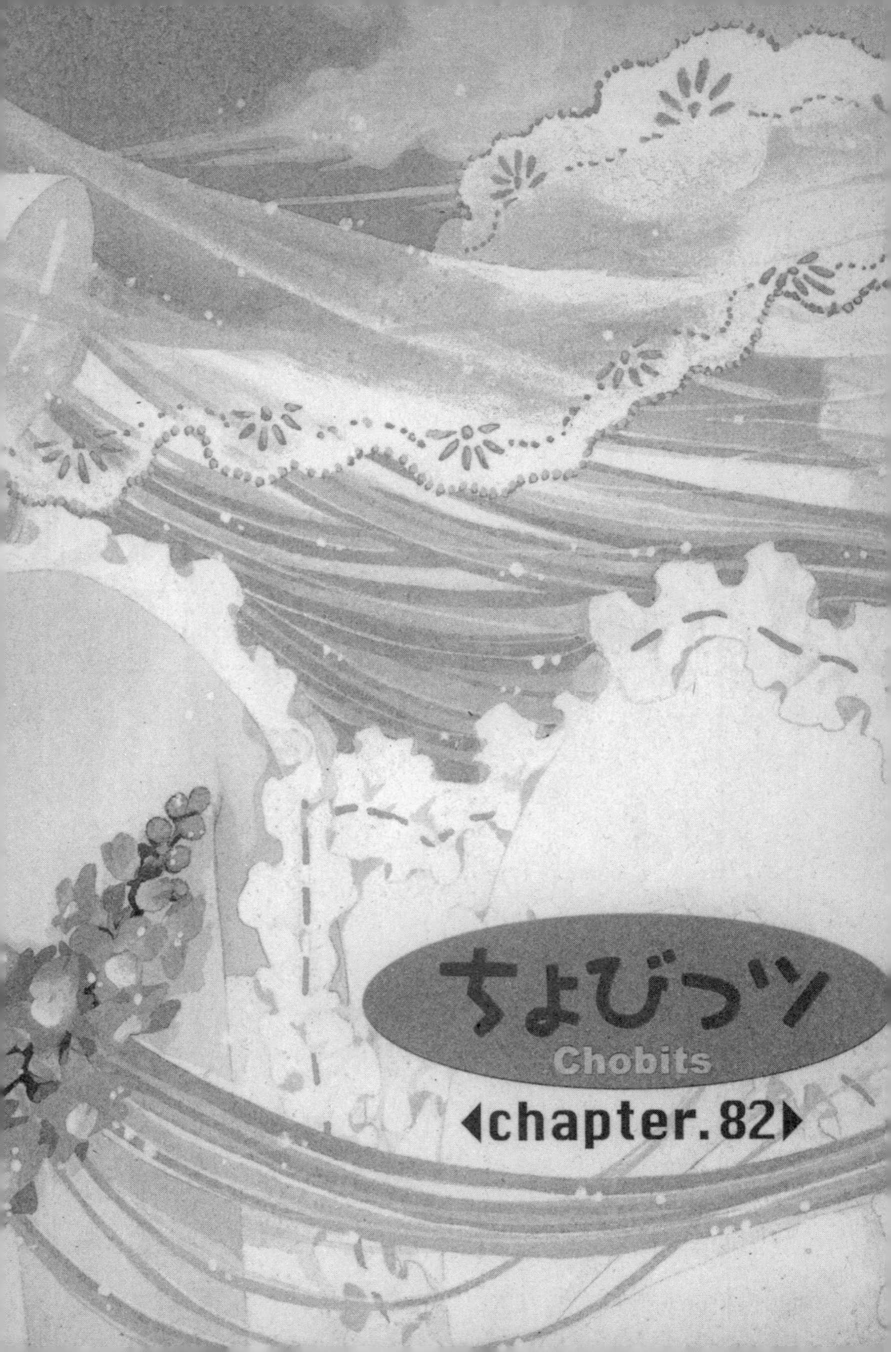
ちょびっツ
Chobits
chapter. 82

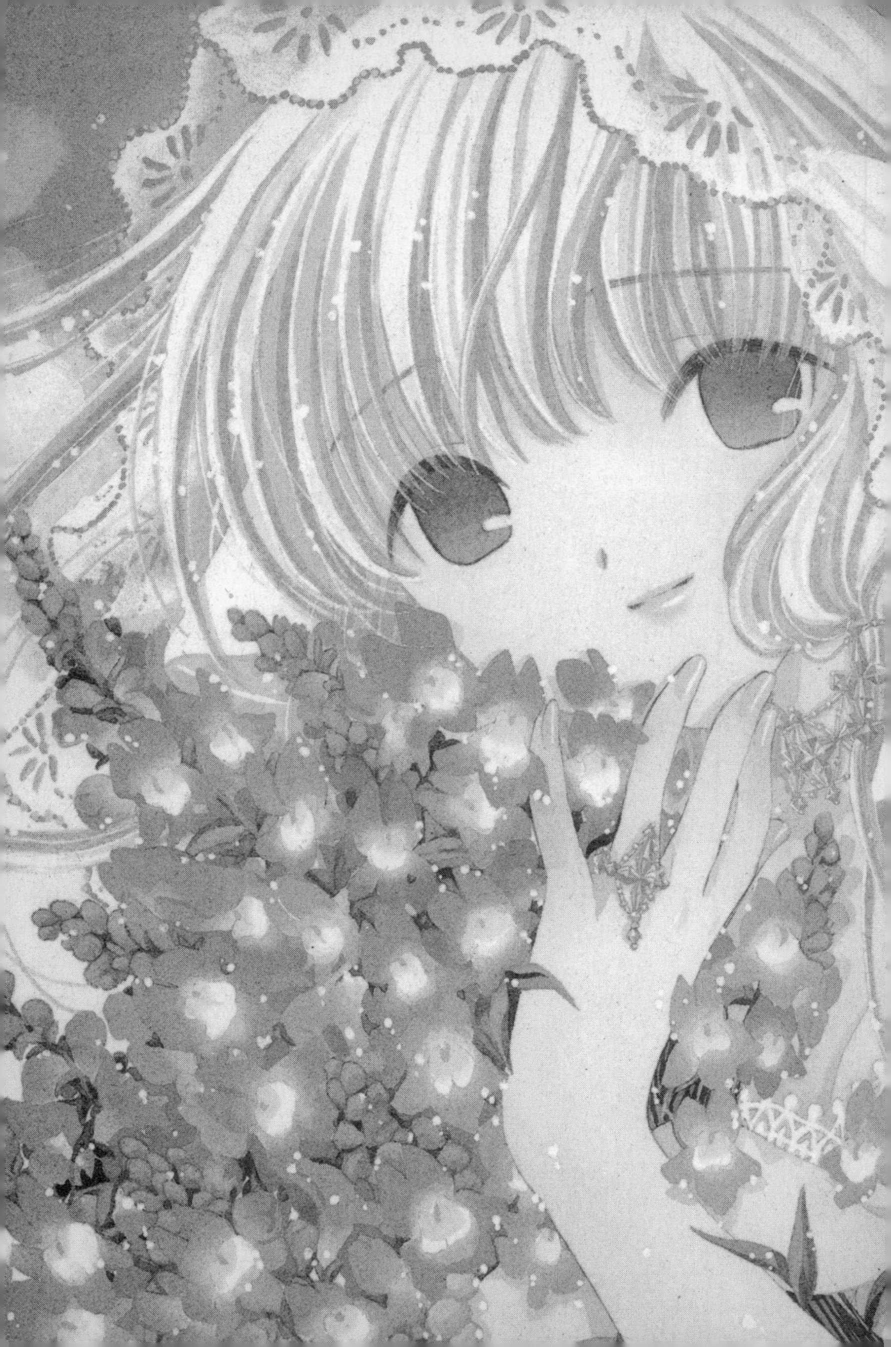

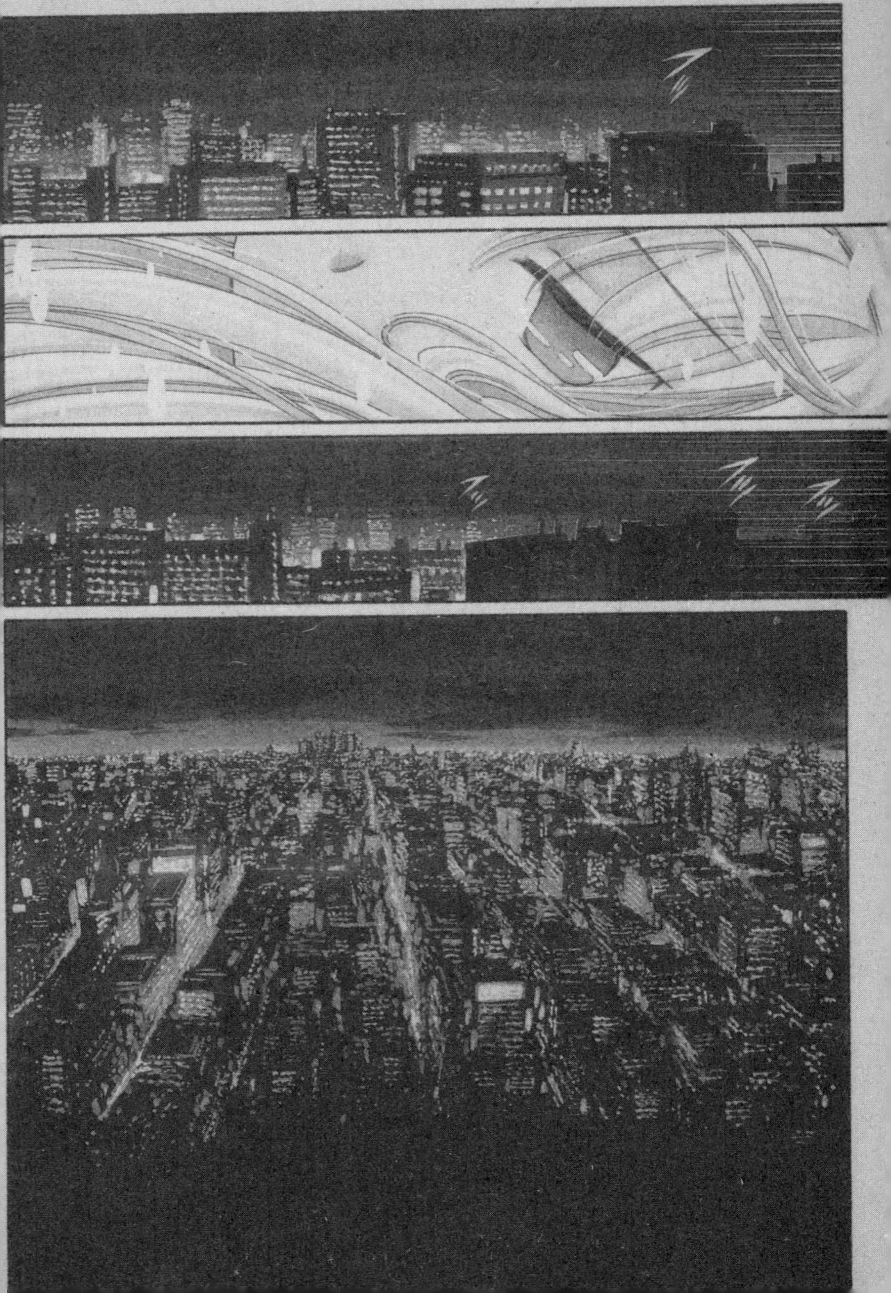
フッ
フッ
フッ
フッ

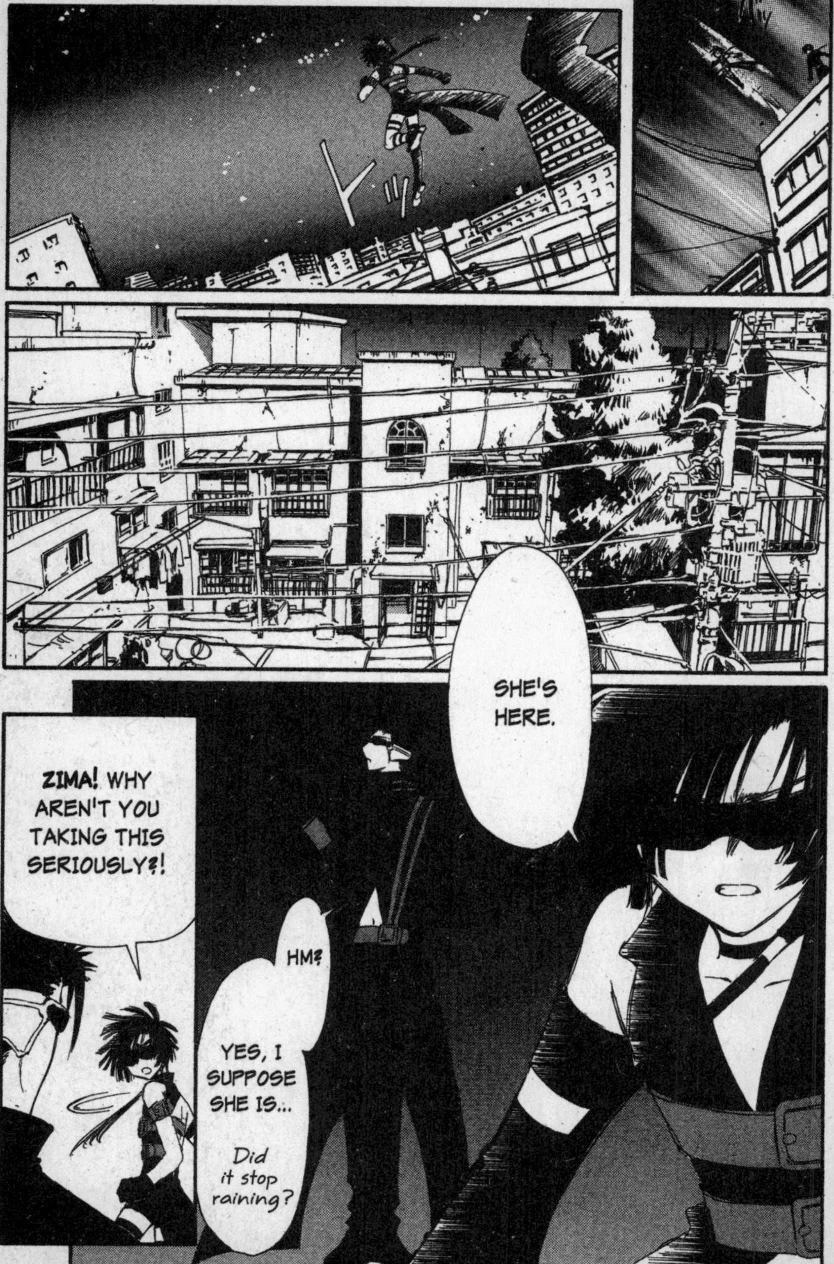
SHE'S HERE.
HM?
YES, I SUPPOSE SHE IS...
Did it stop raining?
ZIMA! WHY AREN'T YOU TAKING THIS SERIOUSLY?!

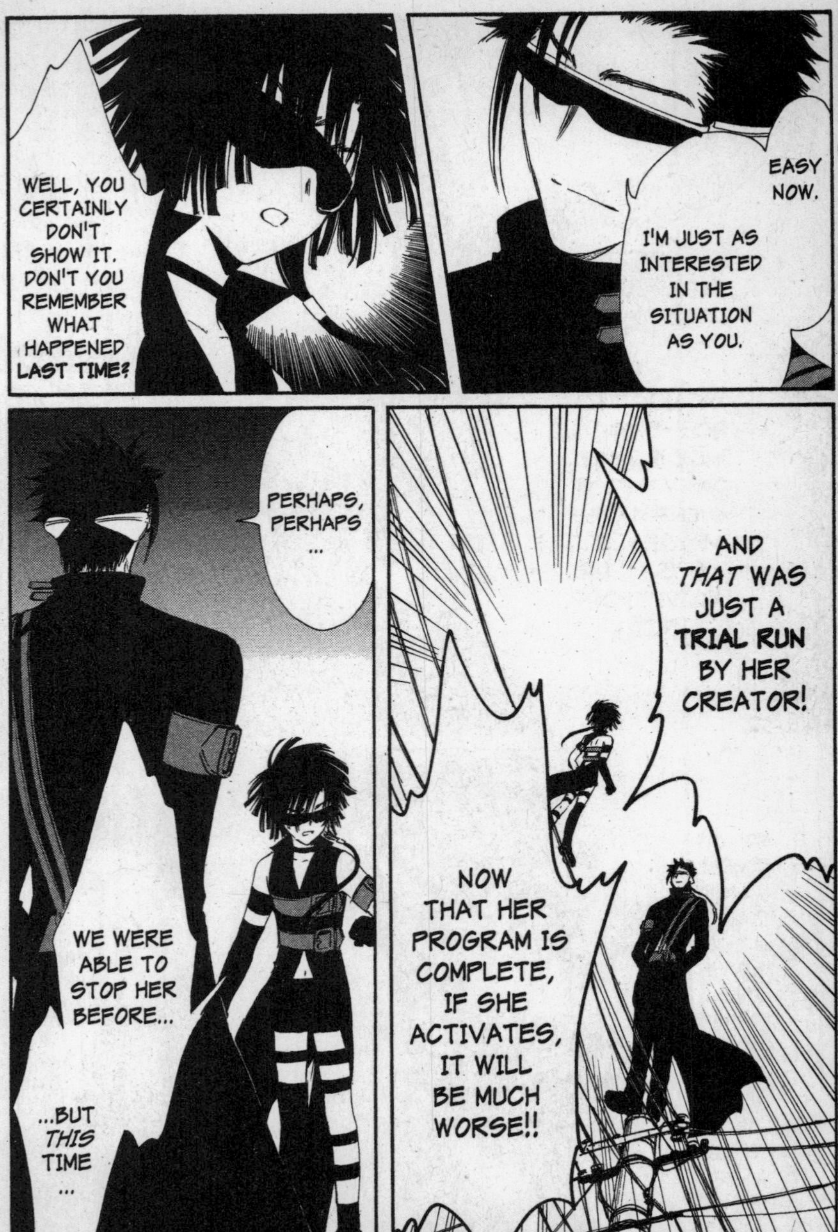
EASY NOW.
I'M JUST AS INTERESTED IN THE SITUATION AS YOU.
WELL, YOU CERTAINLY DON'T SHOW IT. DON'T YOU REMEMBER WHAT HAPPENED **LAST TIME?**
AND *THAT* WAS JUST A **TRIAL RUN** BY HER CREATOR!
NOW THAT HER PROGRAM IS COMPLETE, IF SHE ACTIVATES, IT WILL BE MUCH WORSE!!
PERHAPS, PERHAPS ...
WE WERE ABLE TO STOP HER BEFORE...
...BUT *THIS* TIME ...

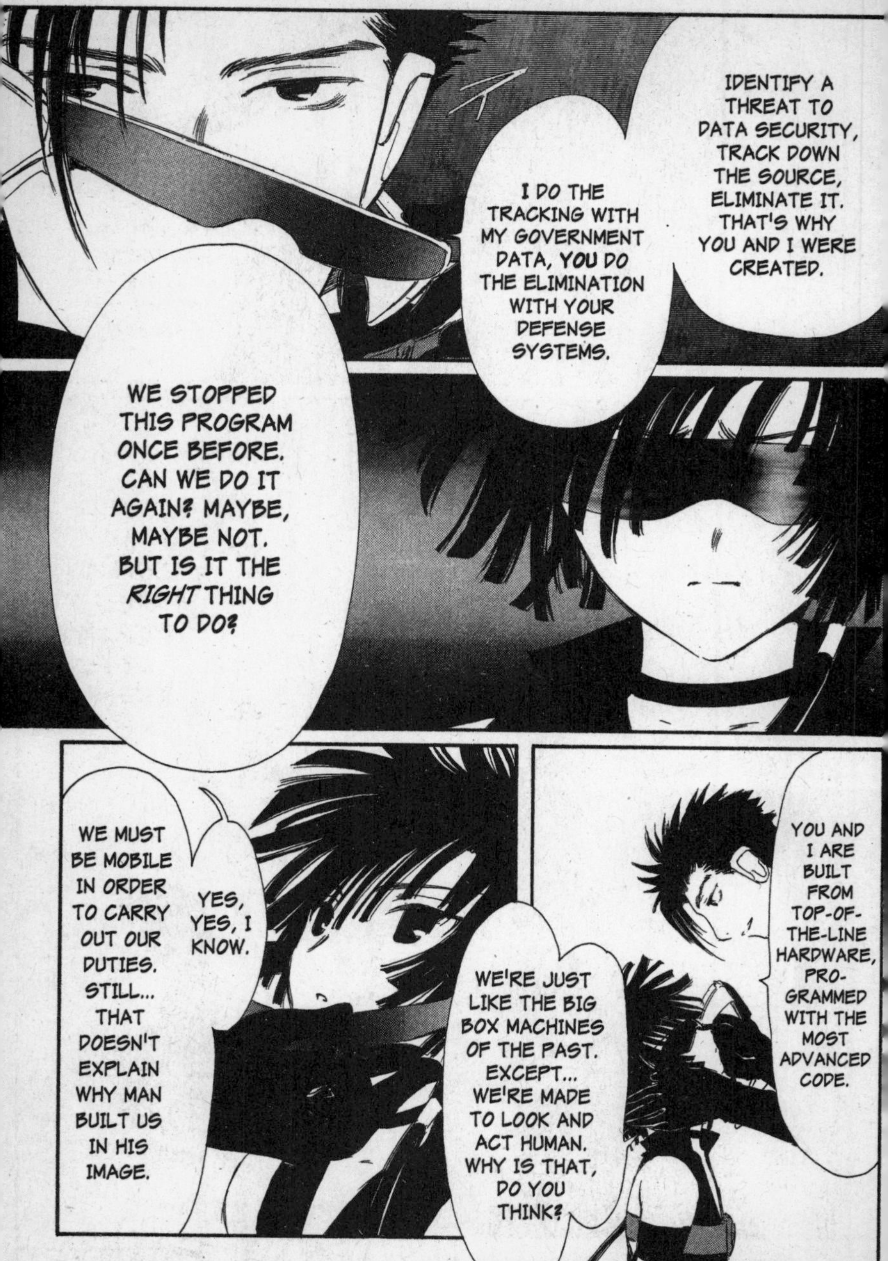
IDENTIFY A THREAT TO DATA SECURITY, TRACK DOWN THE SOURCE, ELIMINATE IT. THAT'S WHY YOU AND I WERE CREATED.
I DO THE TRACKING WITH MY GOVERNMENT DATA, YOU DO THE ELIMINATION WITH YOUR DEFENSE SYSTEMS.
WE STOPPED THIS PROGRAM ONCE BEFORE. CAN WE DO IT AGAIN? MAYBE, MAYBE NOT. BUT IS IT THE *RIGHT* THING TO DO?
YOU AND I ARE BUILT FROM TOP-OF-THE-LINE HARDWARE, PRO-GRAMMED WITH THE MOST ADVANCED CODE.
WE'RE JUST LIKE THE BIG BOX MACHINES OF THE PAST. EXCEPT... WE'RE MADE TO LOOK AND ACT HUMAN. WHY IS THAT, DO YOU THINK?
WE MUST BE MOBILE IN ORDER TO CARRY OUT OUR DUTIES. STILL... THAT DOESN'T EXPLAIN WHY MAN BUILT US IN HIS IMAGE.
YES, YES, I KNOW.

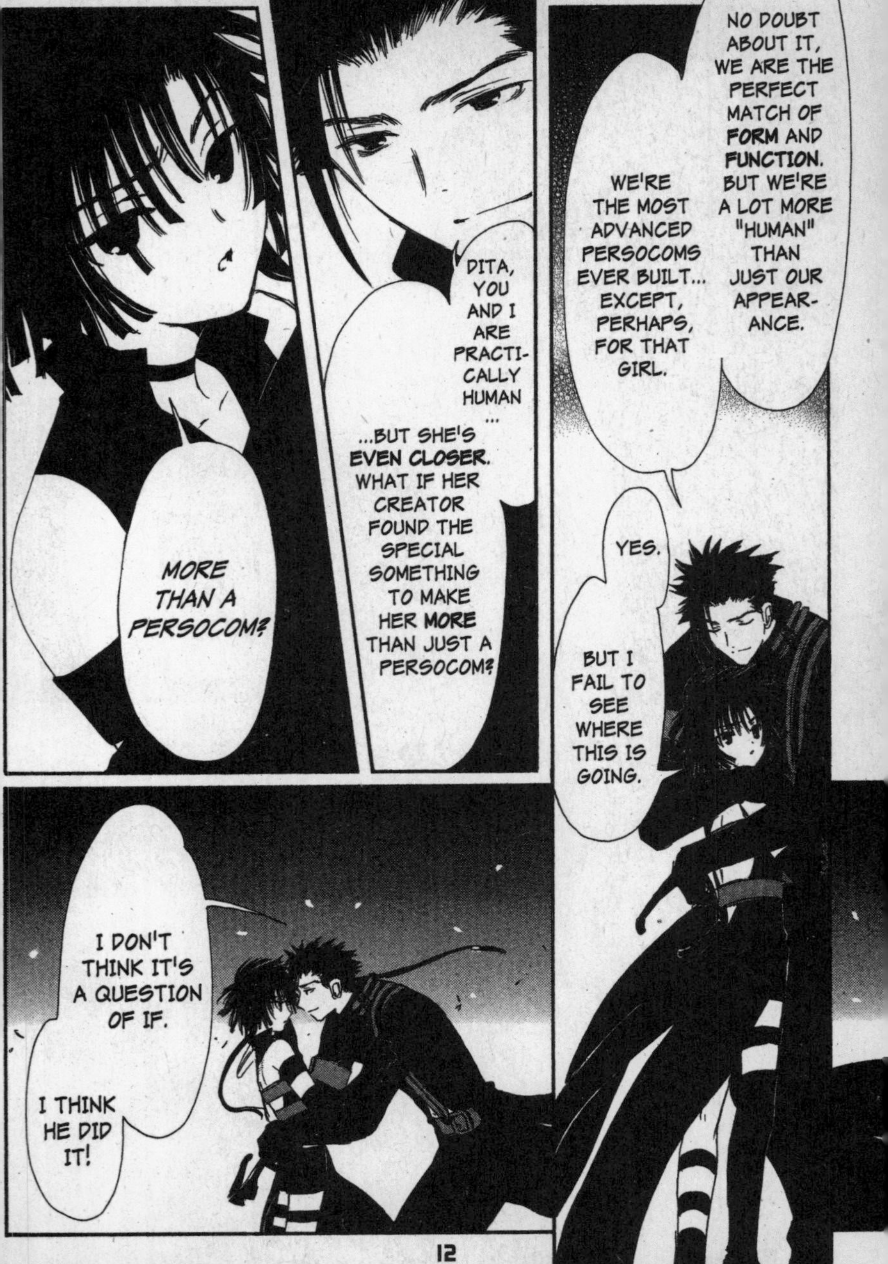
NO DOUBT ABOUT IT, WE ARE THE PERFECT MATCH OF **FORM** AND **FUNCTION**. BUT WE'RE A LOT MORE "HUMAN" THAN JUST OUR APPEARANCE.
WE'RE THE MOST ADVANCED PERSOCOMS EVER BUILT... EXCEPT, PERHAPS, FOR THAT GIRL.
YES.
BUT I FAIL TO SEE WHERE THIS IS GOING.
DITA, YOU AND I ARE PRACTICALLY HUMAN...
...BUT SHE'S **EVEN CLOSER**. WHAT IF HER CREATOR FOUND THE SPECIAL SOMETHING TO MAKE HER **MORE** THAN JUST A PERSOCOM?
*MORE THAN A PERSOCOM?*
I DON'T THINK IT'S A QUESTION OF IF.
I THINK HE DID IT!

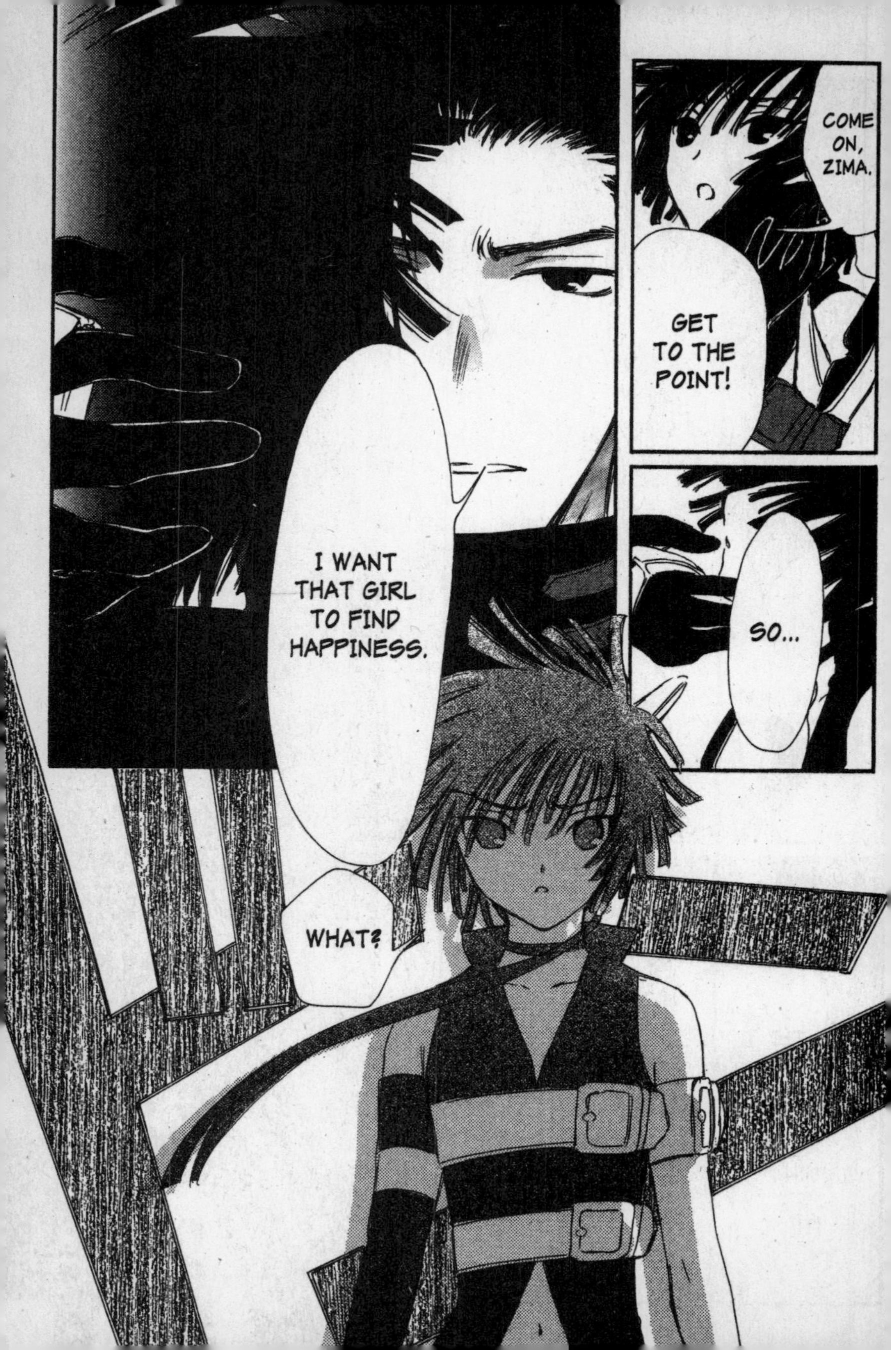
COME ON, ZIMA.
GET TO THE POINT!
SO...
I WANT THAT GIRL TO FIND HAPPINESS.
WHAT?

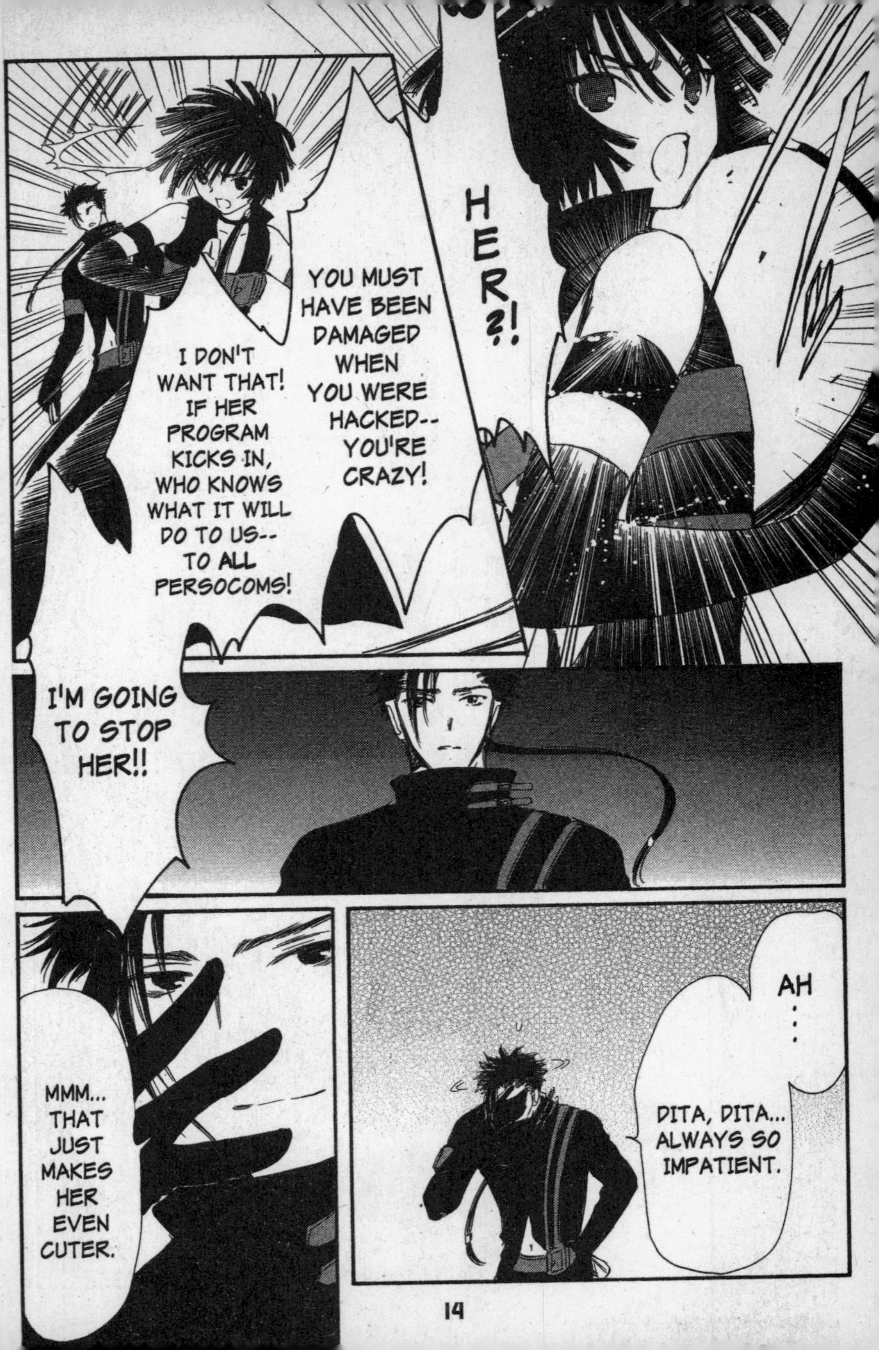
HER?!
YOU MUST HAVE BEEN DAMAGED WHEN YOU WERE HACKED-- YOU'RE CRAZY!
I DON'T WANT THAT! IF HER PROGRAM KICKS IN, WHO KNOWS WHAT IT WILL DO TO US-- TO ALL PERSOCOMS!
I'M GOING TO STOP HER!!
AH...
DITA, DITA... ALWAYS SO IMPATIENT.
MMM... THAT JUST MAKES HER EVEN CUTER.

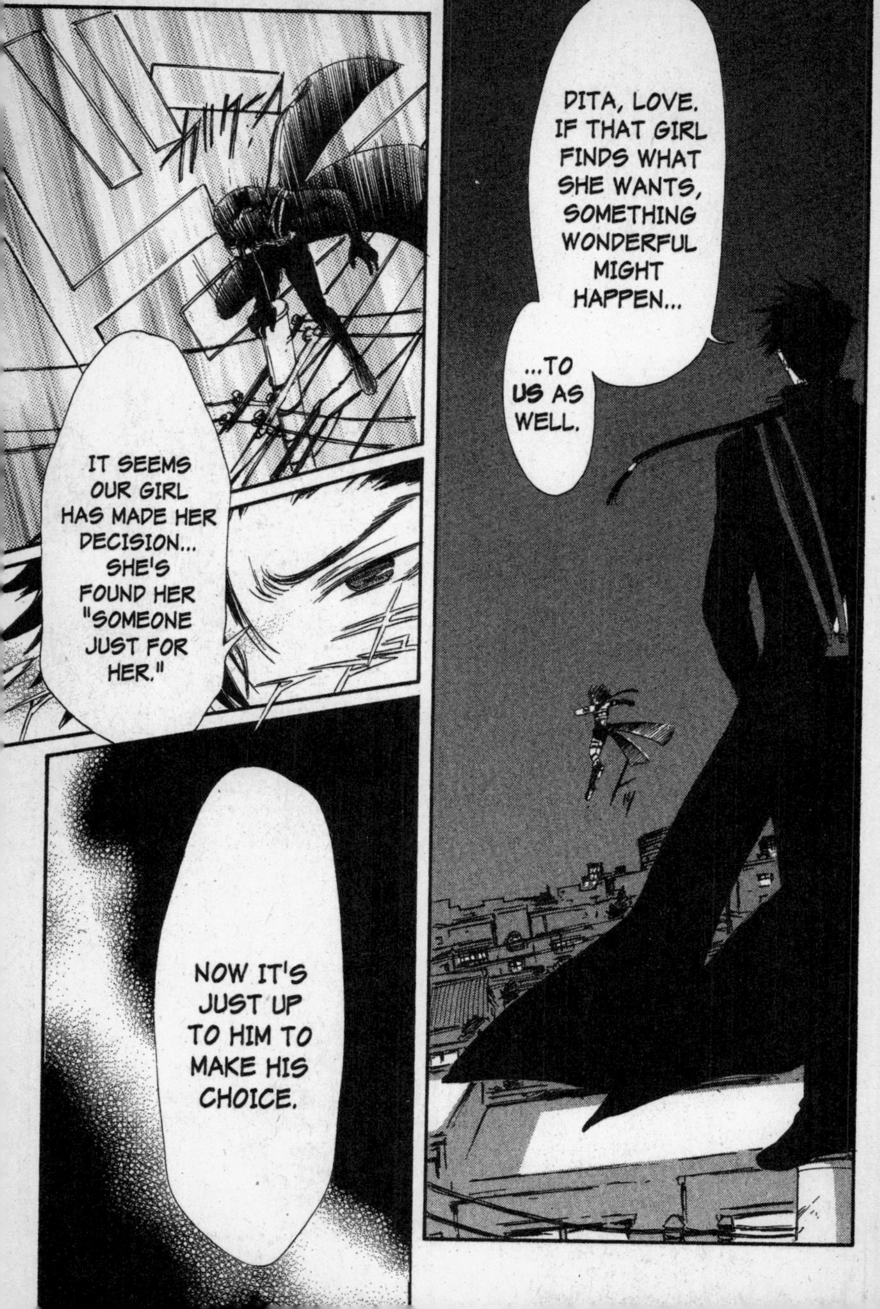
DITA, LOVE. IF THAT GIRL FINDS WHAT SHE WANTS, SOMETHING WONDERFUL MIGHT HAPPEN...
...TO US AS WELL.
IT SEEMS OUR GIRL HAS MADE HER DECISION... SHE'S FOUND HER "SOMEONE JUST FOR HER."
NOW IT'S JUST UP TO HIM TO MAKE HIS CHOICE.

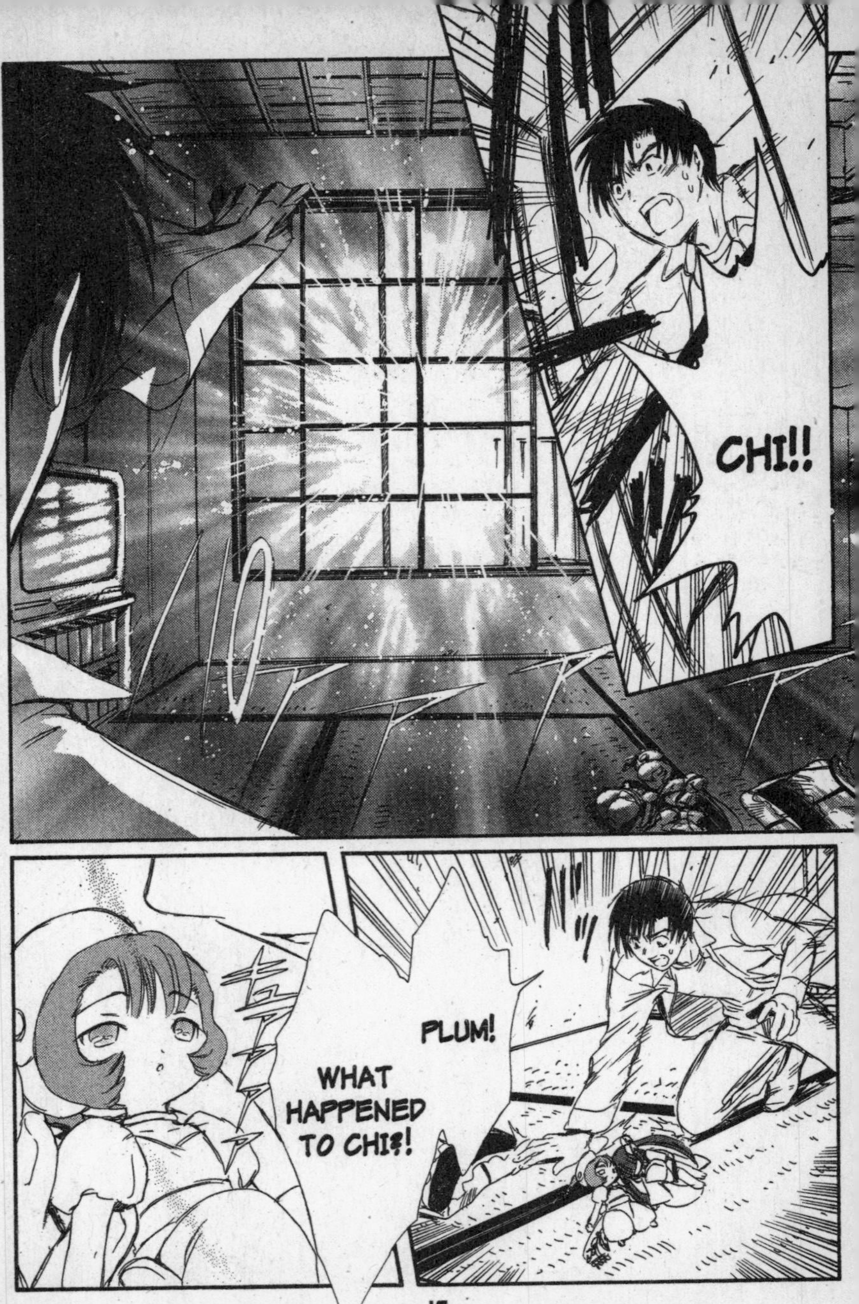
CHI!!
PLUM!
WHAT HAPPENED TO CHI?!

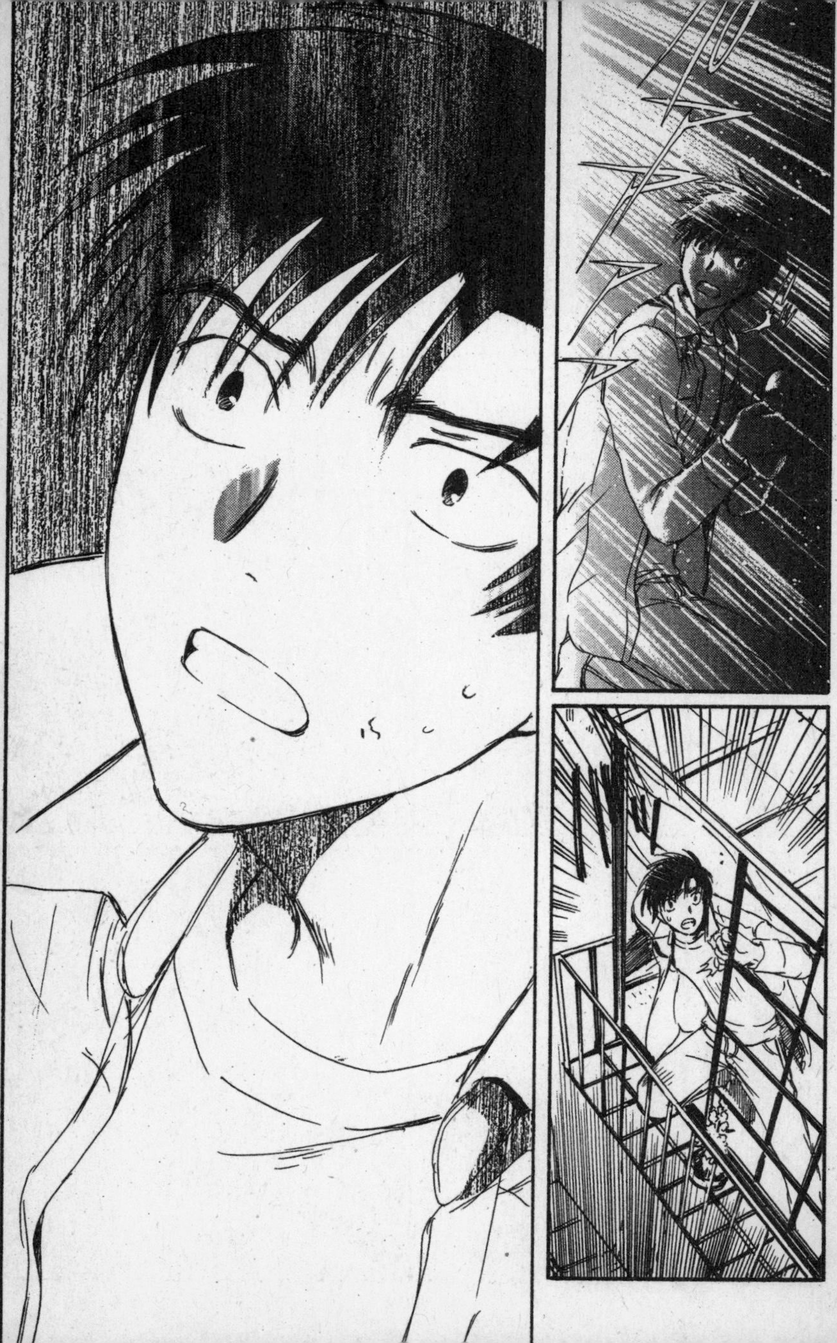

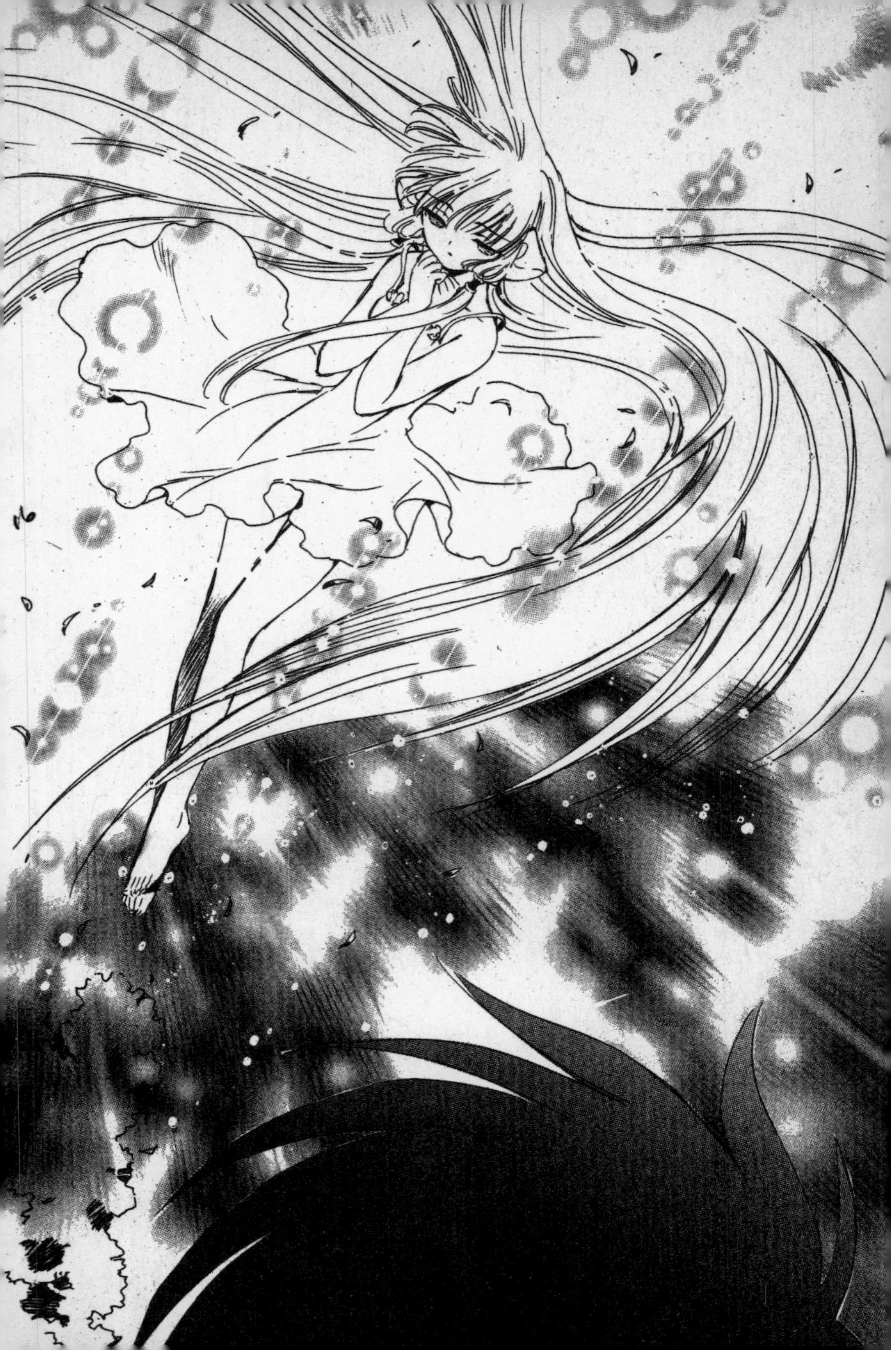

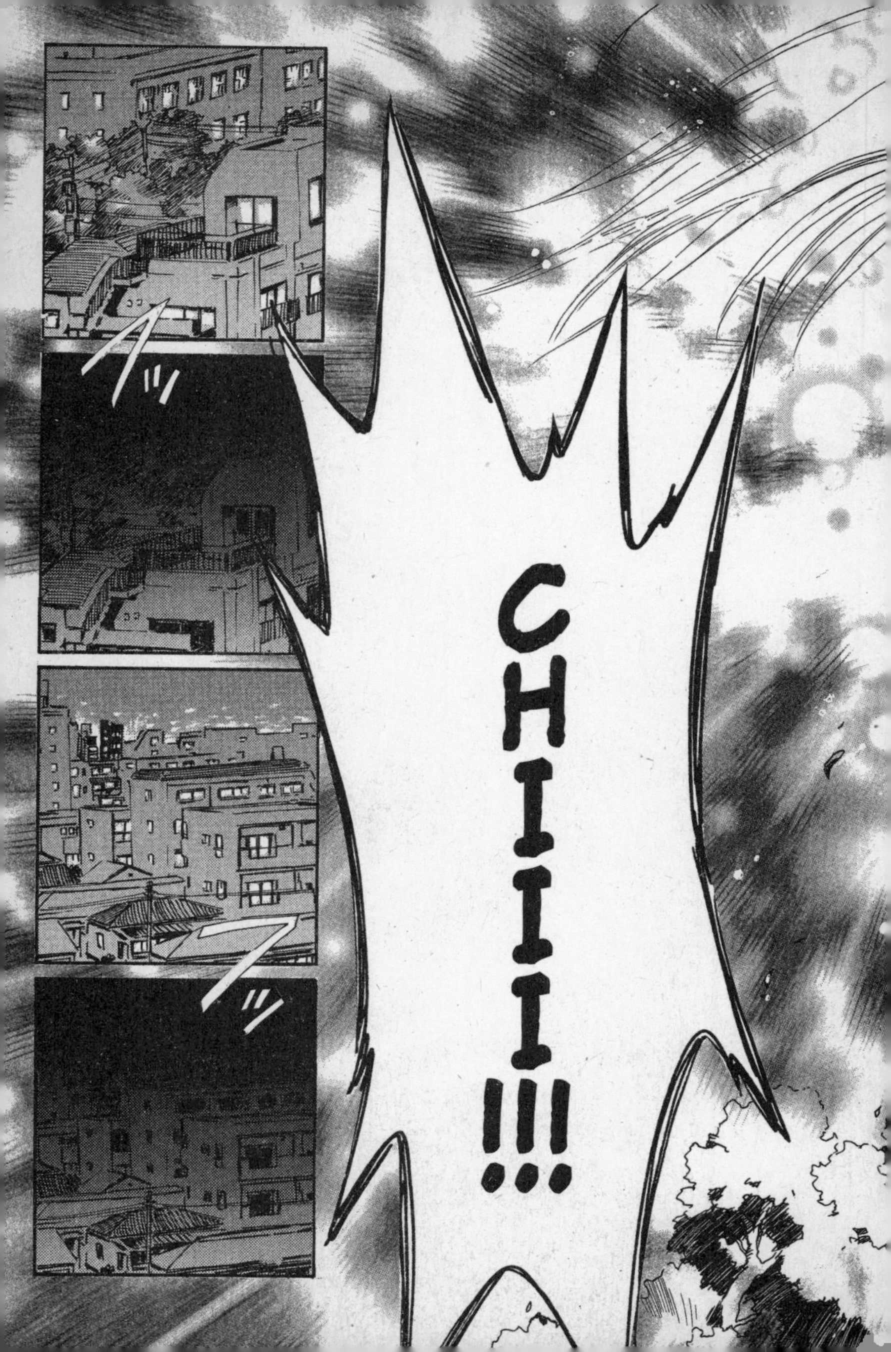
CHIIII!!!

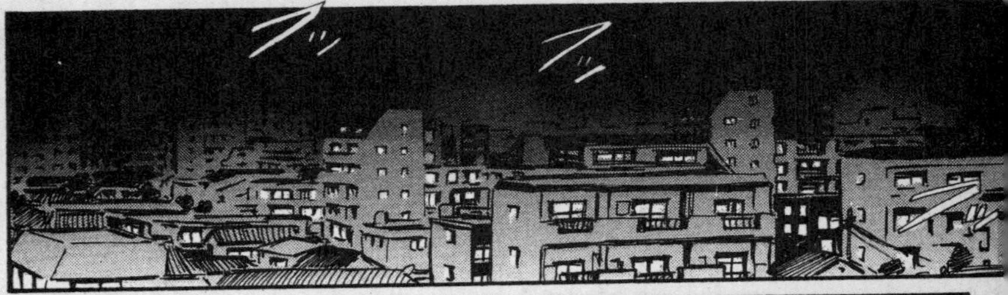
ブン
ブン
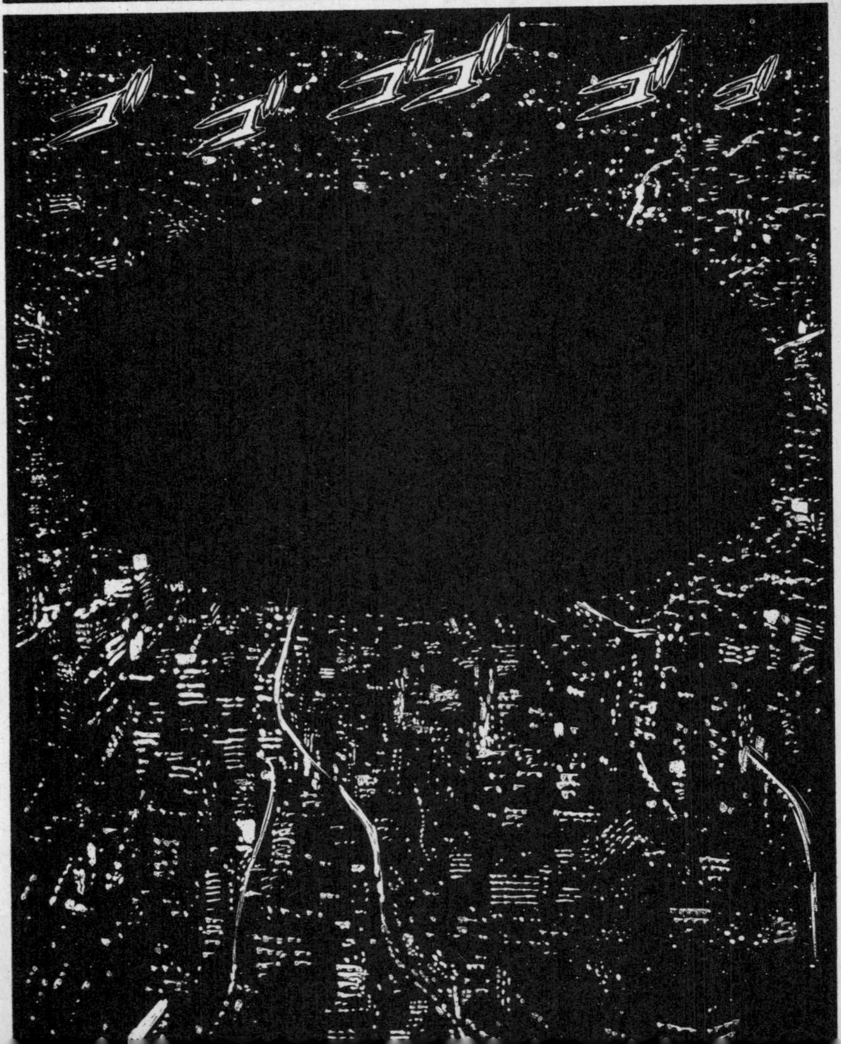
ゴゴゴゴゴゴ

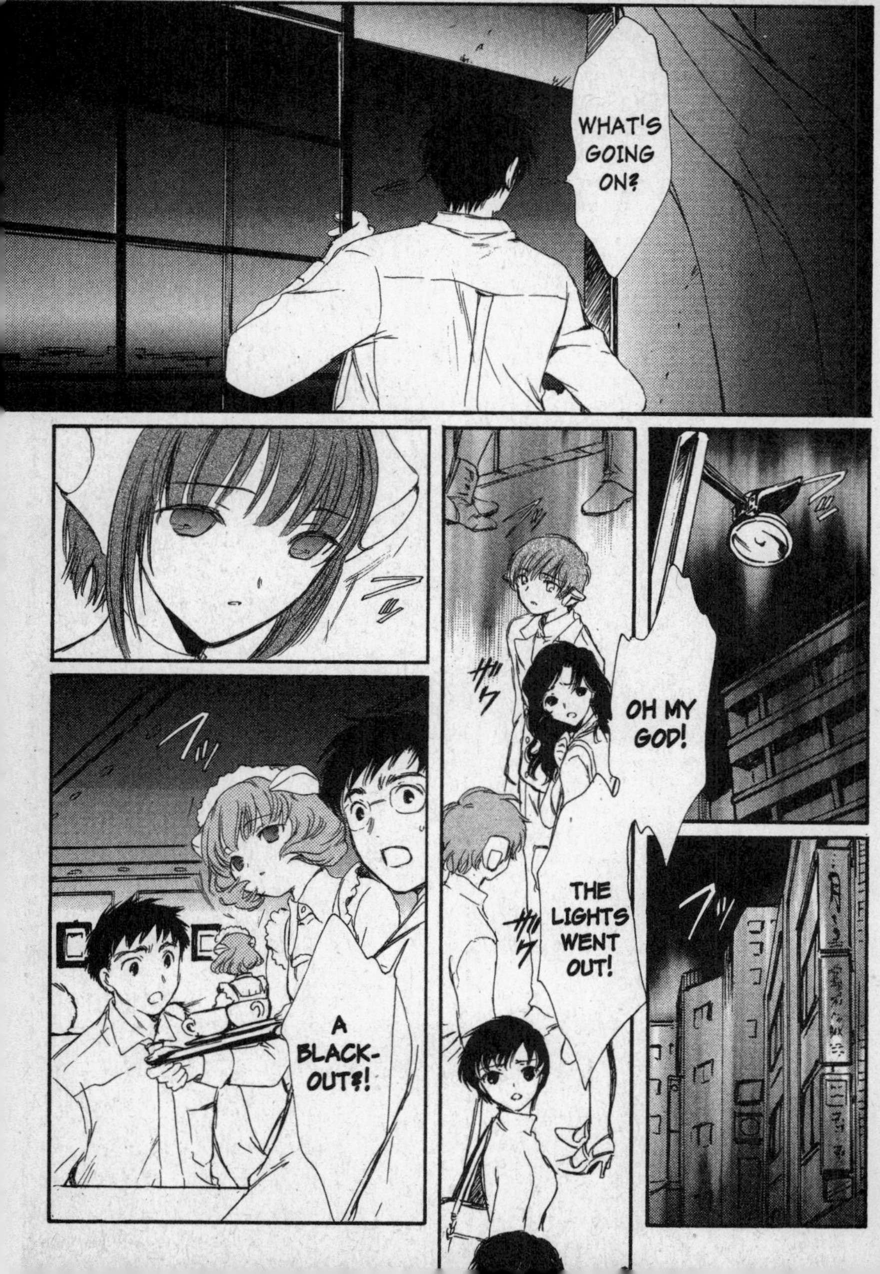
WHAT'S GOING ON?
OH MY GOD!
THE LIGHTS WENT OUT!
A BLACK-OUT?!

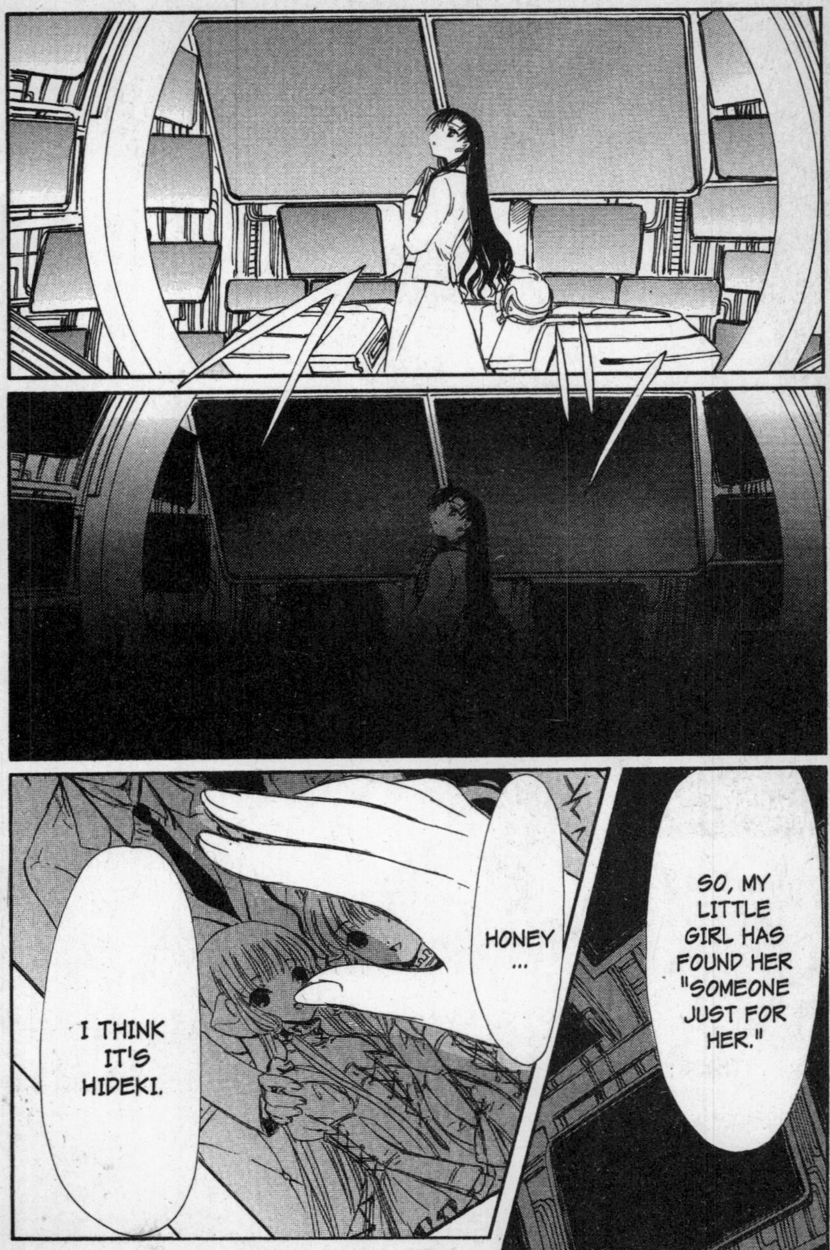
SO, MY LITTLE GIRL HAS FOUND HER "SOMEONE JUST FOR HER."
HONEY ...
I THINK IT'S HIDEKI.

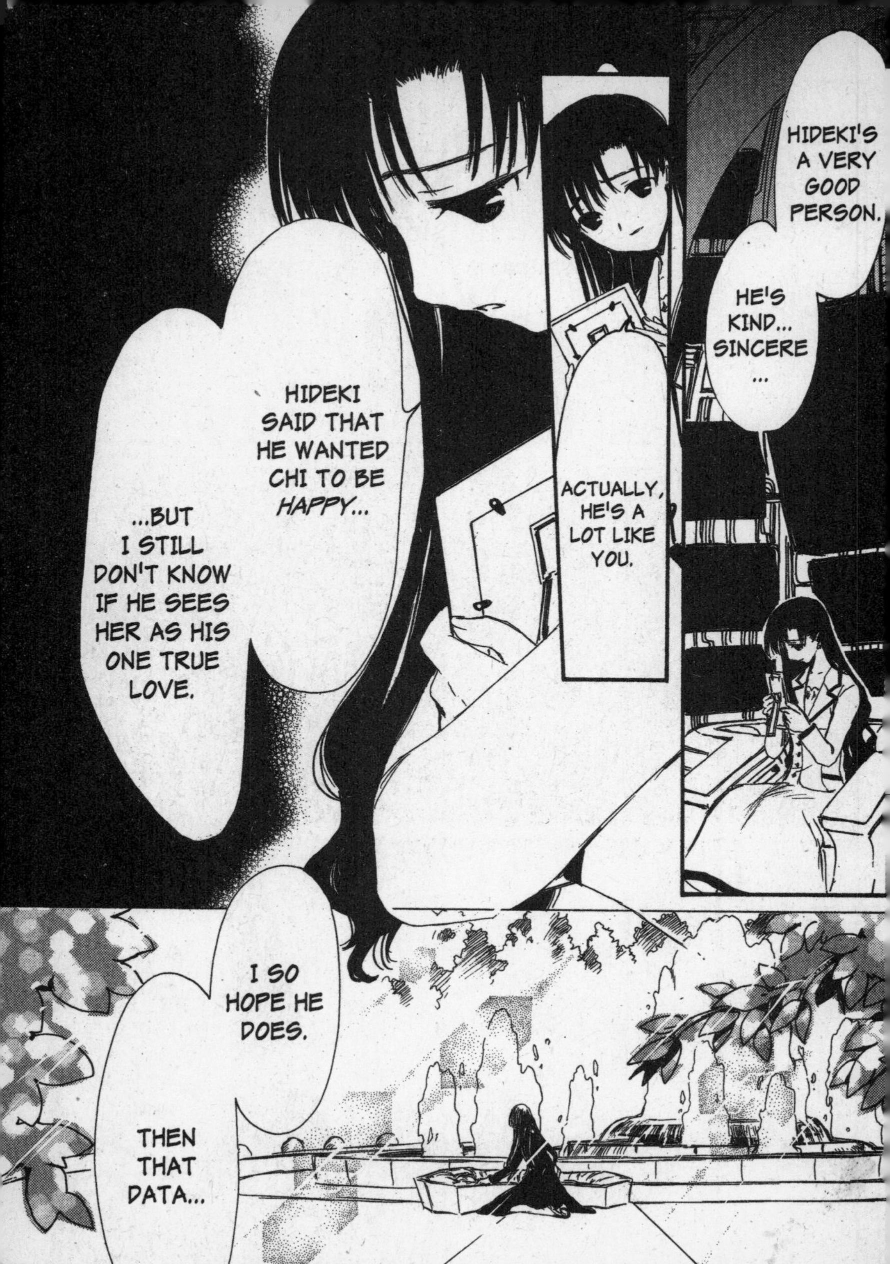

HIDEKI'S A VERY GOOD PERSON.
HE'S KIND... SINCERE...
ACTUALLY, HE'S A LOT LIKE YOU.
HIDEKI SAID THAT HE WANTED CHI TO BE *HAPPY*...
...BUT I STILL DON'T KNOW IF HE SEES HER AS HIS ONE TRUE LOVE.
I SO HOPE HE DOES.
THEN THAT DATA...

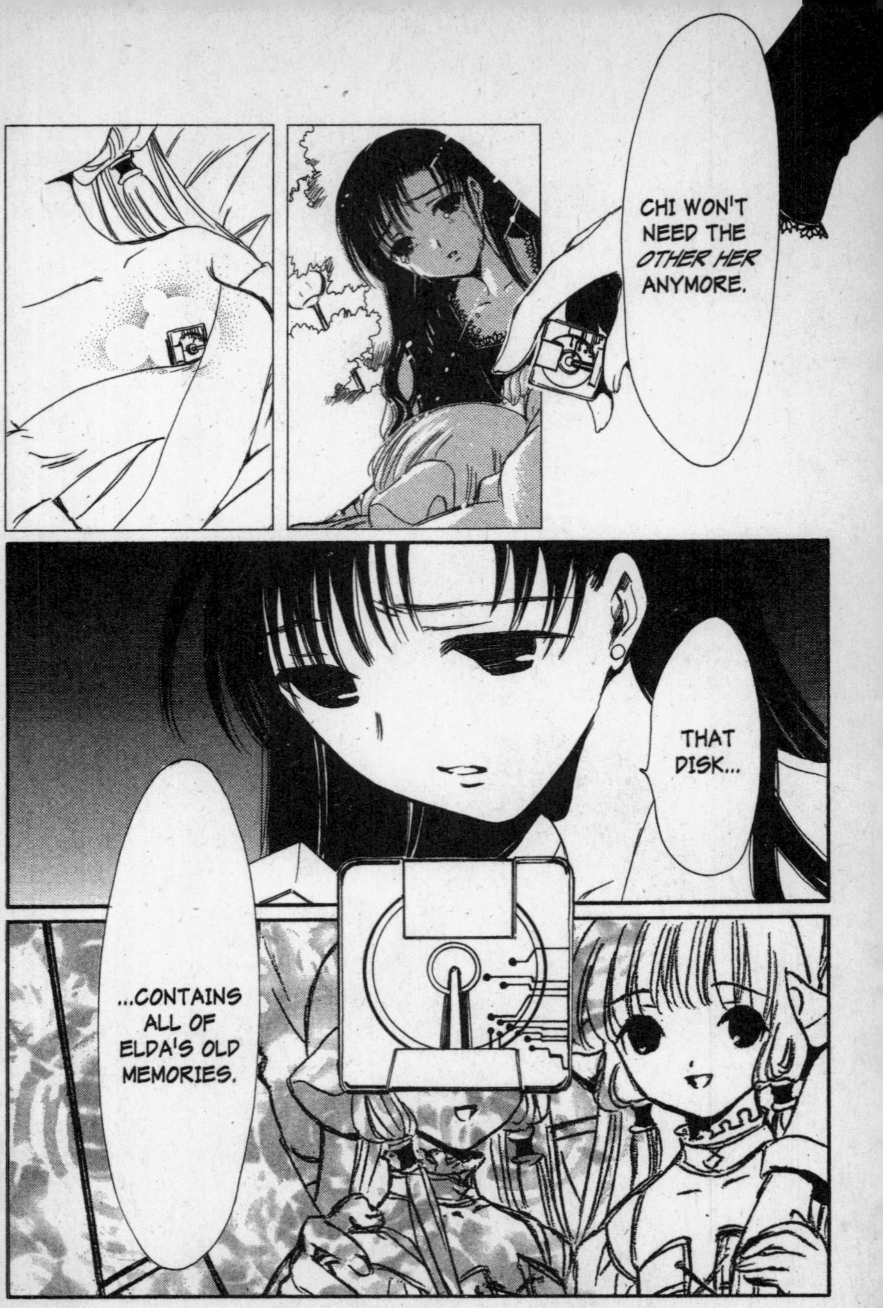
CHI WON'T NEED THE *OTHER HER* ANYMORE.
THAT DISK...
...CONTAINS ALL OF ELDA'S OLD MEMORIES.

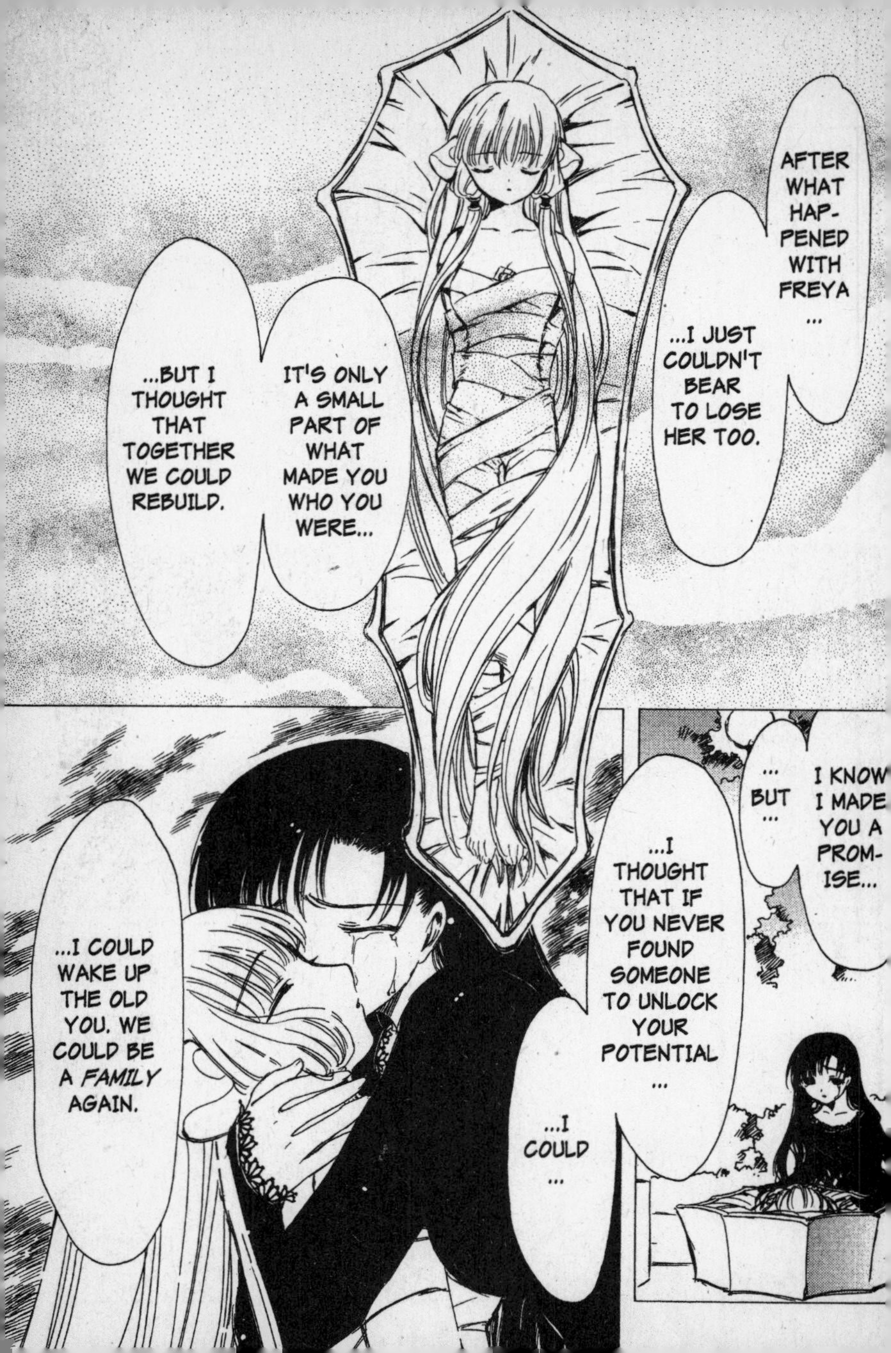
AFTER WHAT HAP-PENED WITH FREYA ...
...I JUST COULDN'T BEAR TO LOSE HER TOO.
IT'S ONLY A SMALL PART OF WHAT MADE YOU WHO YOU WERE...
...BUT I THOUGHT THAT TOGETHER WE COULD REBUILD.
I KNOW I MADE YOU A PROM-ISE...
... BUT ...
...I THOUGHT THAT IF YOU NEVER FOUND SOMEONE TO UNLOCK YOUR POTENTIAL ...
...I COULD ...
...I COULD WAKE UP THE OLD YOU. WE COULD BE A *FAMILY* AGAIN.

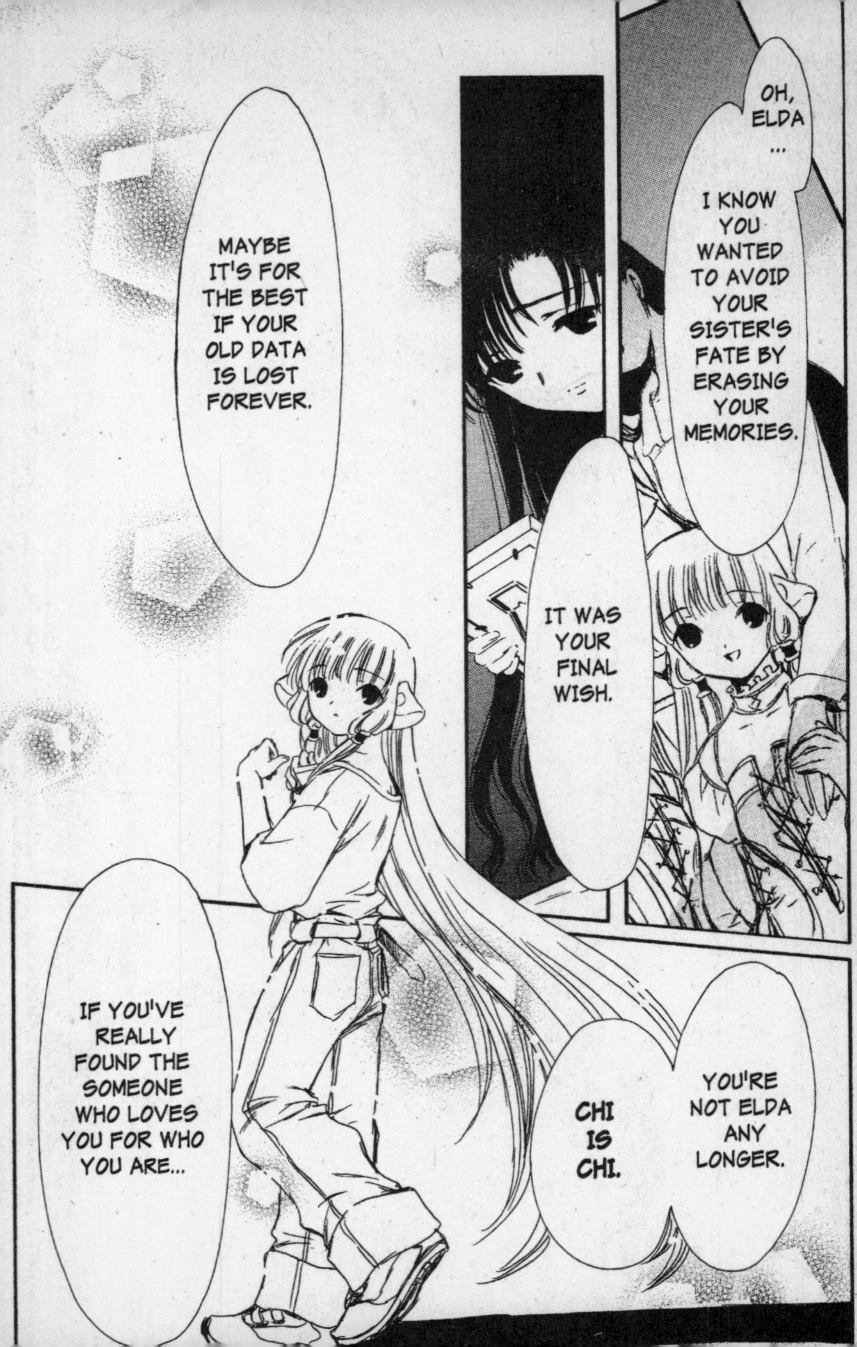
OH, ELDA ...
I KNOW YOU WANTED TO AVOID YOUR SISTER'S FATE BY ERASING YOUR MEMORIES.
IT WAS YOUR FINAL WISH.
MAYBE IT'S FOR THE BEST IF YOUR OLD DATA IS LOST FOREVER.
YOU'RE NOT ELDA ANY LONGER.
CHI IS CHI.
IF YOU'VE REALLY FOUND THE SOMEONE WHO LOVES YOU FOR WHO YOU ARE...

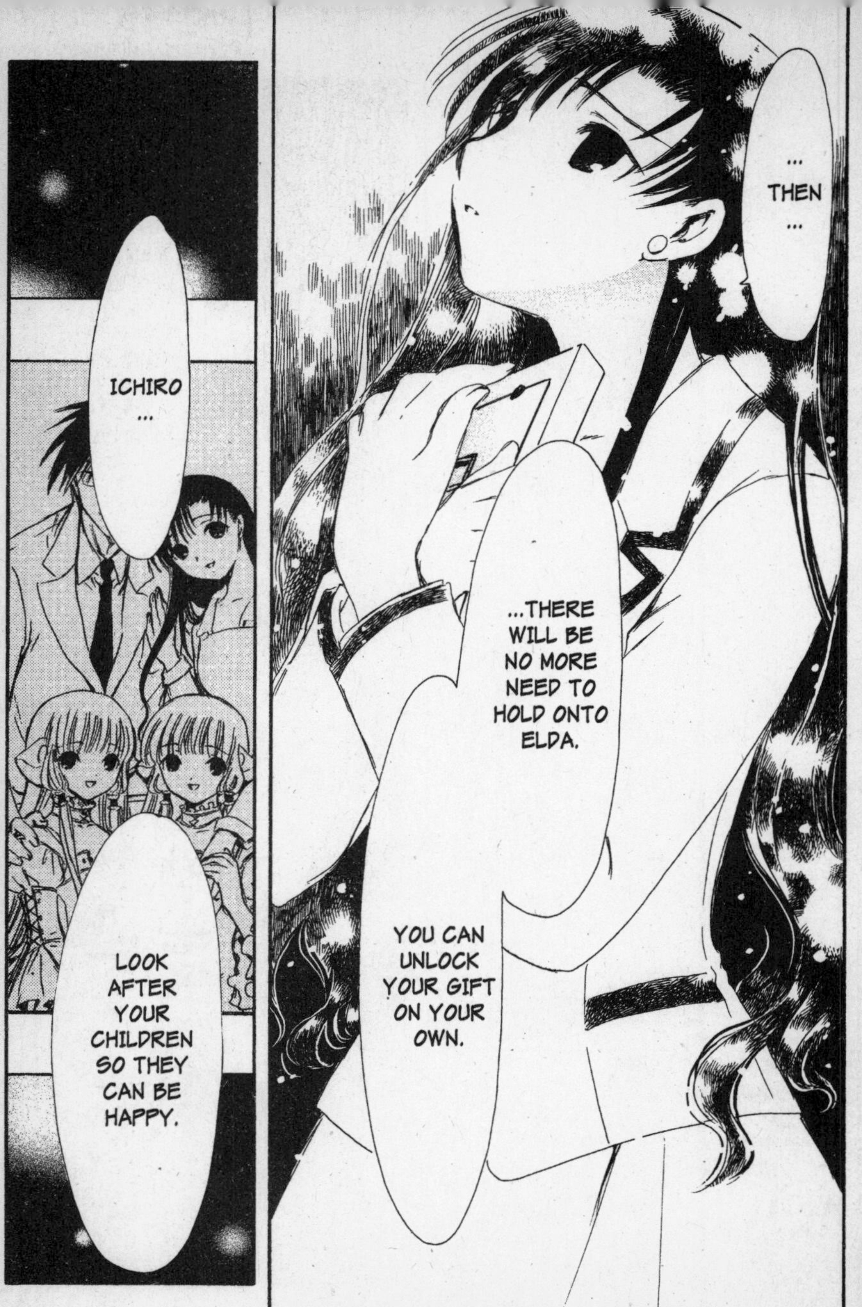
... THEN ...
...THERE WILL BE NO MORE NEED TO HOLD ONTO ELDA.
YOU CAN UNLOCK YOUR GIFT ON YOUR OWN.
ICHIRO ...
LOOK AFTER YOUR CHILDREN SO THEY CAN BE HAPPY.

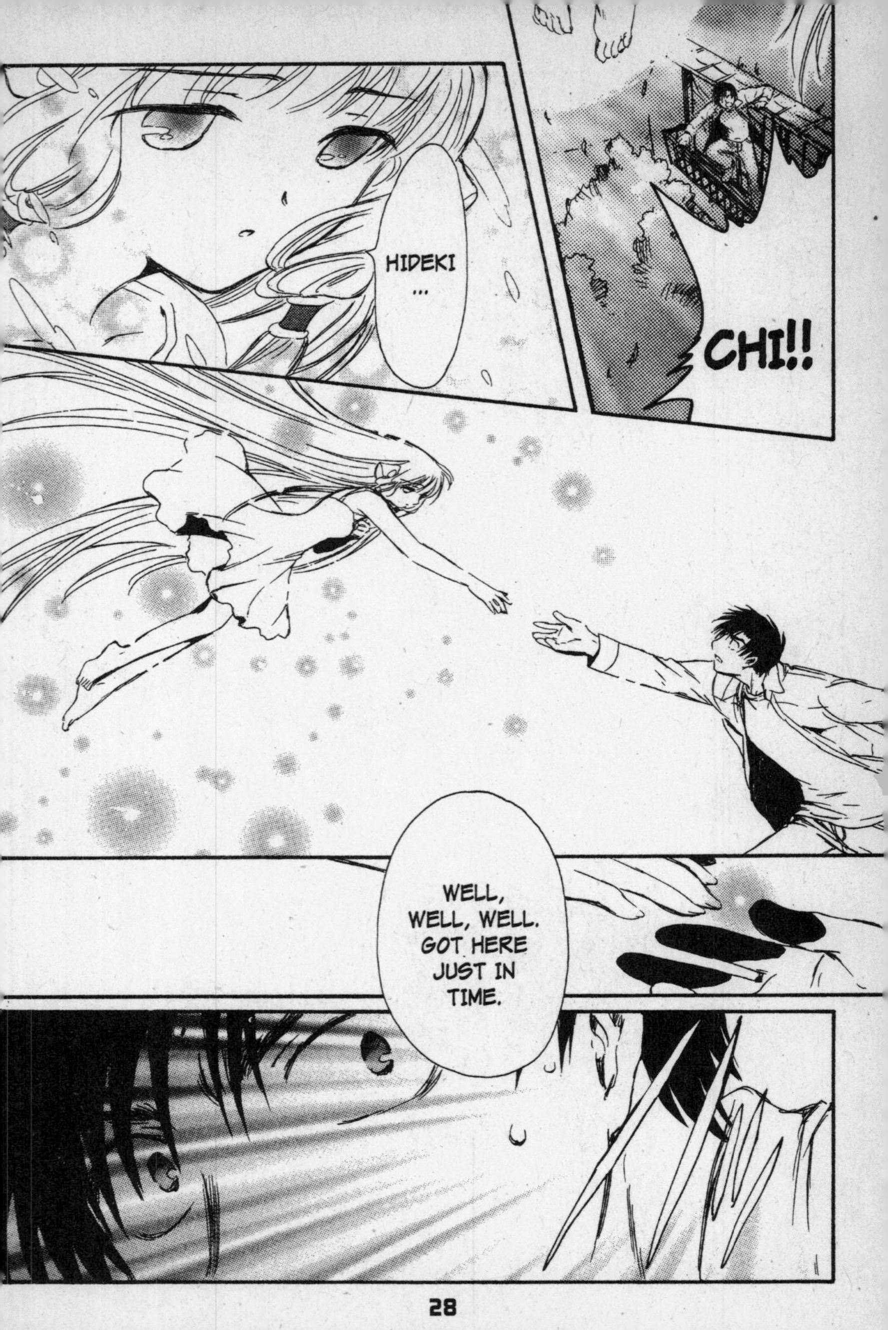
CHI!!
HIDEKI ...
WELL, WELL, WELL. GOT HERE JUST IN TIME.

ちょびっツ
Chobits

◀chapter.83▶

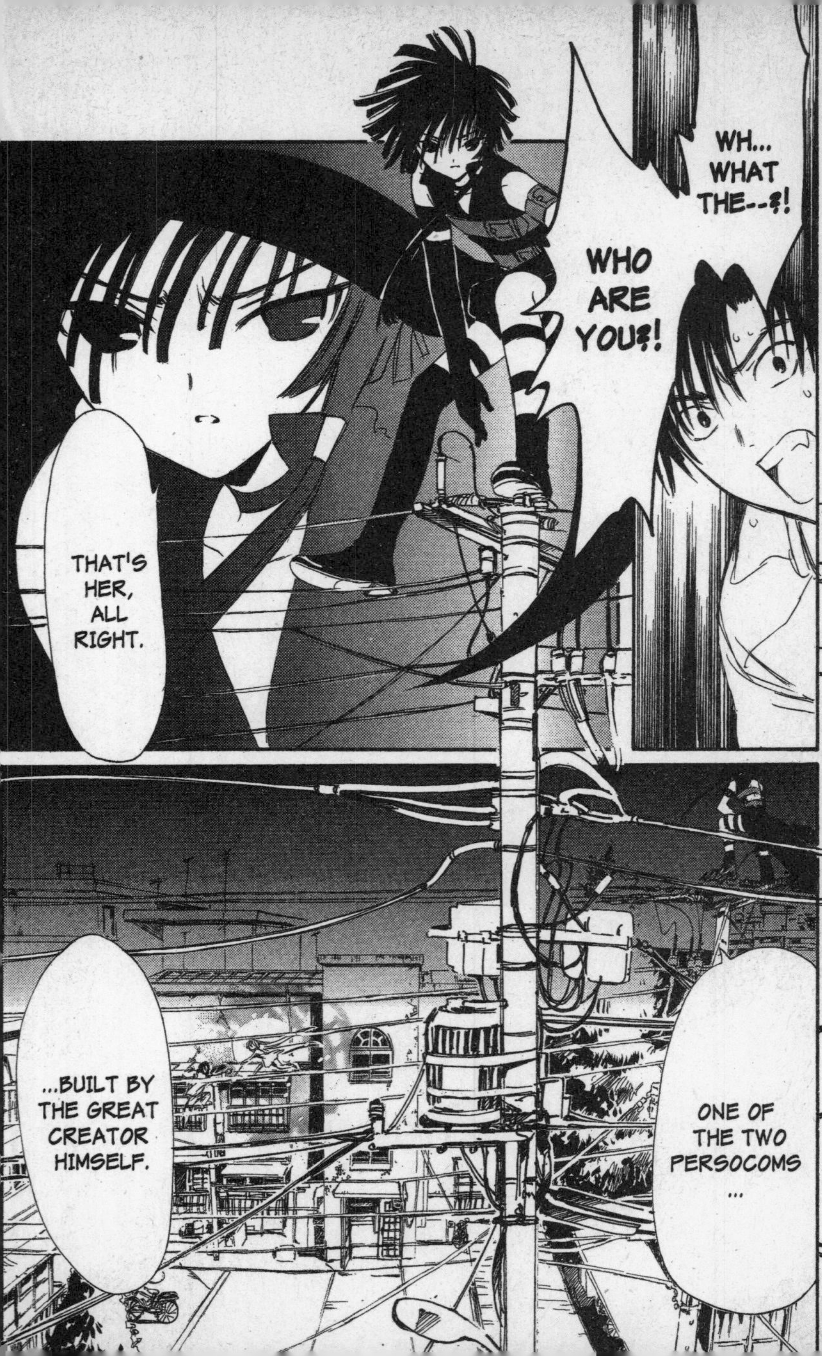
WH... WHAT THE--?!
WHO ARE YOU?!
THAT'S HER, ALL RIGHT.
ONE OF THE TWO PERSOCOMS ...
...BUILT BY THE GREAT CREATOR HIMSELF.

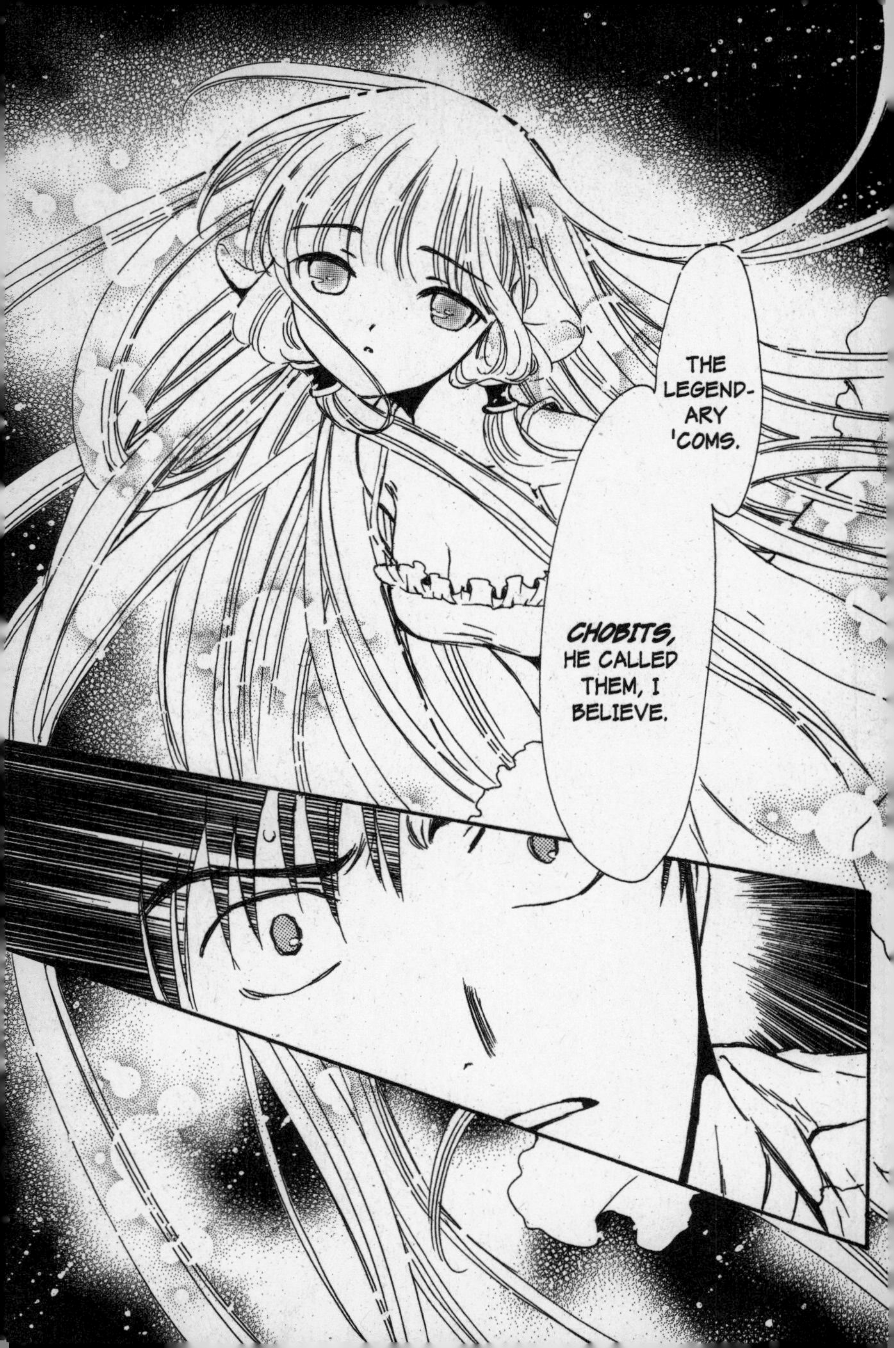
THE LEGEND-ARY 'COMS.
*CHOBITS,* HE CALLED THEM, I BELIEVE.

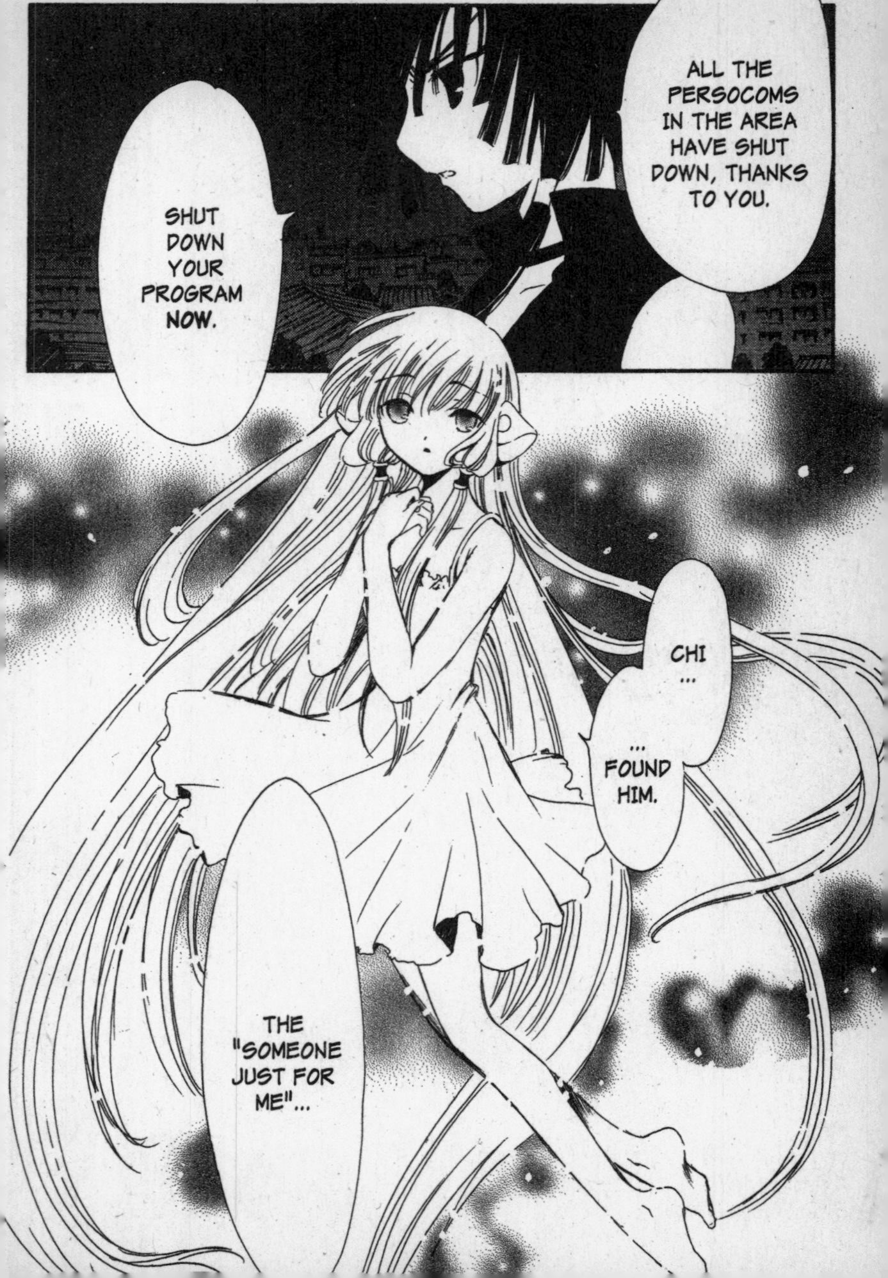
ALL THE PERSOCOMS IN THE AREA HAVE SHUT DOWN, THANKS TO YOU.
SHUT DOWN YOUR PROGRAM NOW.
CHI ...
... FOUND HIM.
THE "SOMEONE JUST FOR ME"...

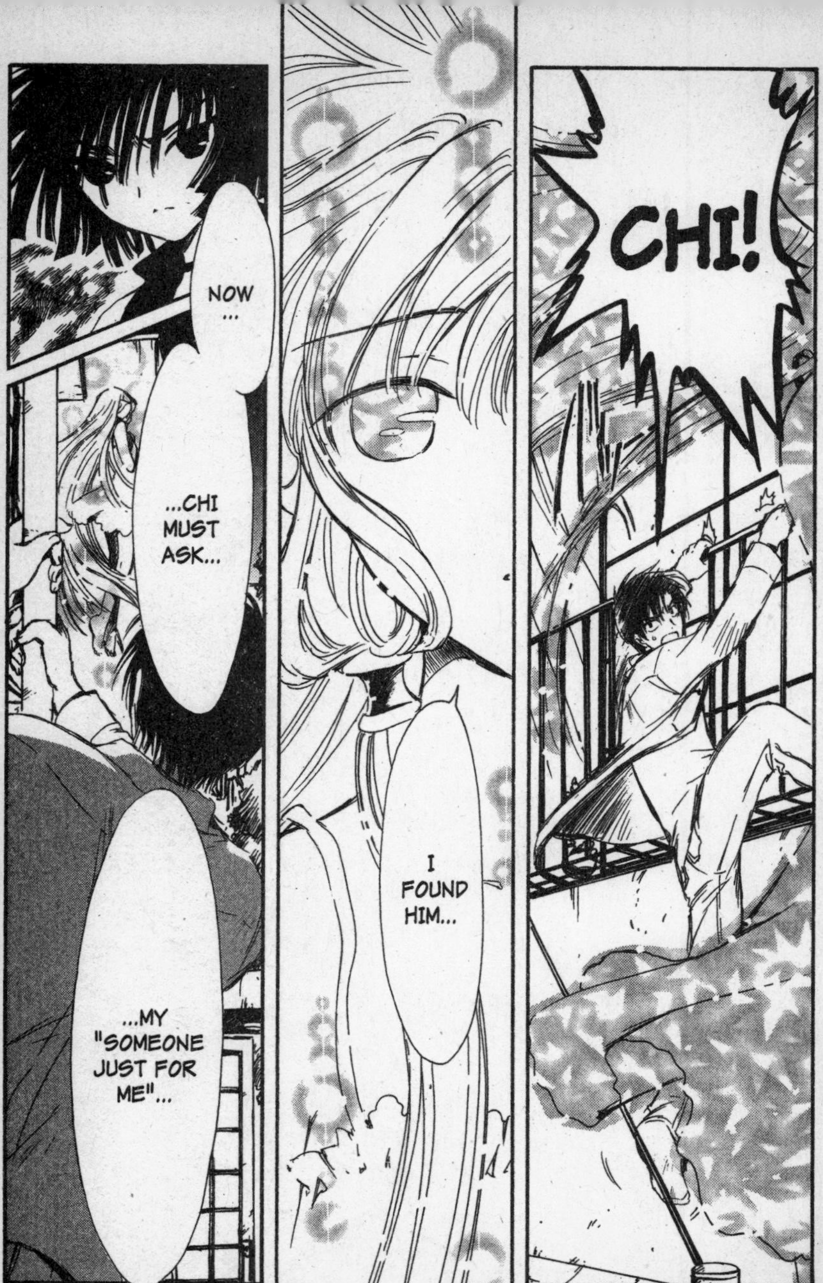
CHI!
I FOUND HIM...
NOW...
...CHI MUST ASK...
...MY "SOMEONE JUST FOR ME"...

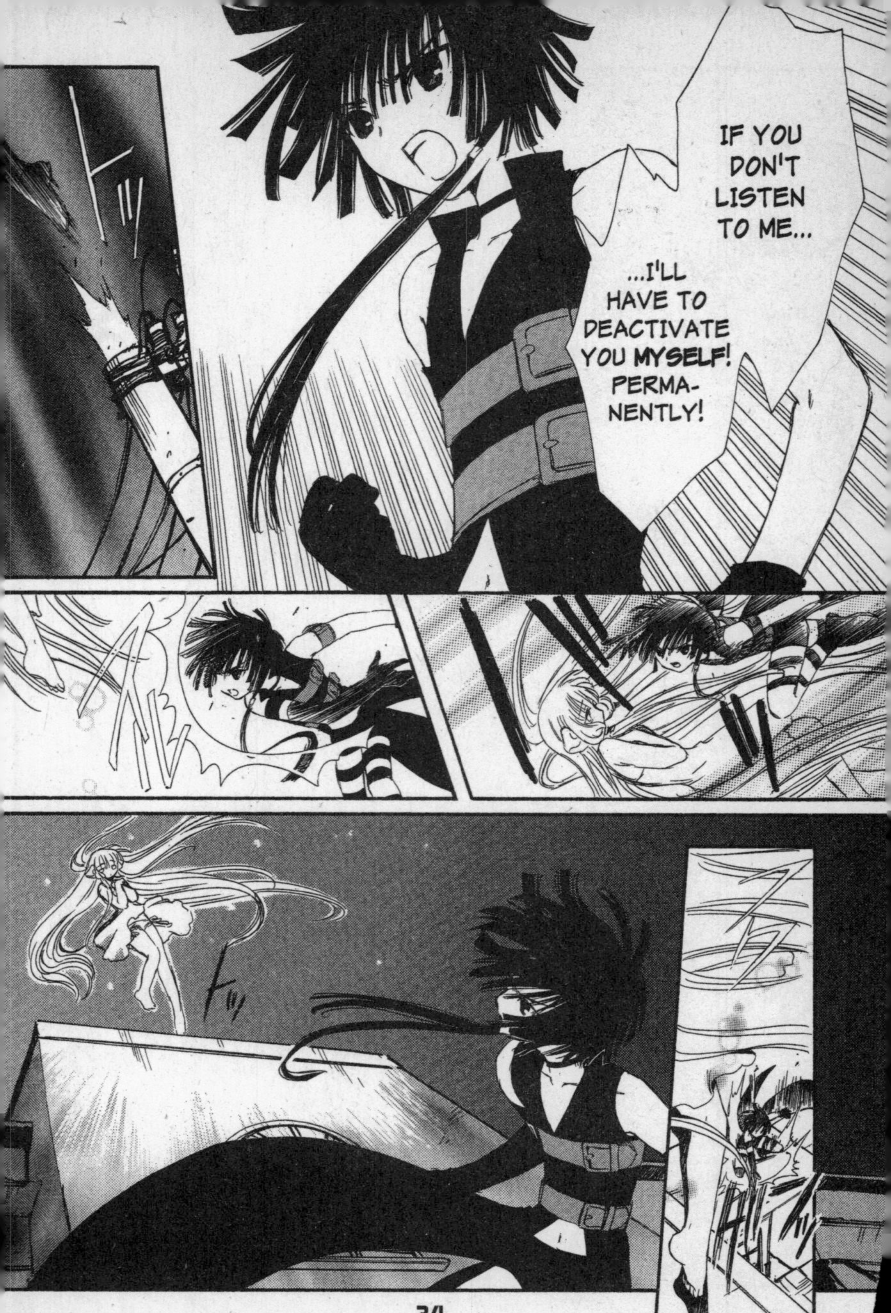
IF YOU DON'T LISTEN TO ME...
...I'LL HAVE TO DEACTIVATE YOU MYSELF! PERMANENTLY!

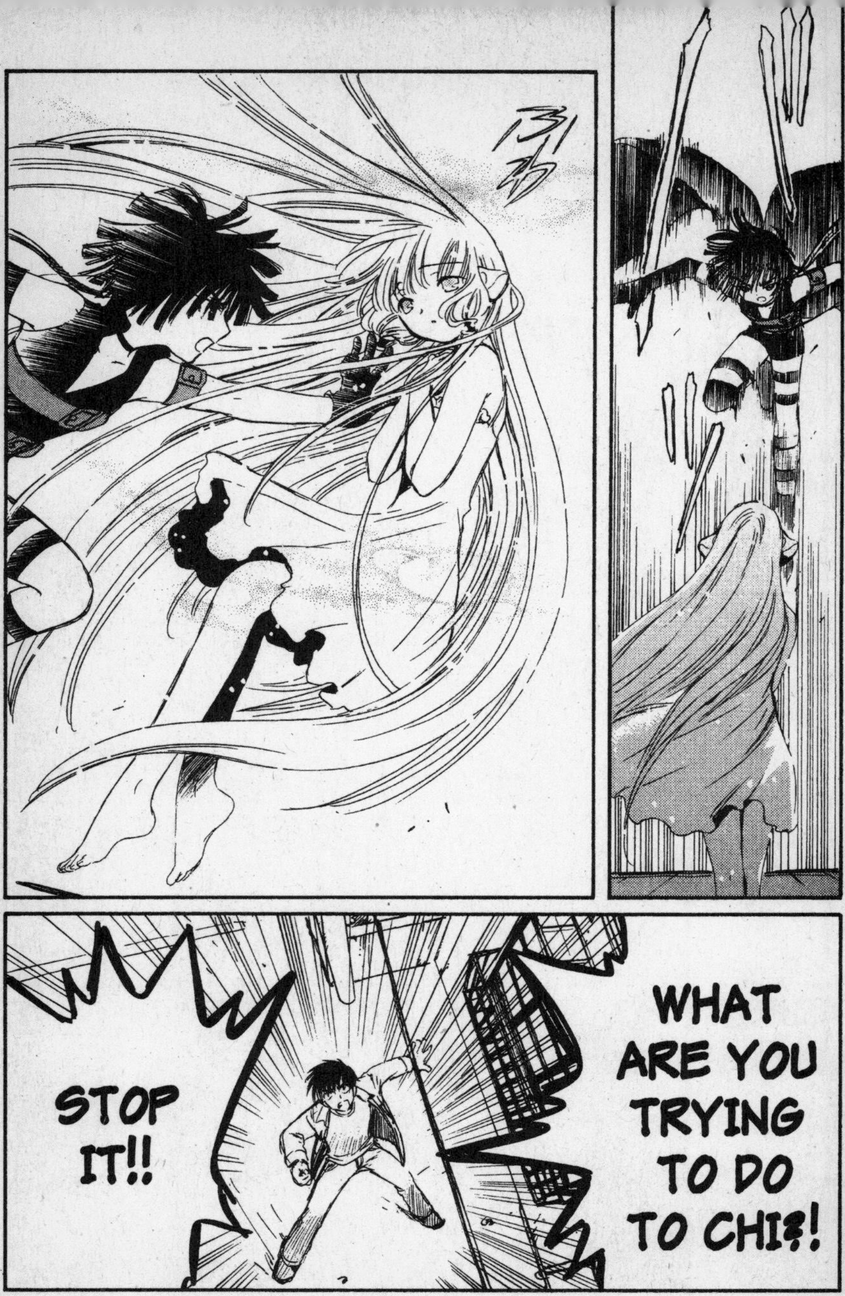
WHAT ARE YOU TRYING TO DO TO CHI?!
STOP IT!!

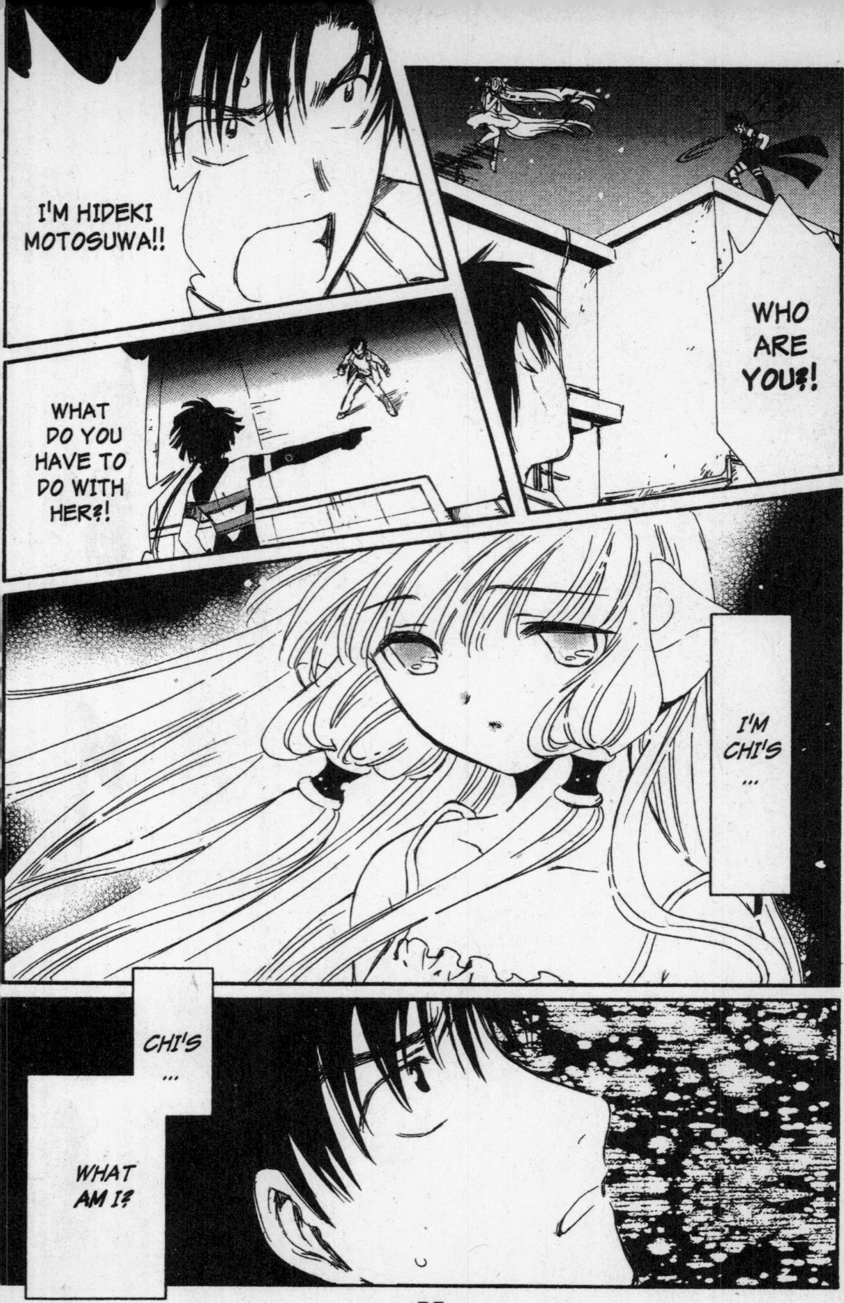
WHO ARE YOU?!
I'M HIDEKI MOTOSUWA!!
WHAT DO YOU HAVE TO DO WITH HER?!
I'M CHI'S ...
CHI'S ...
WHAT AM I?

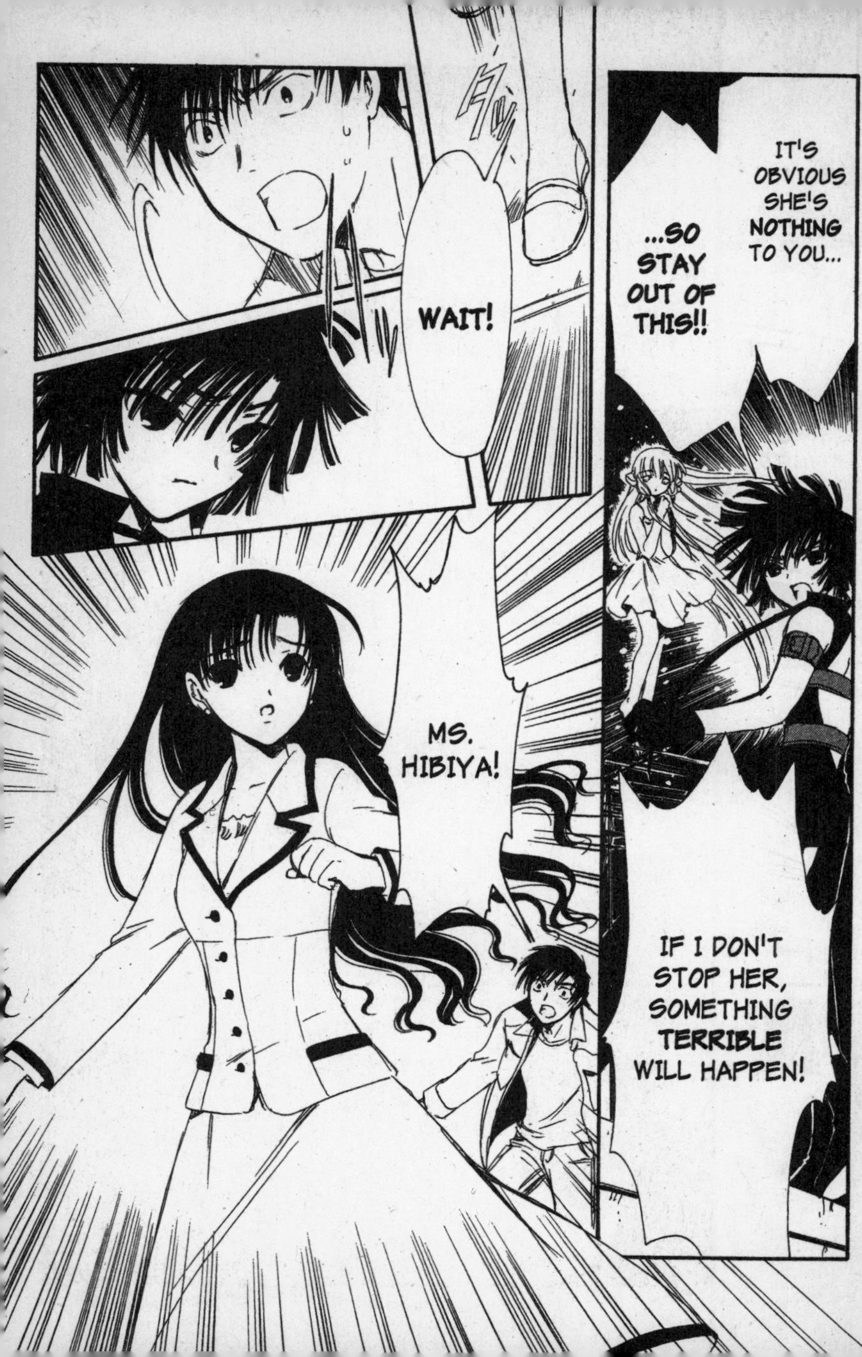
IT'S OBVIOUS SHE'S NOTHING TO YOU...
...SO STAY OUT OF THIS!!
IF I DON'T STOP HER, SOMETHING TERRIBLE WILL HAPPEN!
WAIT!
MS. HIBIYA!

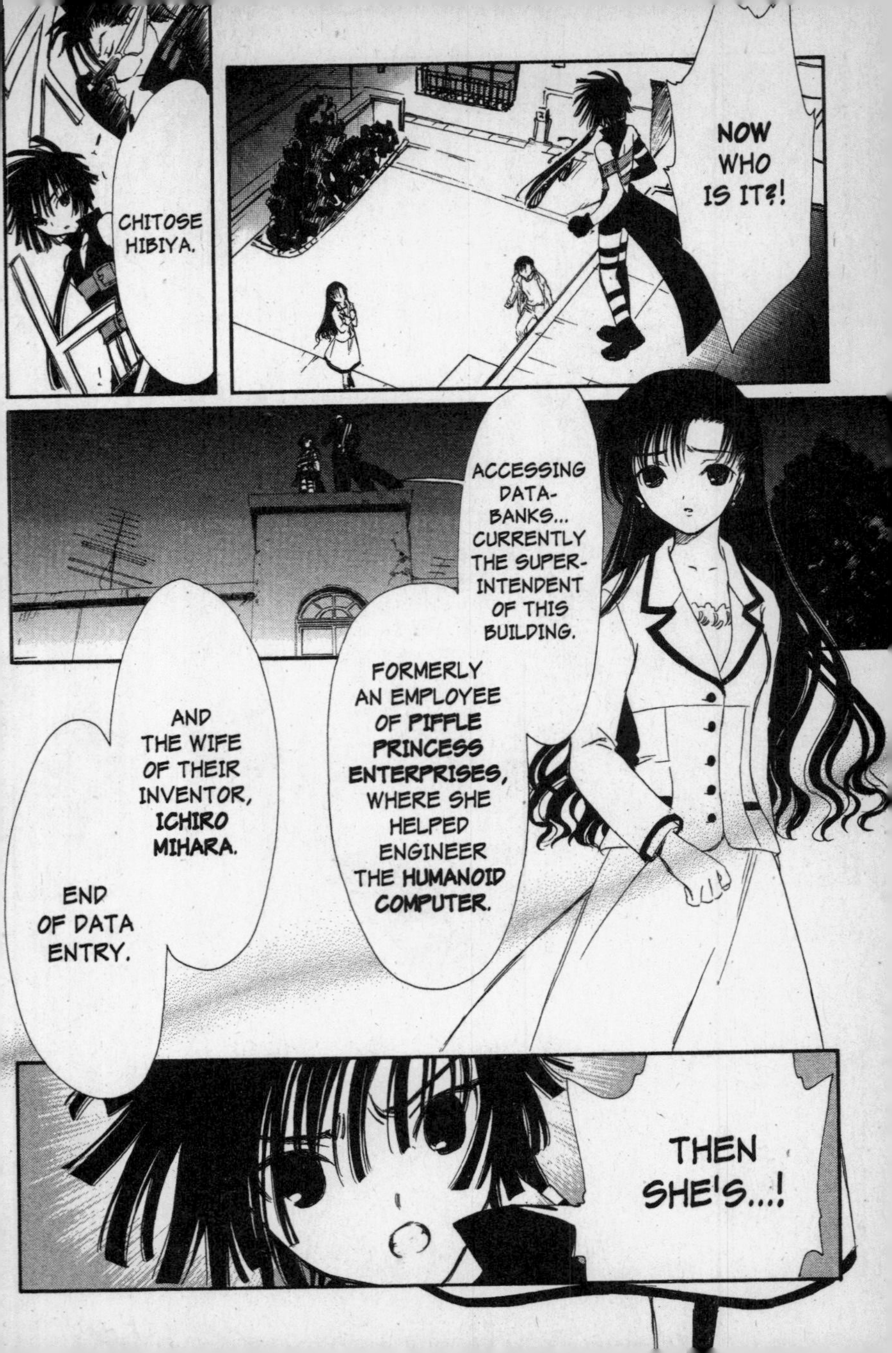
NOW WHO IS IT?!
CHITOSE HIBIYA.
ACCESSING DATA-BANKS... CURRENTLY THE SUPER-INTENDENT OF THIS BUILDING.
FORMERLY AN EMPLOYEE OF PIFFLE PRINCESS ENTERPRISES, WHERE SHE HELPED ENGINEER THE HUMANOID COMPUTER.
AND THE WIFE OF THEIR INVENTOR, ICHIRO MIHARA.
END OF DATA ENTRY.
THEN SHE'S...!

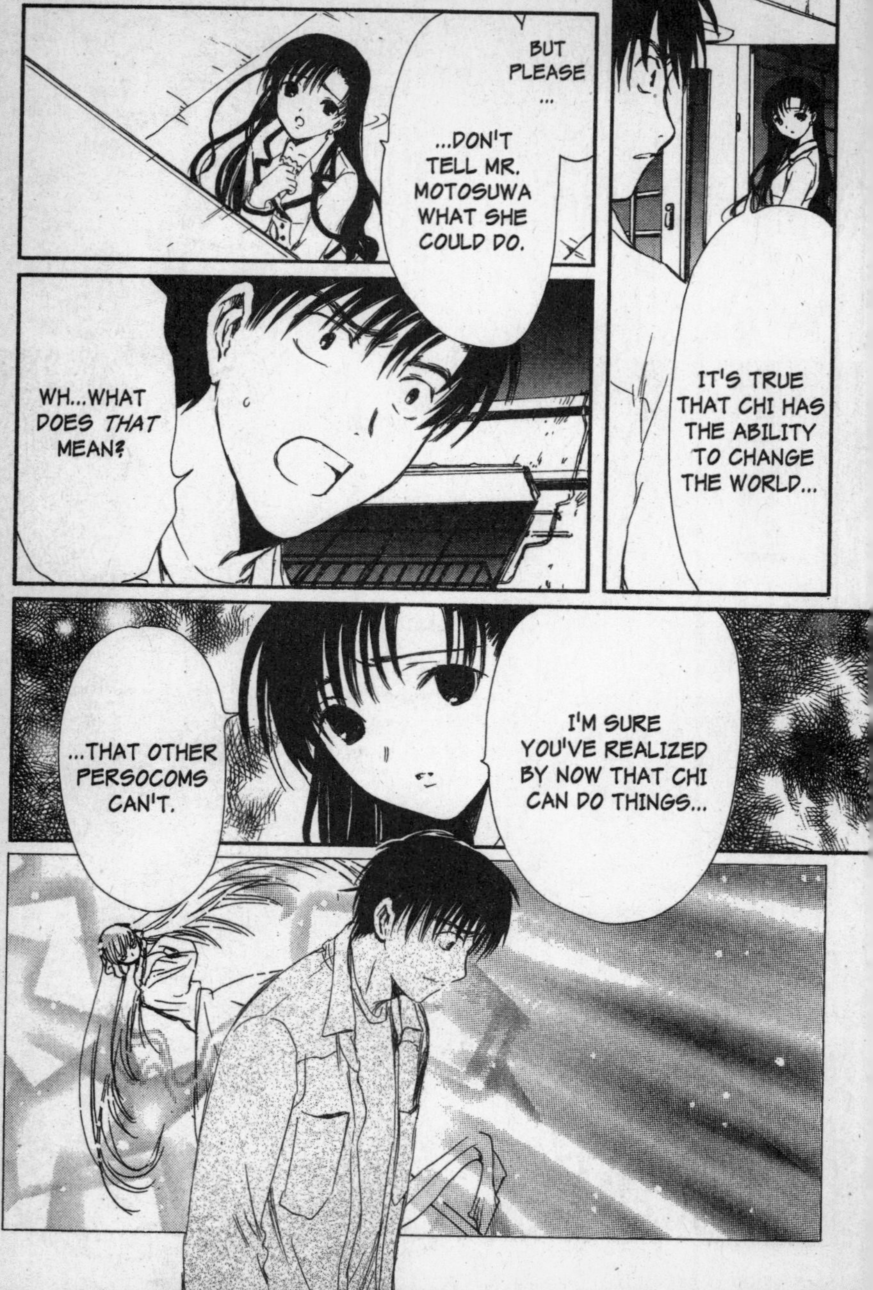
IT'S TRUE THAT CHI HAS THE ABILITY TO CHANGE THE WORLD...
BUT PLEASE ...
...DON'T TELL MR. MOTOSUWA WHAT SHE COULD DO.
WH...WHAT DOES *THAT* MEAN?
I'M SURE YOU'VE REALIZED BY NOW THAT CHI CAN DO THINGS...
...THAT OTHER PERSOCOMS CAN'T.

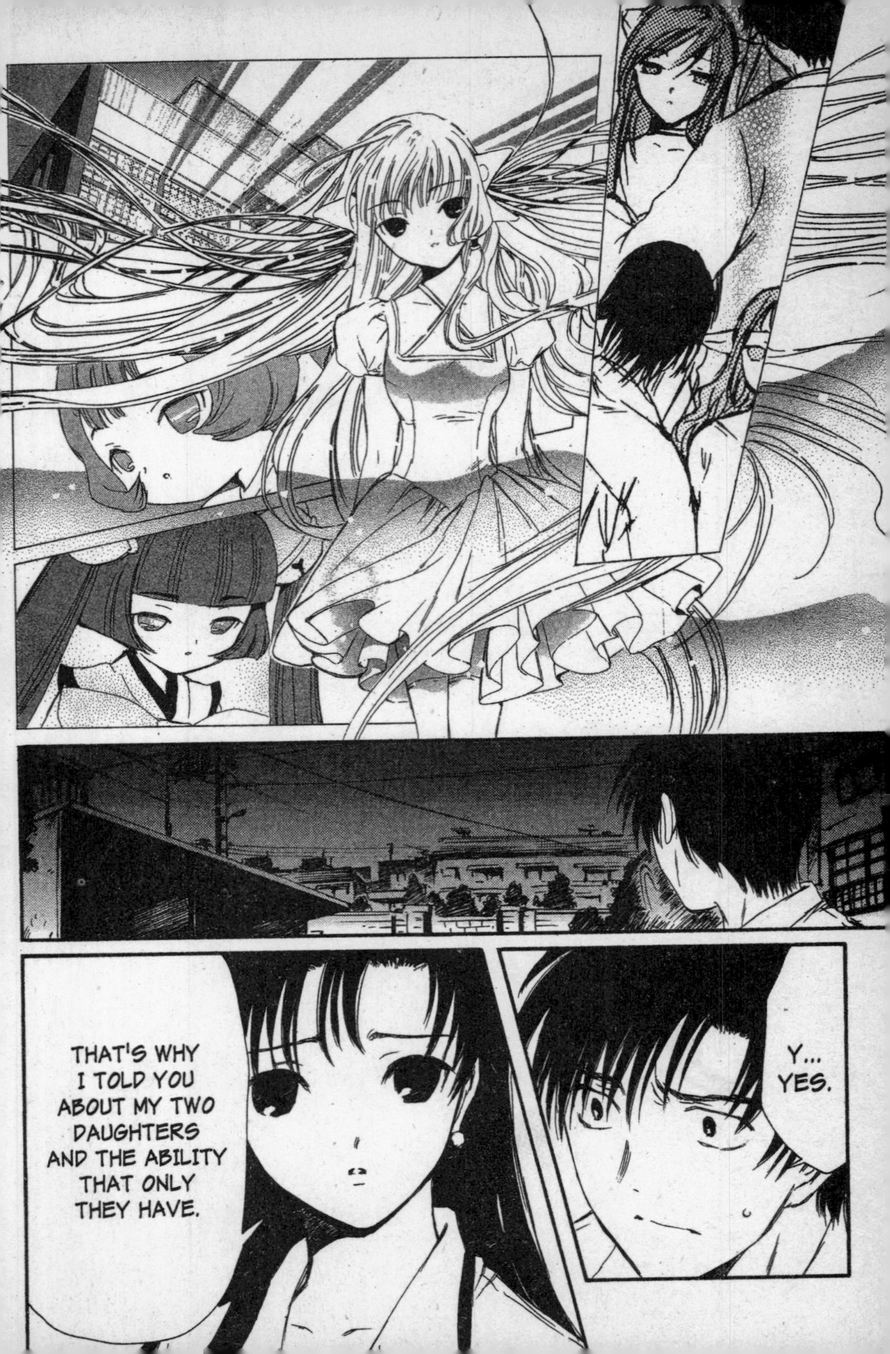
Y... YES.
THAT'S WHY I TOLD YOU ABOUT MY TWO DAUGHTERS AND THE ABILITY THAT ONLY THEY HAVE.

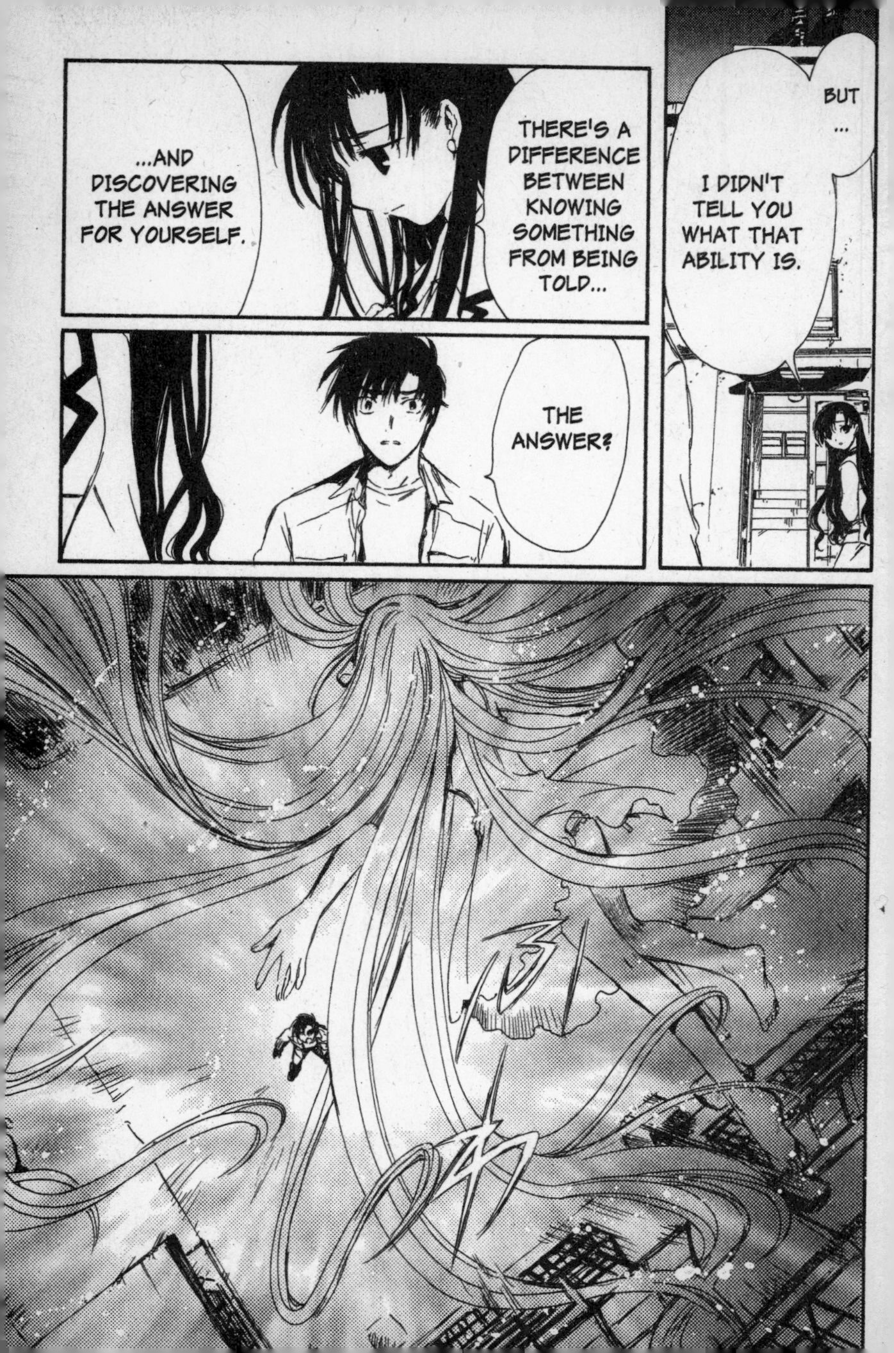

BUT ...
I DIDN'T TELL YOU WHAT THAT ABILITY IS.
THERE'S A DIFFERENCE BETWEEN KNOWING SOMETHING FROM BEING TOLD...
...AND DISCOVERING THE ANSWER FOR YOURSELF.
THE ANSWER?

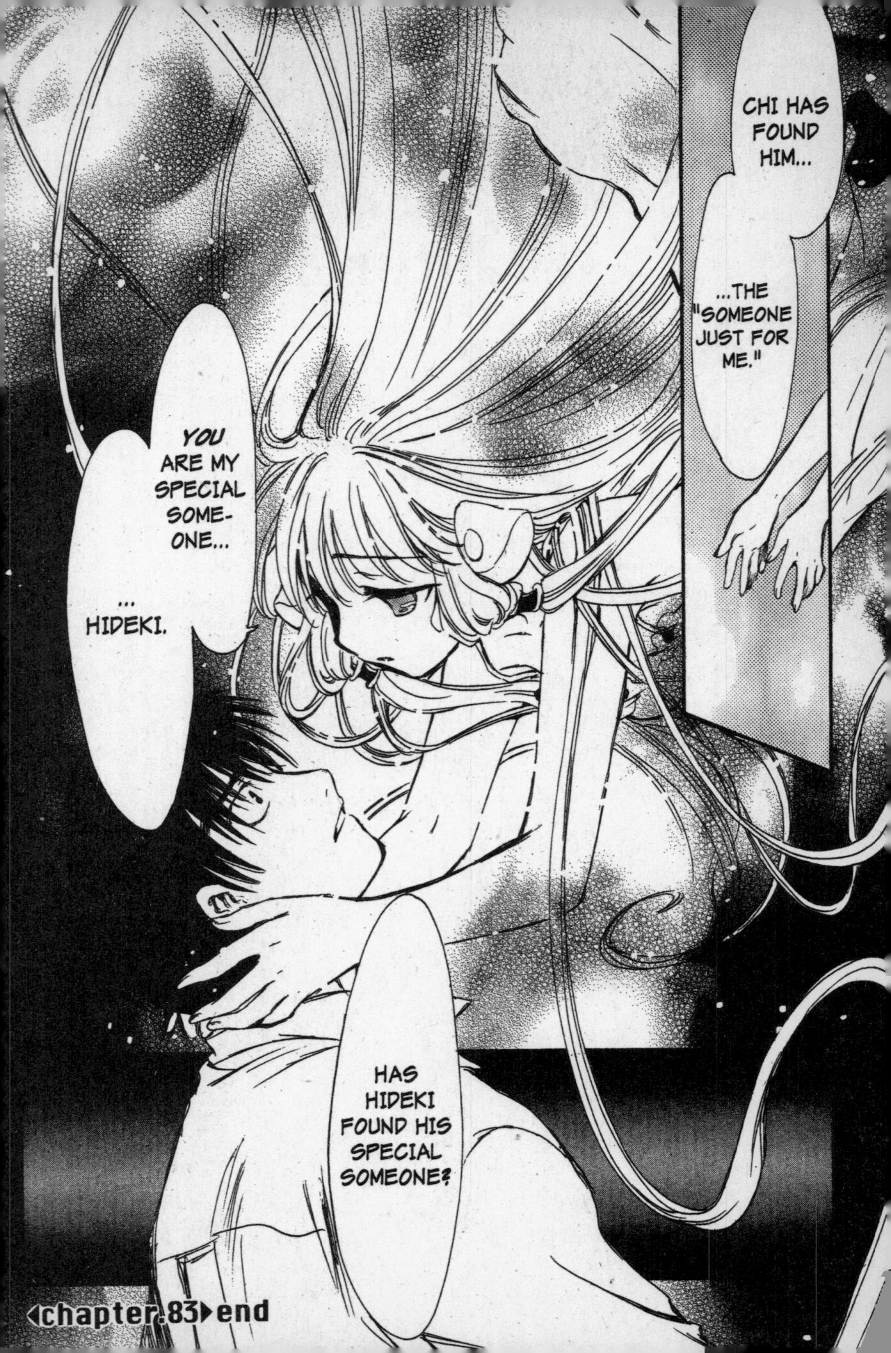
CHI HAS FOUND HIM...
...THE "SOMEONE JUST FOR ME."
YOU ARE MY SPECIAL SOME-ONE...
... HIDEKI.
HAS HIDEKI FOUND HIS SPECIAL SOMEONE?
chapter.83 end

ちょびっツ

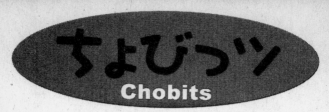

Chobits

# ◀chapter.84▶

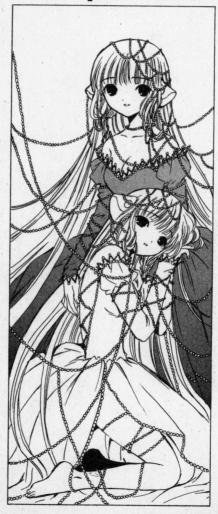

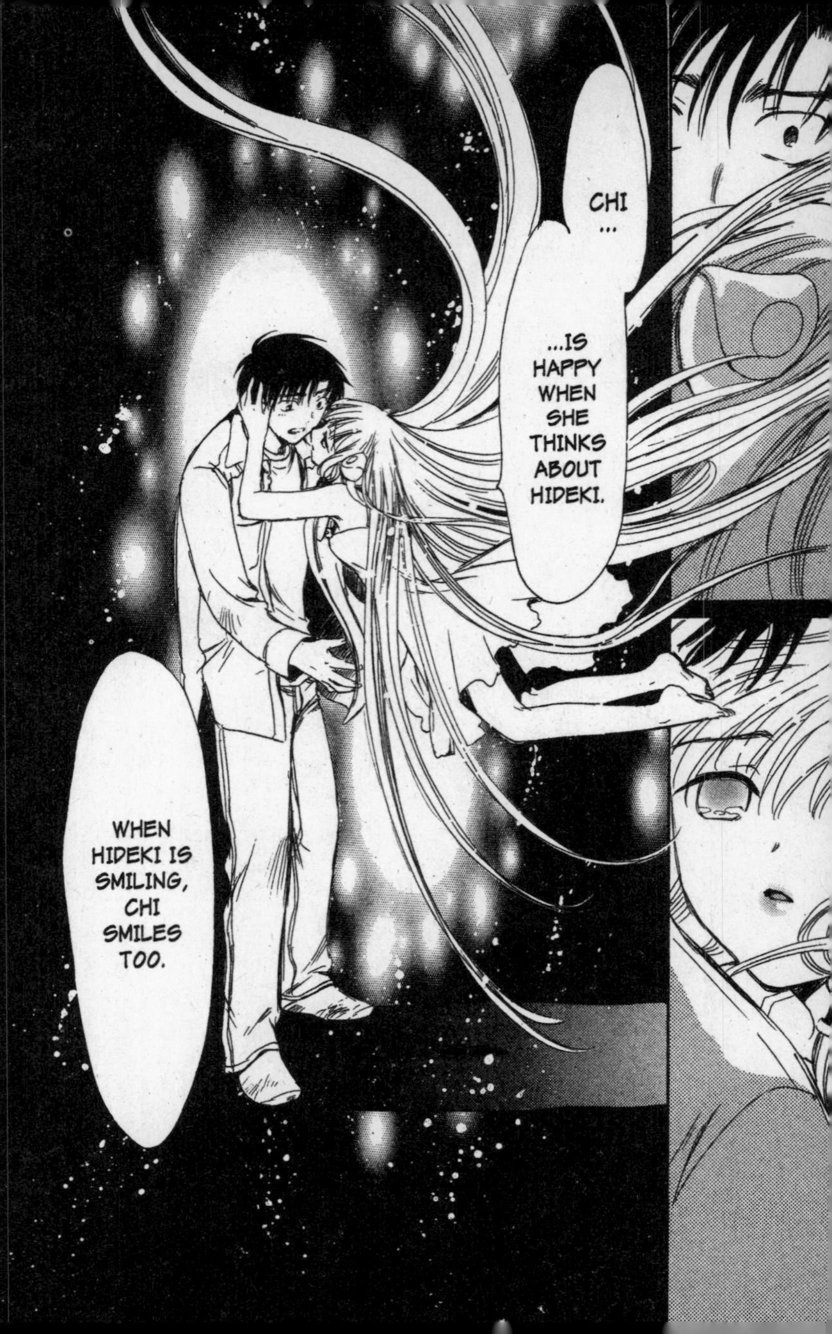
CHI ...
...IS HAPPY WHEN SHE THINKS ABOUT HIDEKI.
WHEN HIDEKI IS SMILING, CHI SMILES TOO.

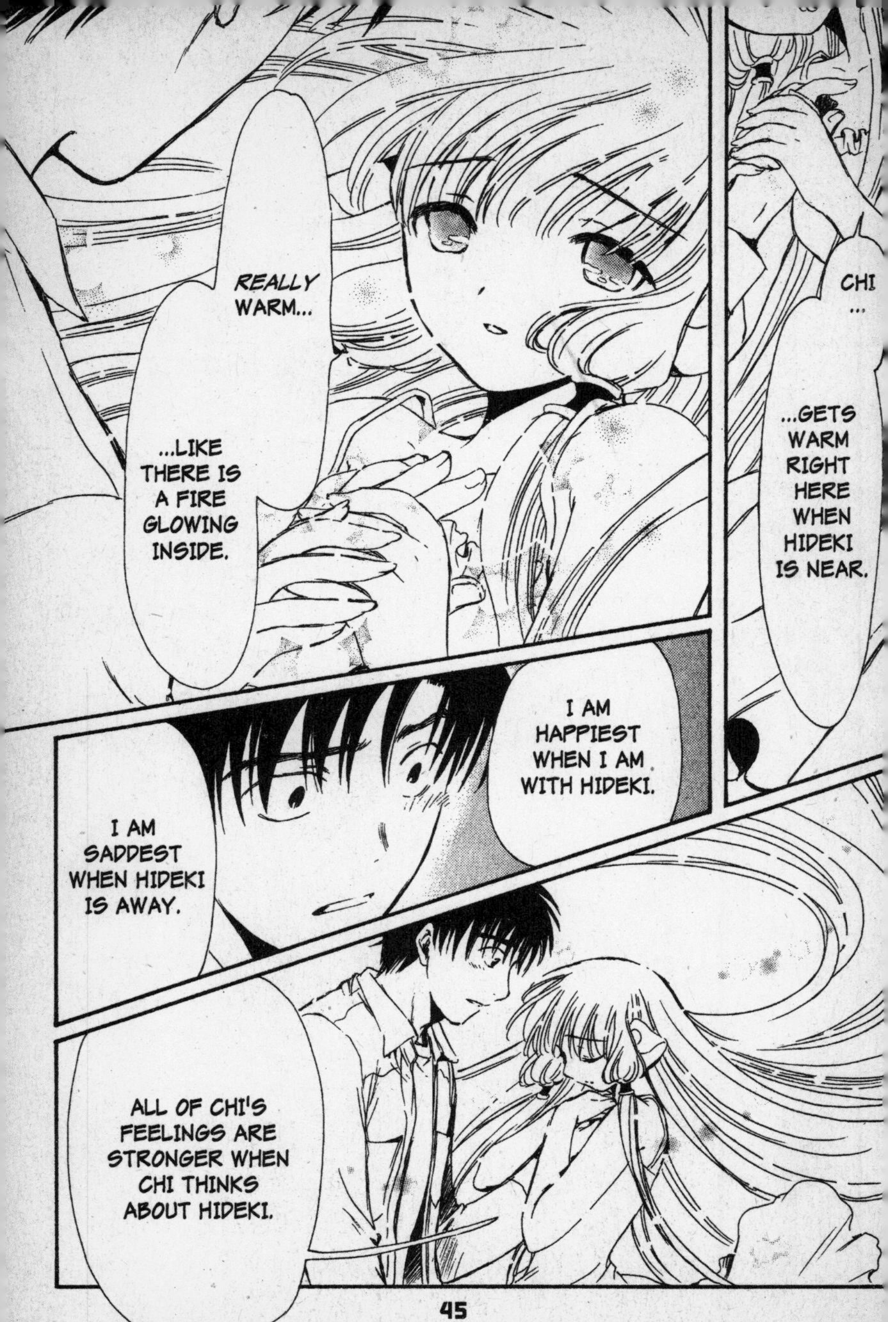
CHI ...
...GETS WARM RIGHT HERE WHEN HIDEKI IS NEAR.
REALLY WARM...
...LIKE THERE IS A FIRE GLOWING INSIDE.
I AM HAPPIEST WHEN I AM WITH HIDEKI.
I AM SADDEST WHEN HIDEKI IS AWAY.
ALL OF CHI'S FEELINGS ARE STRONGER WHEN CHI THINKS ABOUT HIDEKI.

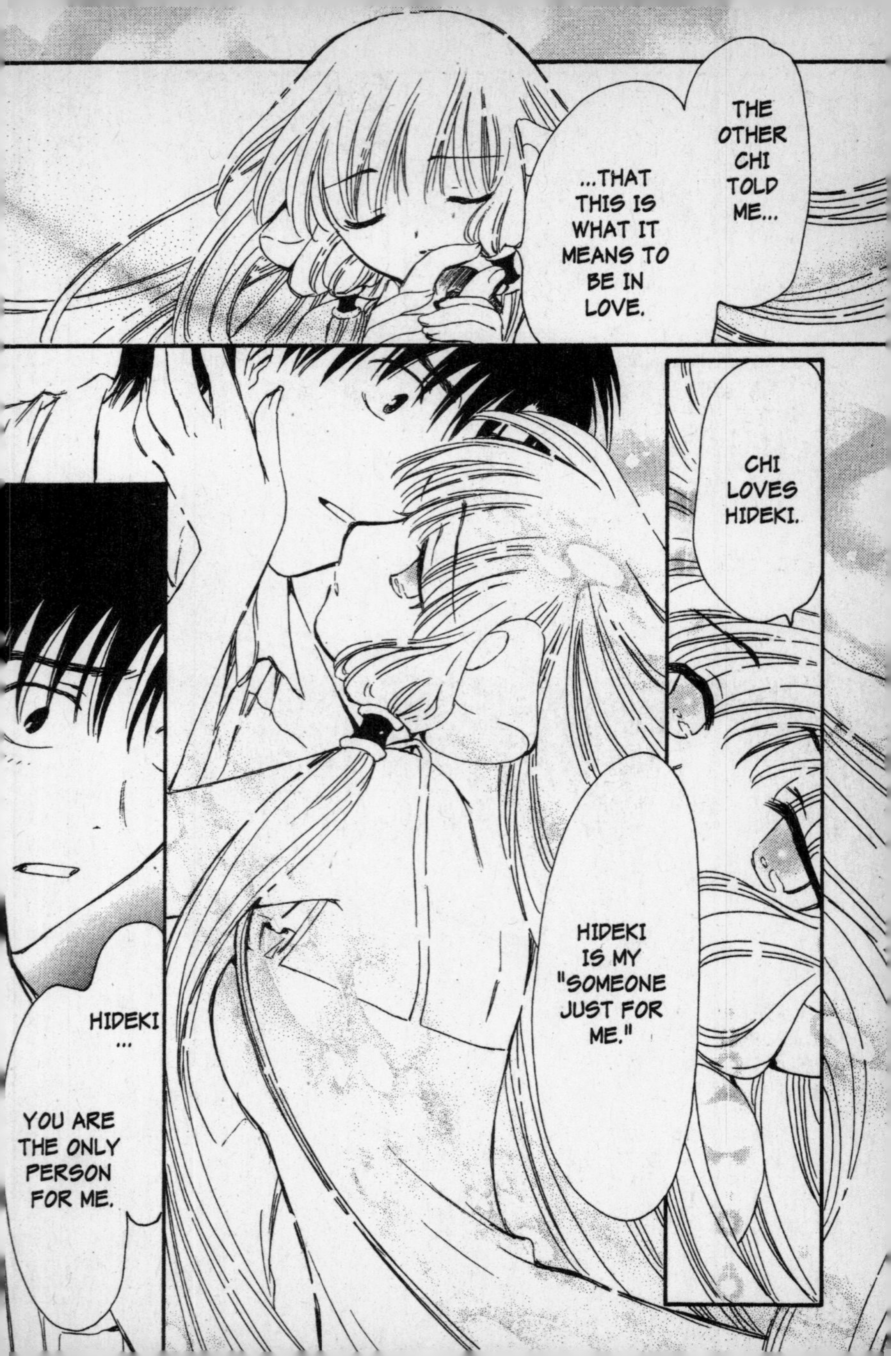
THE OTHER CHI TOLD ME...
...THAT THIS IS WHAT IT MEANS TO BE IN LOVE.
CHI LOVES HIDEKI.
HIDEKI IS MY "SOMEONE JUST FOR ME."
HIDEKI ...
YOU ARE THE ONLY PERSON FOR ME.

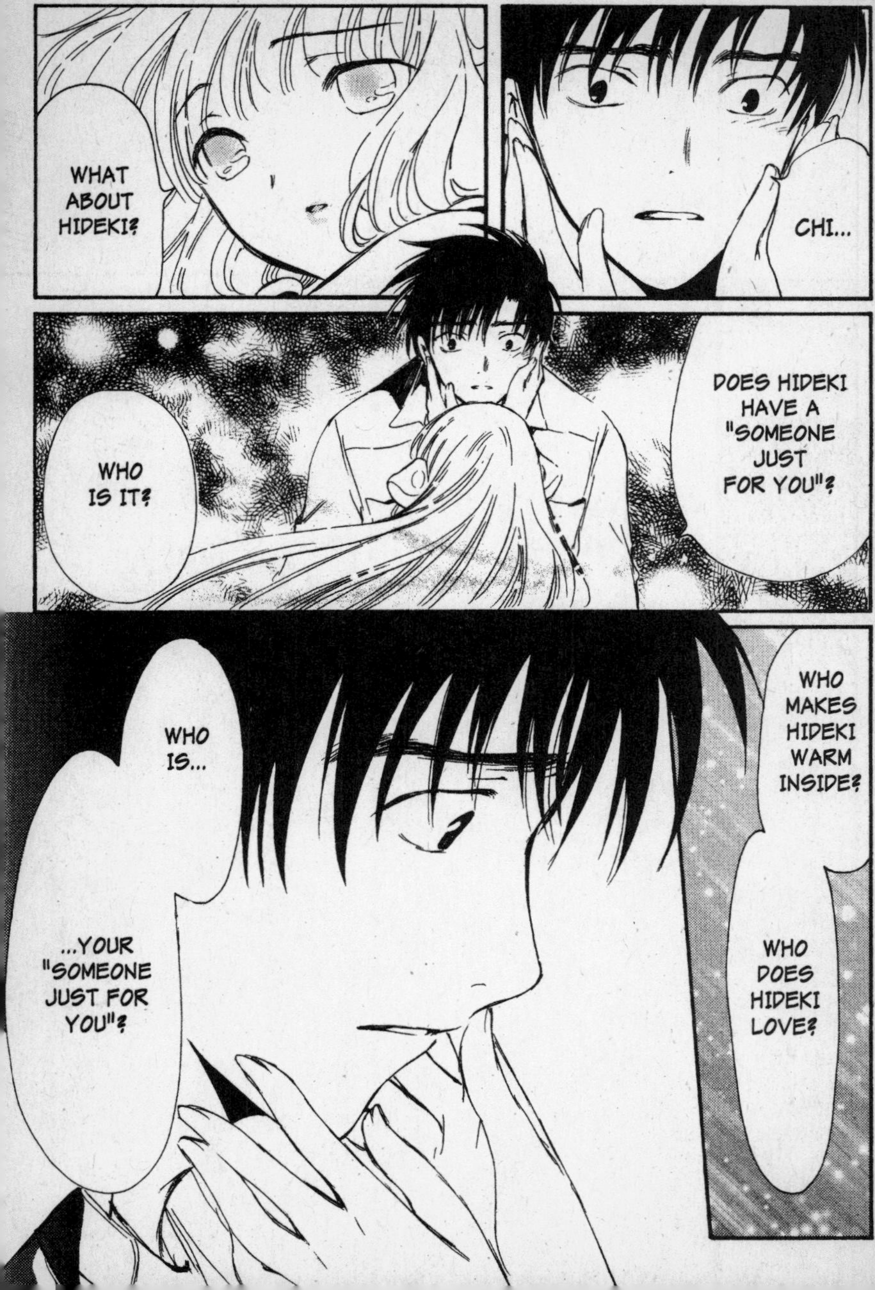
CHI...
WHAT ABOUT HIDEKI?
DOES HIDEKI HAVE A "SOMEONE JUST FOR YOU"?
WHO IS IT?
WHO MAKES HIDEKI WARM INSIDE?
WHO DOES HIDEKI LOVE?
WHO IS...
...YOUR "SOMEONE JUST FOR YOU"?

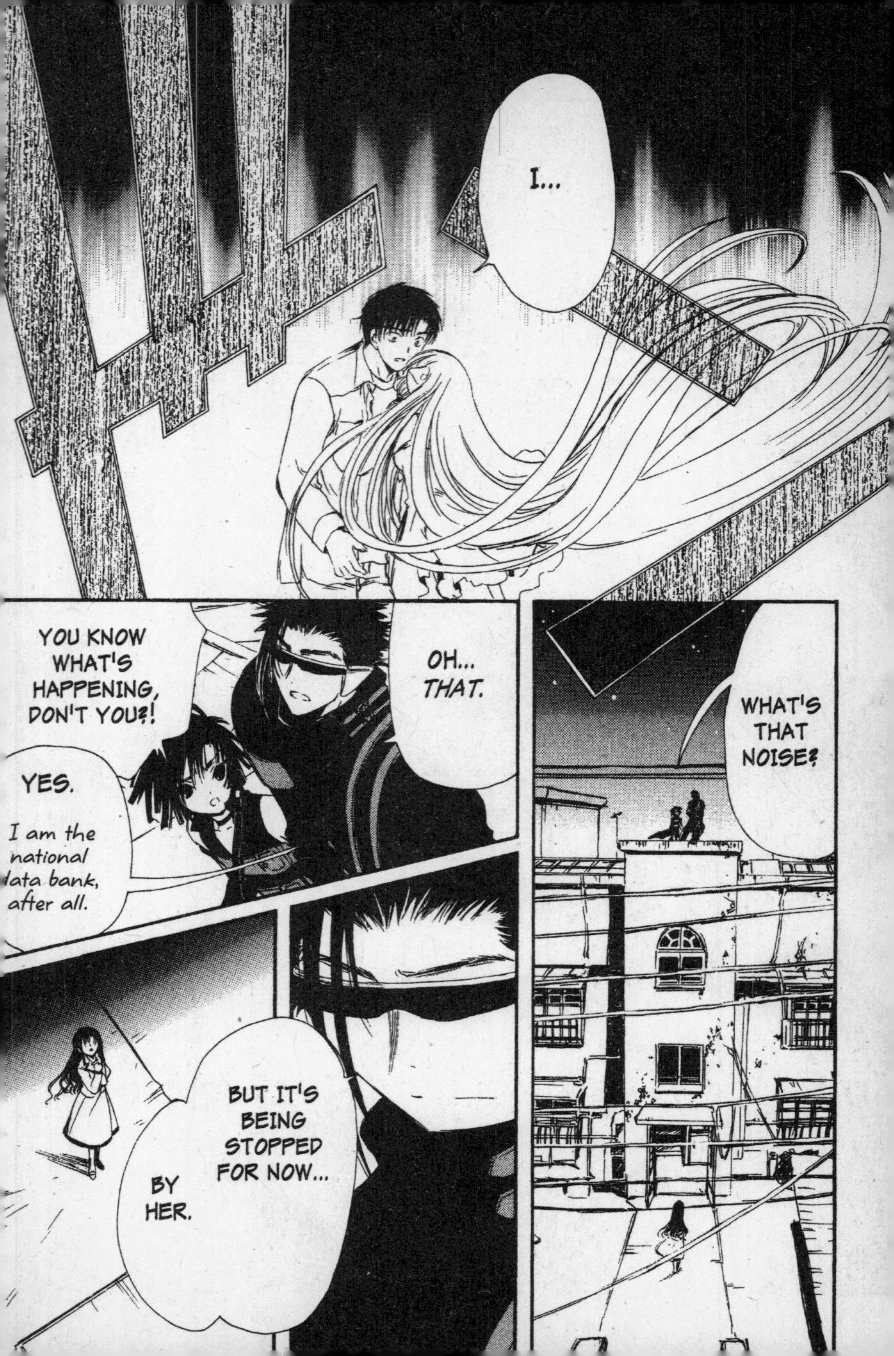
I...
WHAT'S THAT NOISE?
OH... THAT.
YOU KNOW WHAT'S HAPPENING, DON'T YOU?!
YES.
I am the national data bank, after all.
BUT IT'S BEING STOPPED FOR NOW...
BY HER.

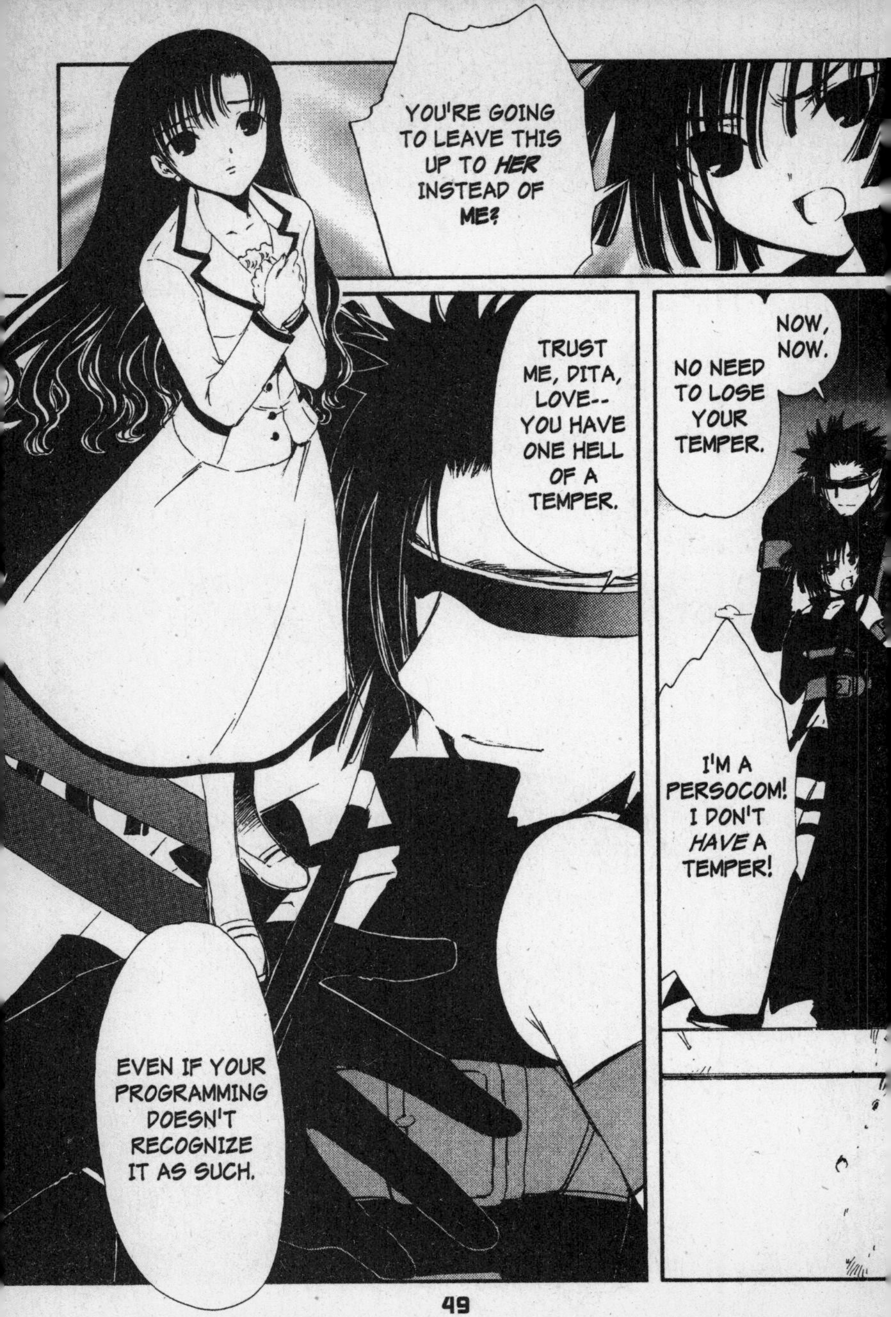
YOU'RE GOING TO LEAVE THIS UP TO *HER* INSTEAD OF ME?
NOW, NOW.
NO NEED TO LOSE YOUR TEMPER.
I'M A PERSOCOM! I DON'T *HAVE* A TEMPER!
TRUST ME, DITA, LOVE-- YOU HAVE ONE HELL OF A TEMPER.
EVEN IF YOUR PROGRAMMING DOESN'T RECOGNIZE IT AS SUCH.

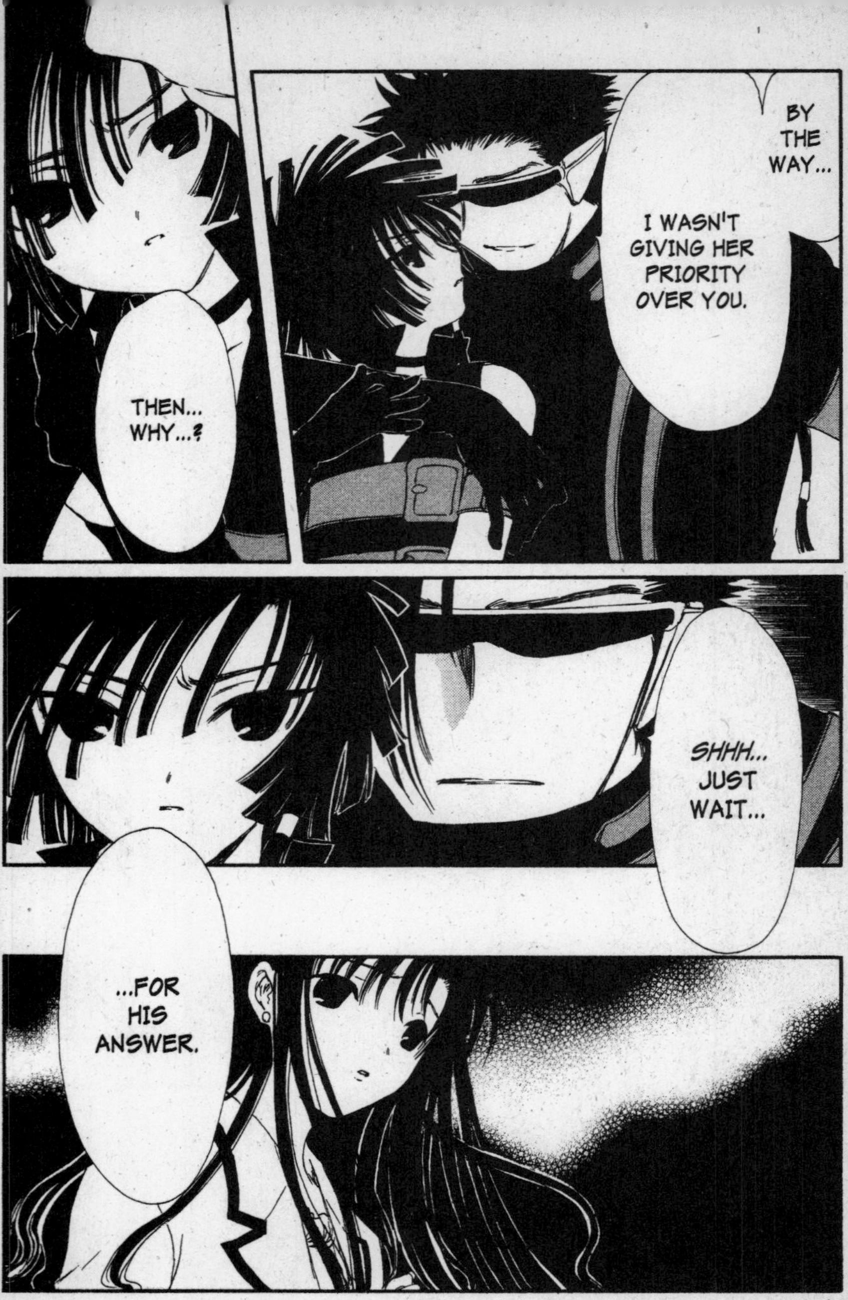
BY THE WAY...
I WASN'T GIVING HER PRIORITY OVER YOU.
THEN... WHY...?
SHHH... JUST WAIT...
...FOR HIS ANSWER.

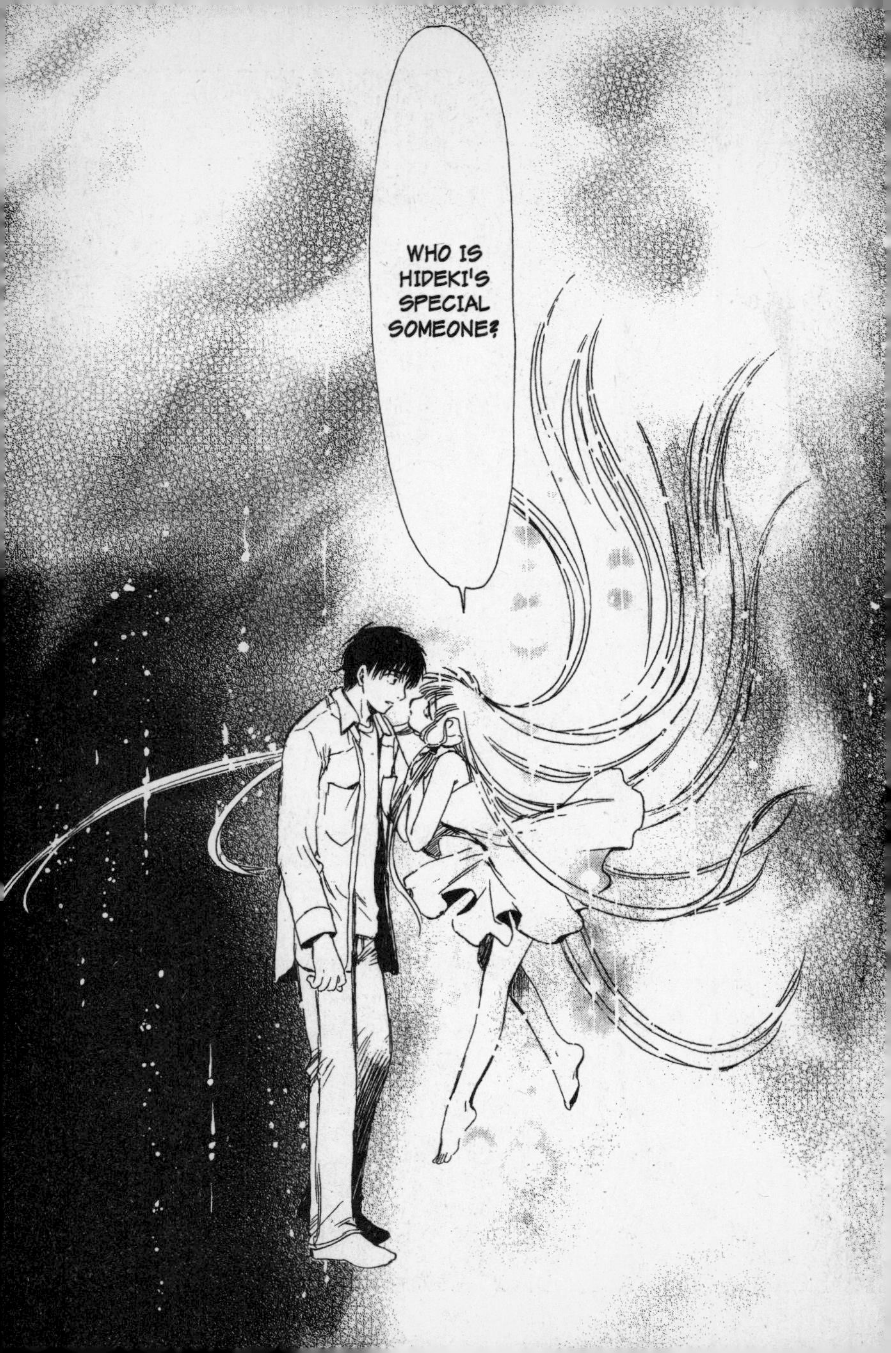
WHO IS HIDEKI'S SPECIAL SOMEONE?

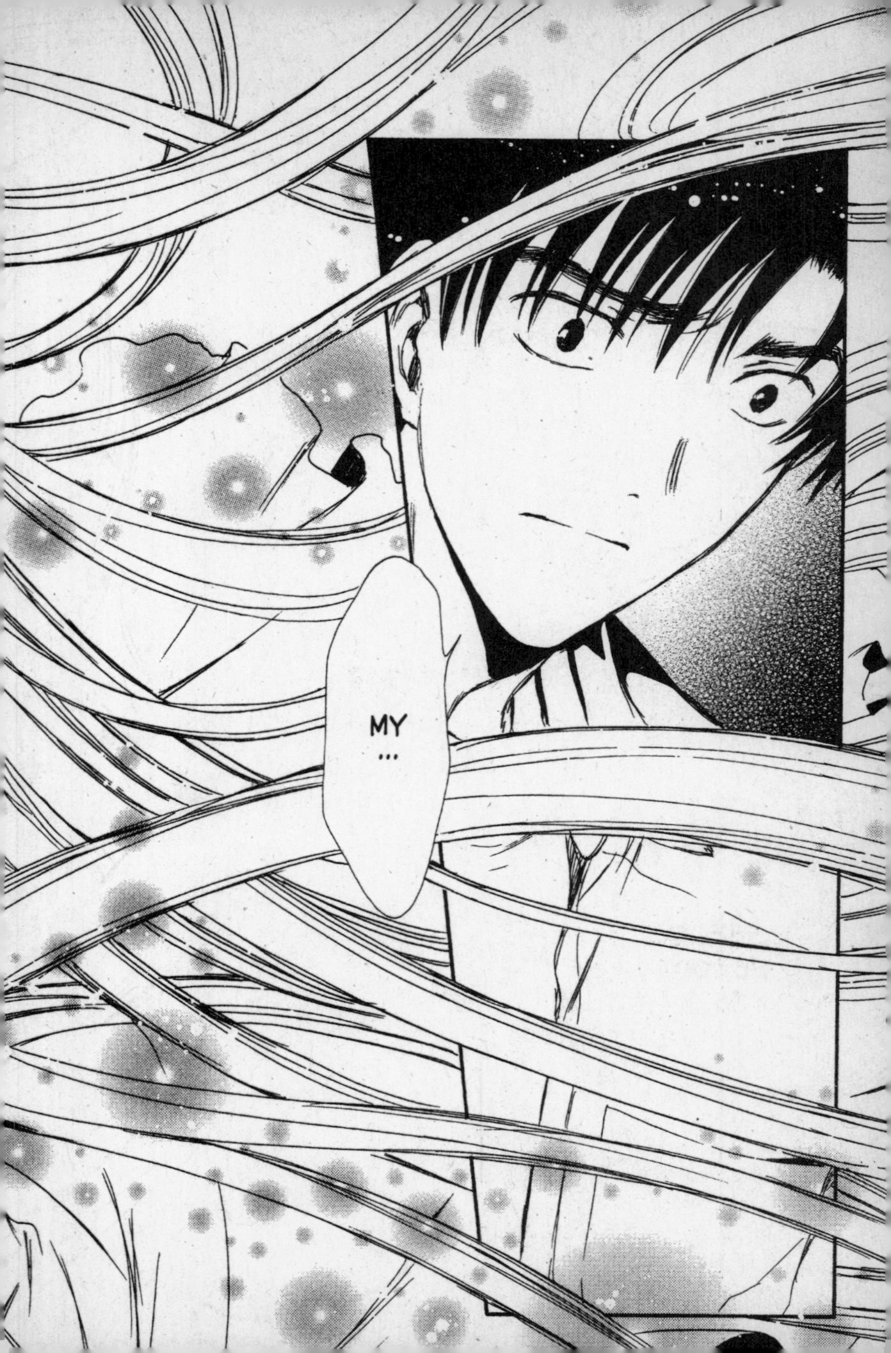
MY ...

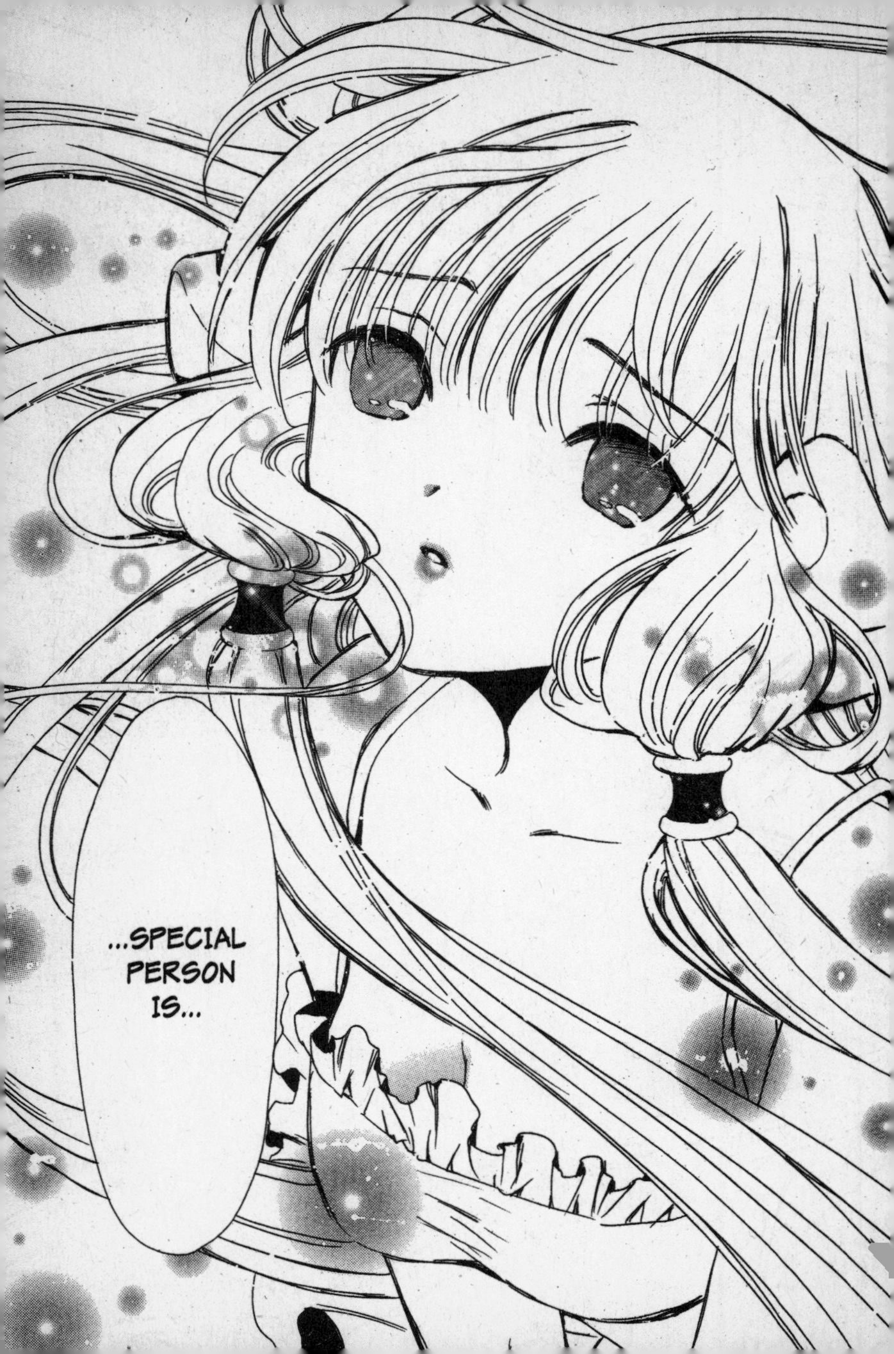
...SPECIAL PERSON IS...

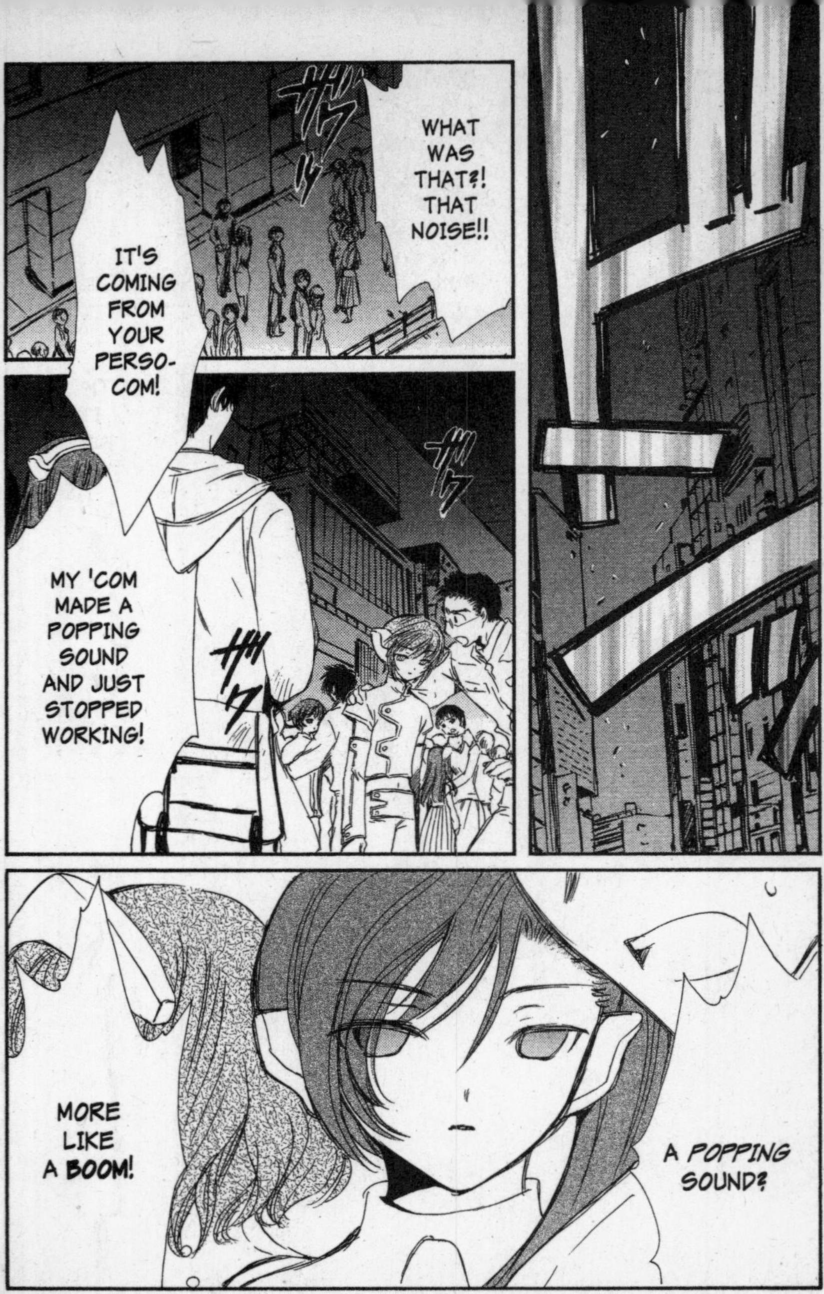
WHAT WAS THAT?! THAT NOISE!!
IT'S COMING FROM YOUR PERSO-COM!
MY 'COM MADE A POPPING SOUND AND JUST STOPPED WORKING!
A *POPPING* SOUND?
MORE LIKE A **BOOM**!

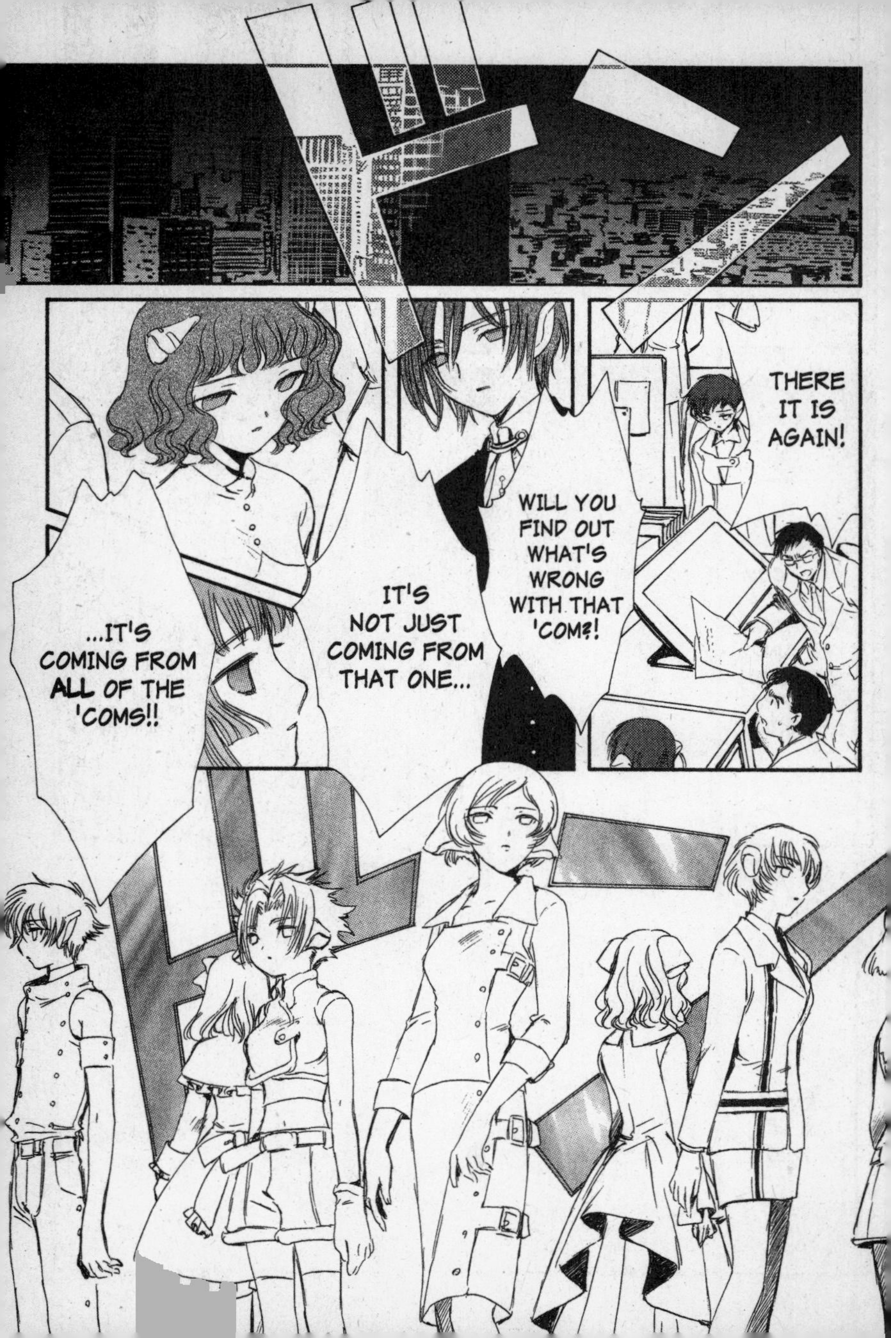
THERE IT IS AGAIN!
WILL YOU FIND OUT WHAT'S WRONG WITH THAT 'COM?!
IT'S NOT JUST COMING FROM THAT ONE...
...IT'S COMING FROM **ALL** OF THE 'COMS!!

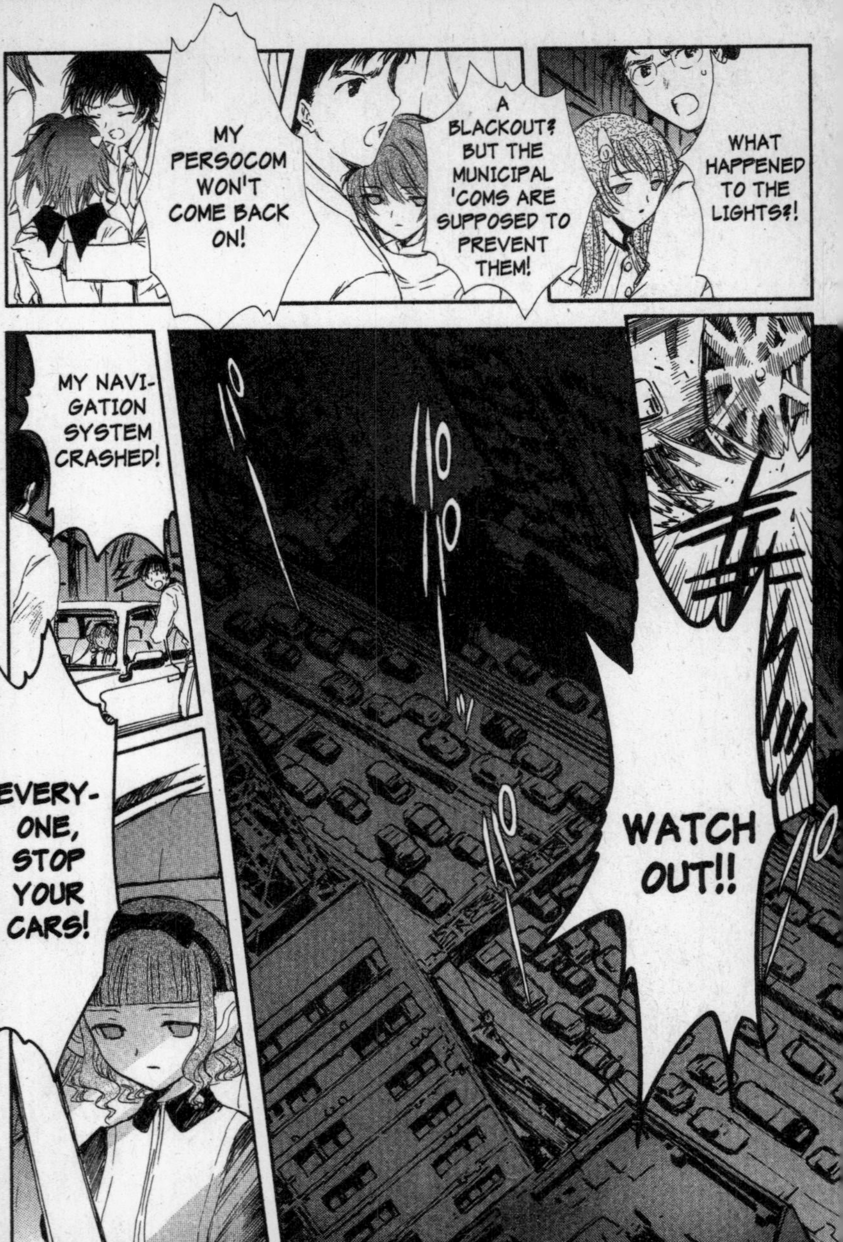
WHAT HAPPENED TO THE LIGHTS?!
A BLACKOUT? BUT THE MUNICIPAL 'COMS ARE SUPPOSED TO PREVENT THEM!
MY PERSOCOM WON'T COME BACK ON!
WATCH OUT!!
MY NAVI-GATION SYSTEM CRASHED!
EVERY-ONE, STOP YOUR CARS!

◀chapter.84▶ end

# ちょびっツ
## Chobits

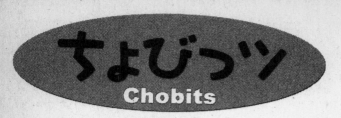

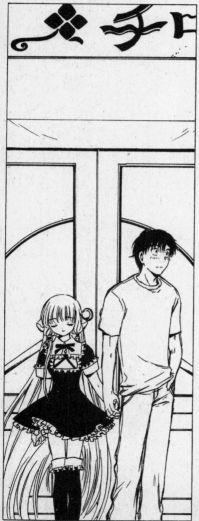

◀chapter.85▶

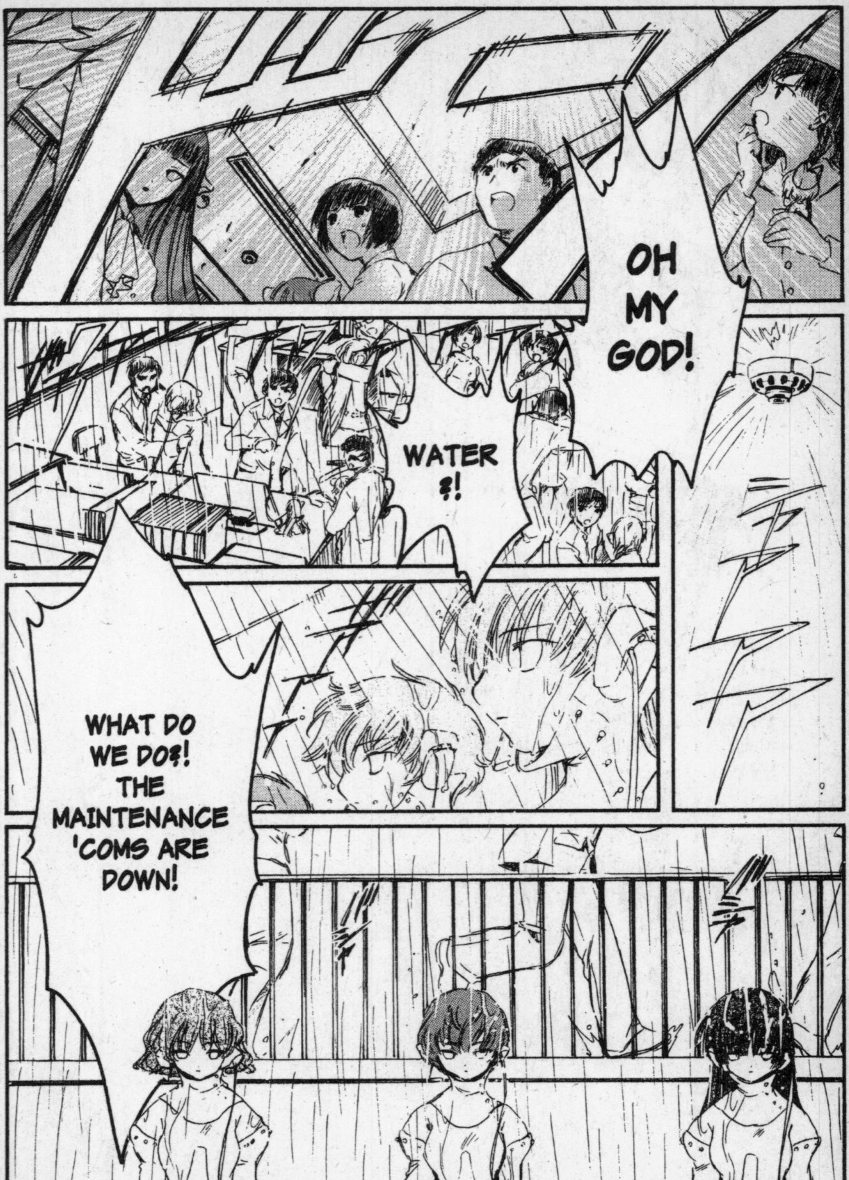
OH MY GOD!
WATER ?!
WHAT DO WE DO?! THE MAINTENANCE 'COMS ARE DOWN!

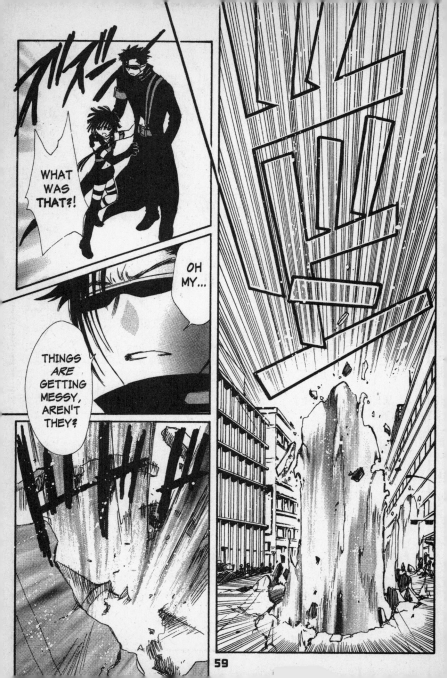

WHAT WAS THAT?!

OH MY...

THINGS ARE GETTING MESSY, AREN'T THEY?

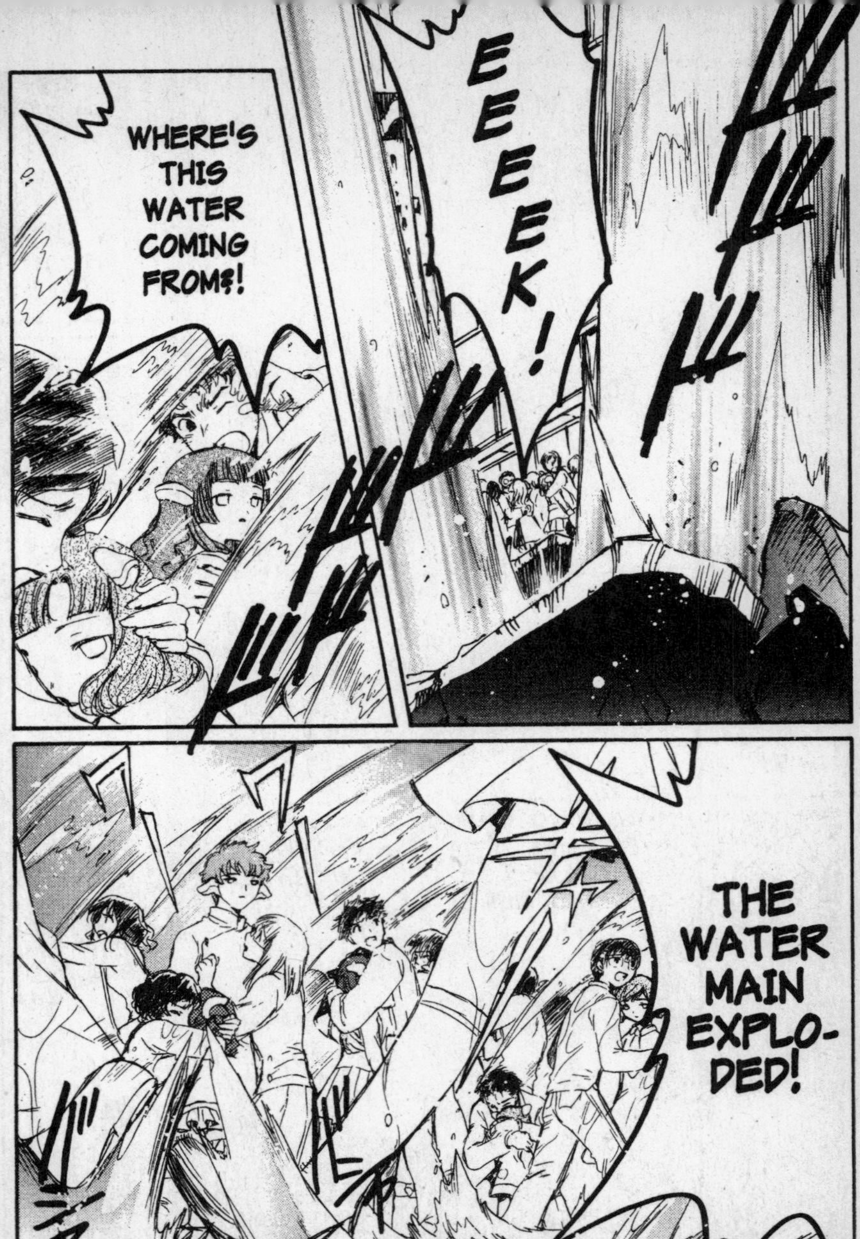
EEEEEK!
WHERE'S THIS WATER COMING FROM?!
THE WATER MAIN EXPLODED!

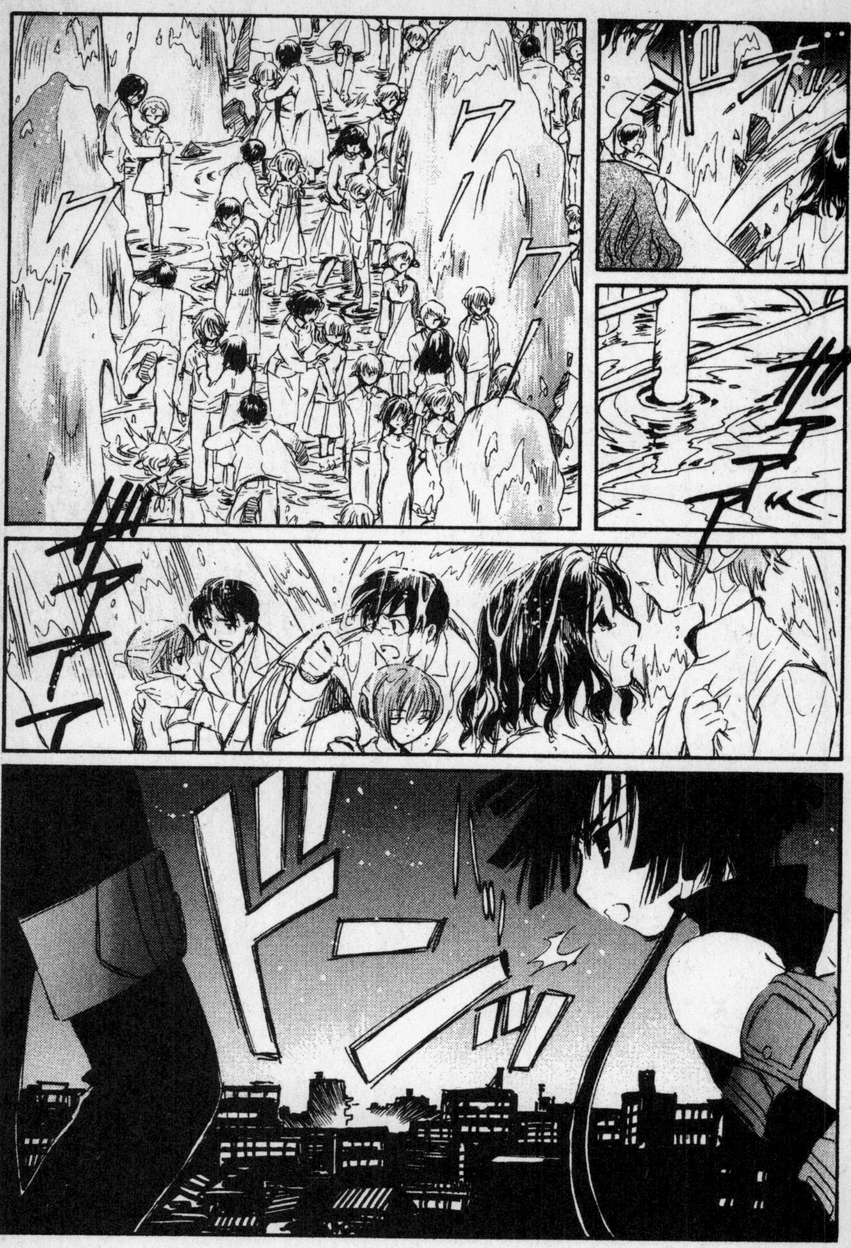
ドオッ
ザアアア

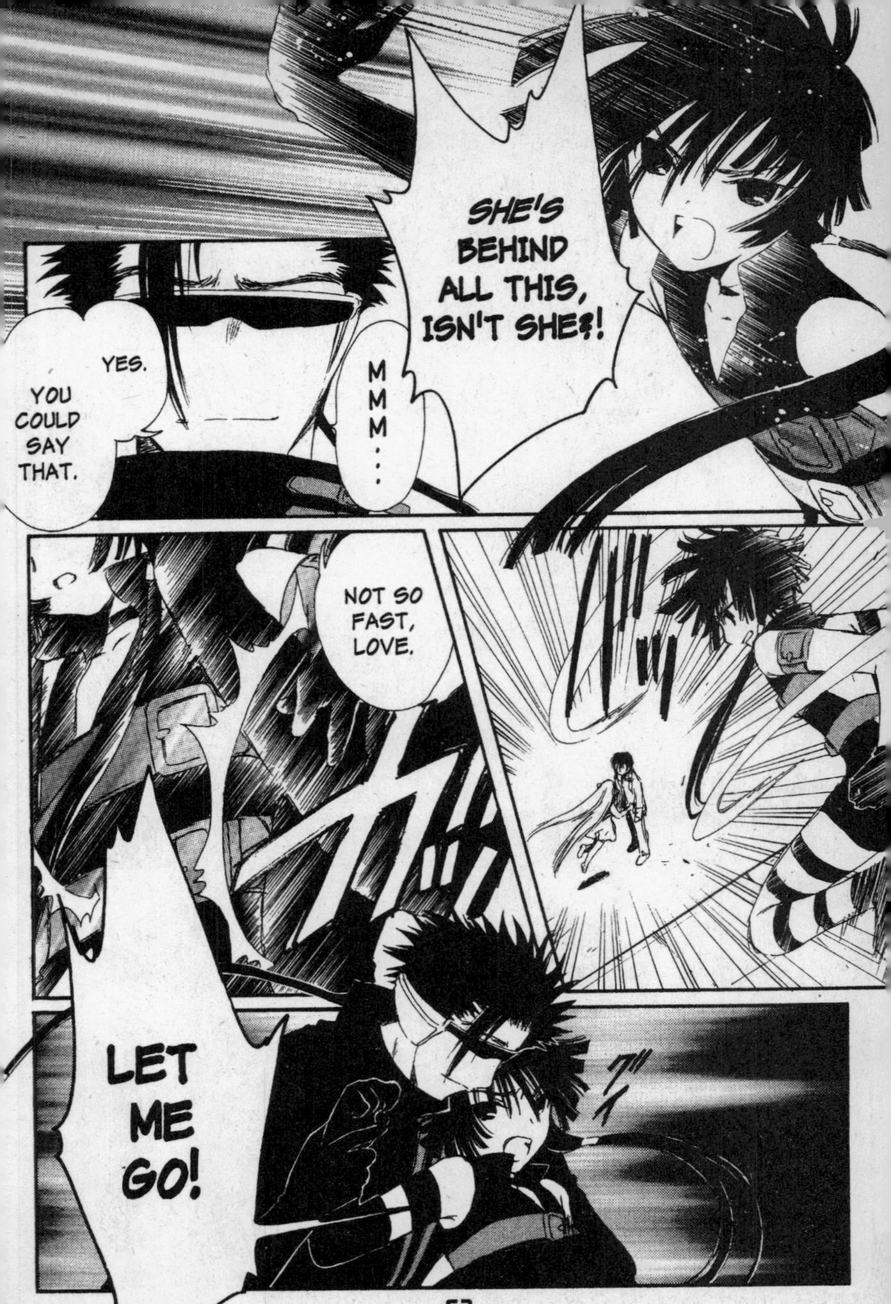
SHE'S BEHIND ALL THIS, ISN'T SHE?!
MMM...
YES. YOU COULD SAY THAT.
NOT SO FAST, LOVE.
LET ME GO!

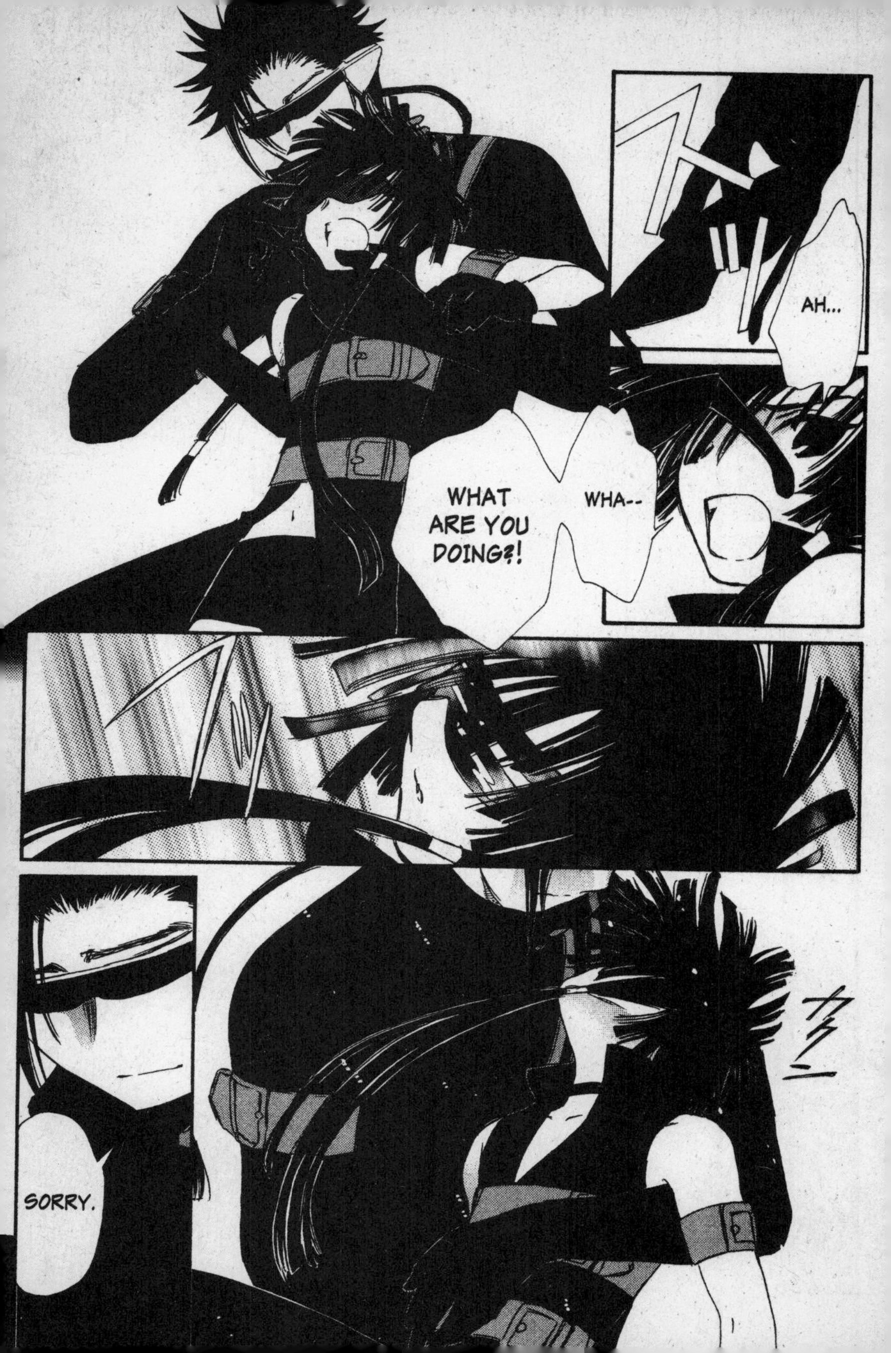
AH...
WHA--
WHAT ARE YOU DOING?!
SORRY.

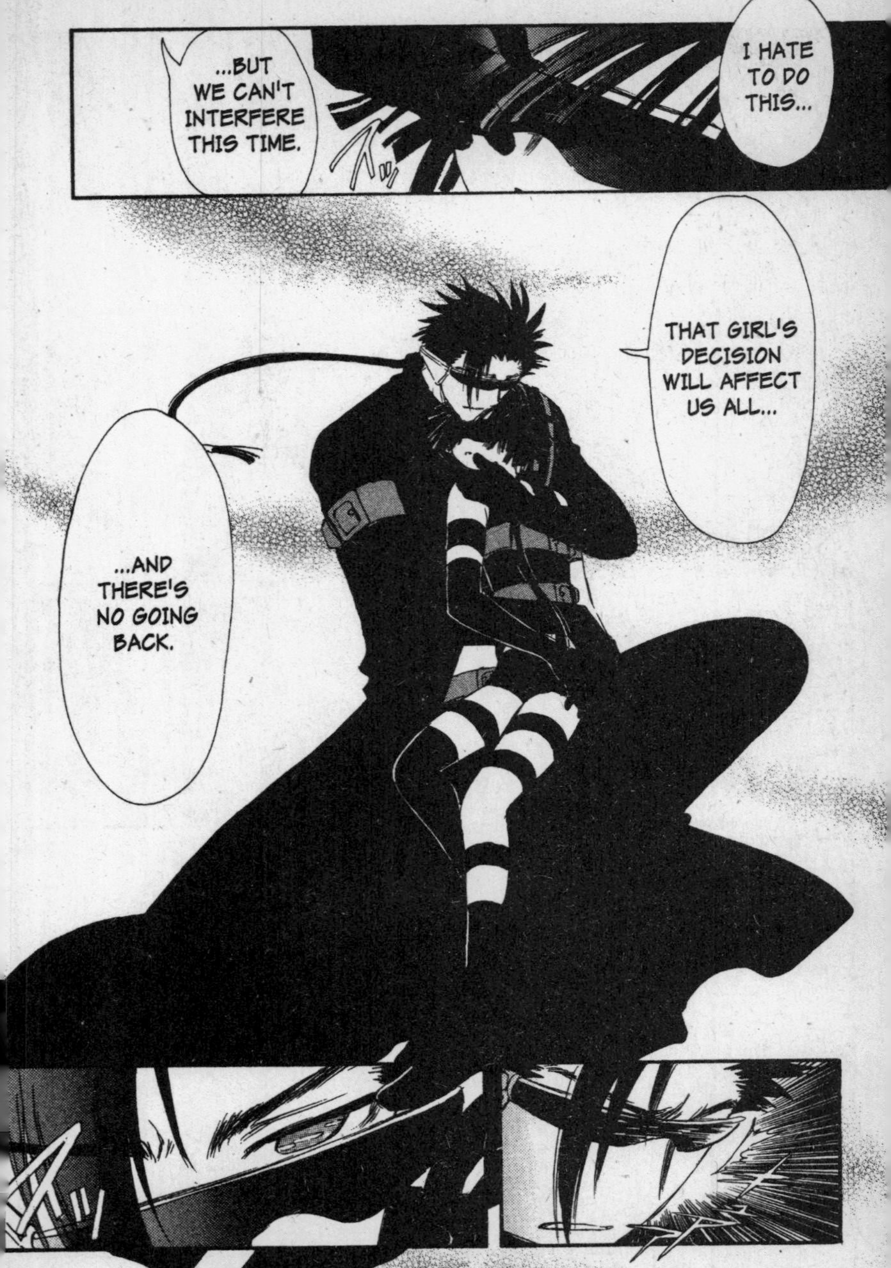
I HATE TO DO THIS...
...BUT WE CAN'T INTERFERE THIS TIME.
THAT GIRL'S DECISION WILL AFFECT US ALL...
...AND THERE'S NO GOING BACK.

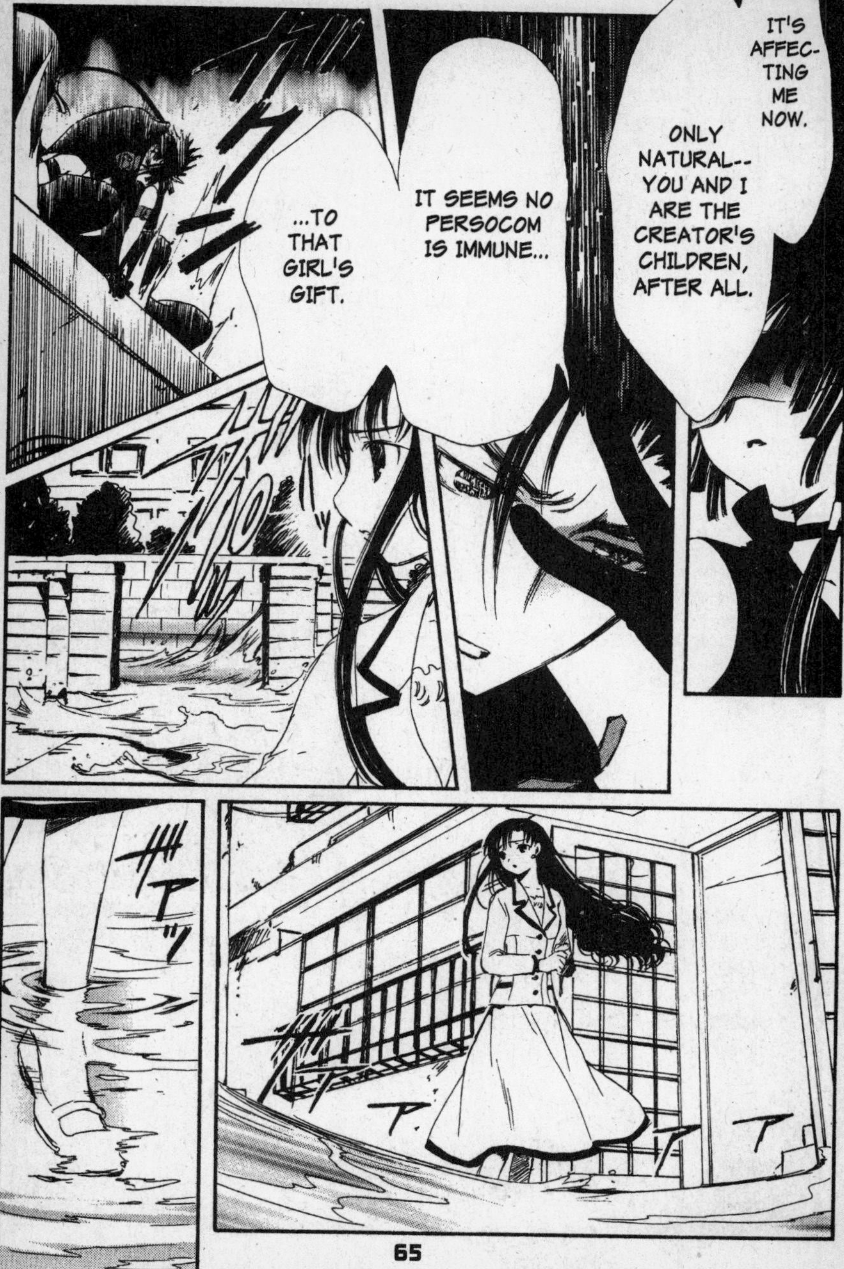
IT'S AFFECTING ME NOW.
ONLY NATURAL-- YOU AND I ARE THE CREATOR'S CHILDREN, AFTER ALL.
IT SEEMS NO PERSOCOM IS IMMUNE...
...TO THAT GIRL'S GIFT.

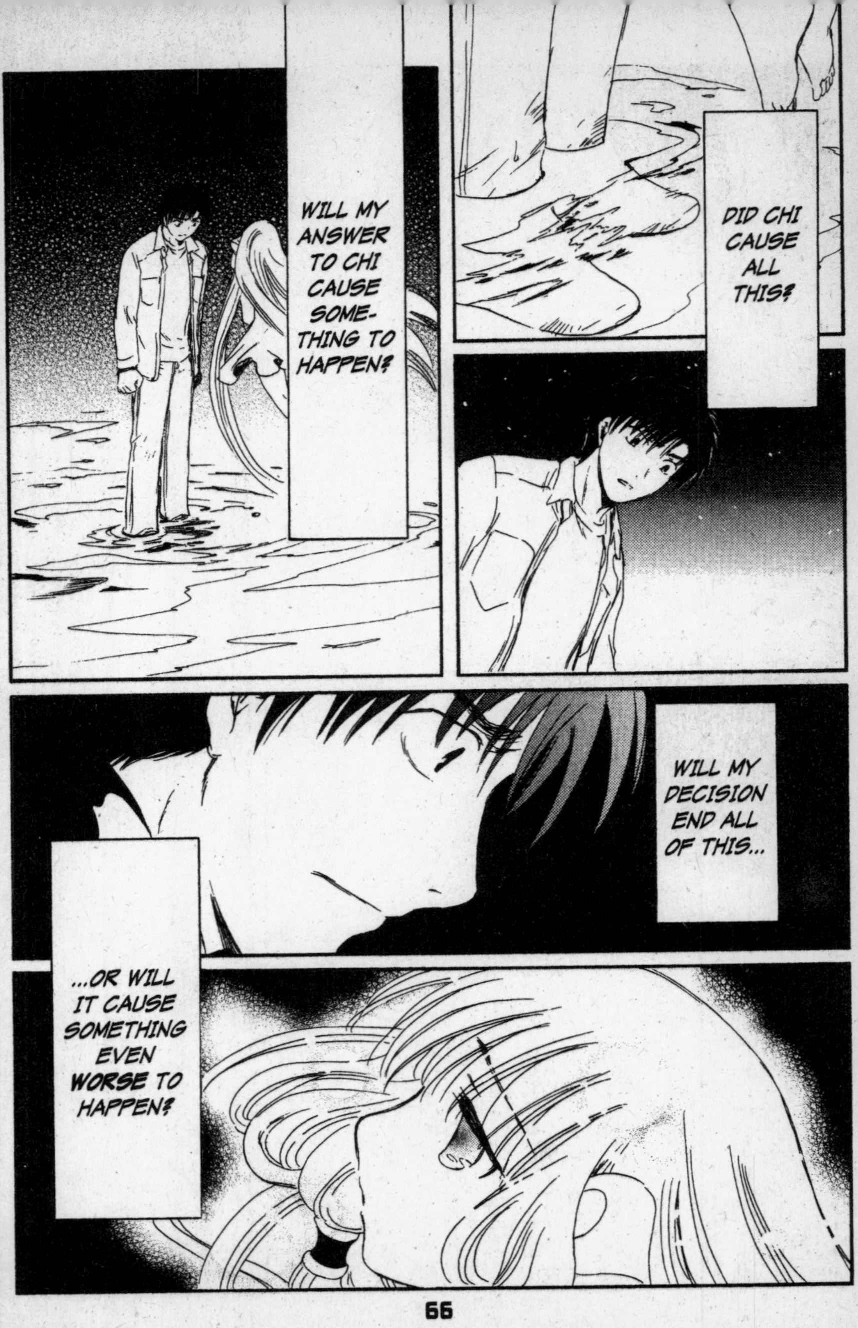
DID CHI CAUSE ALL THIS?
WILL MY ANSWER TO CHI CAUSE SOME-THING TO HAPPEN?
WILL MY DECISION END ALL OF THIS...
...OR WILL IT CAUSE SOMETHING EVEN WORSE TO HAPPEN?

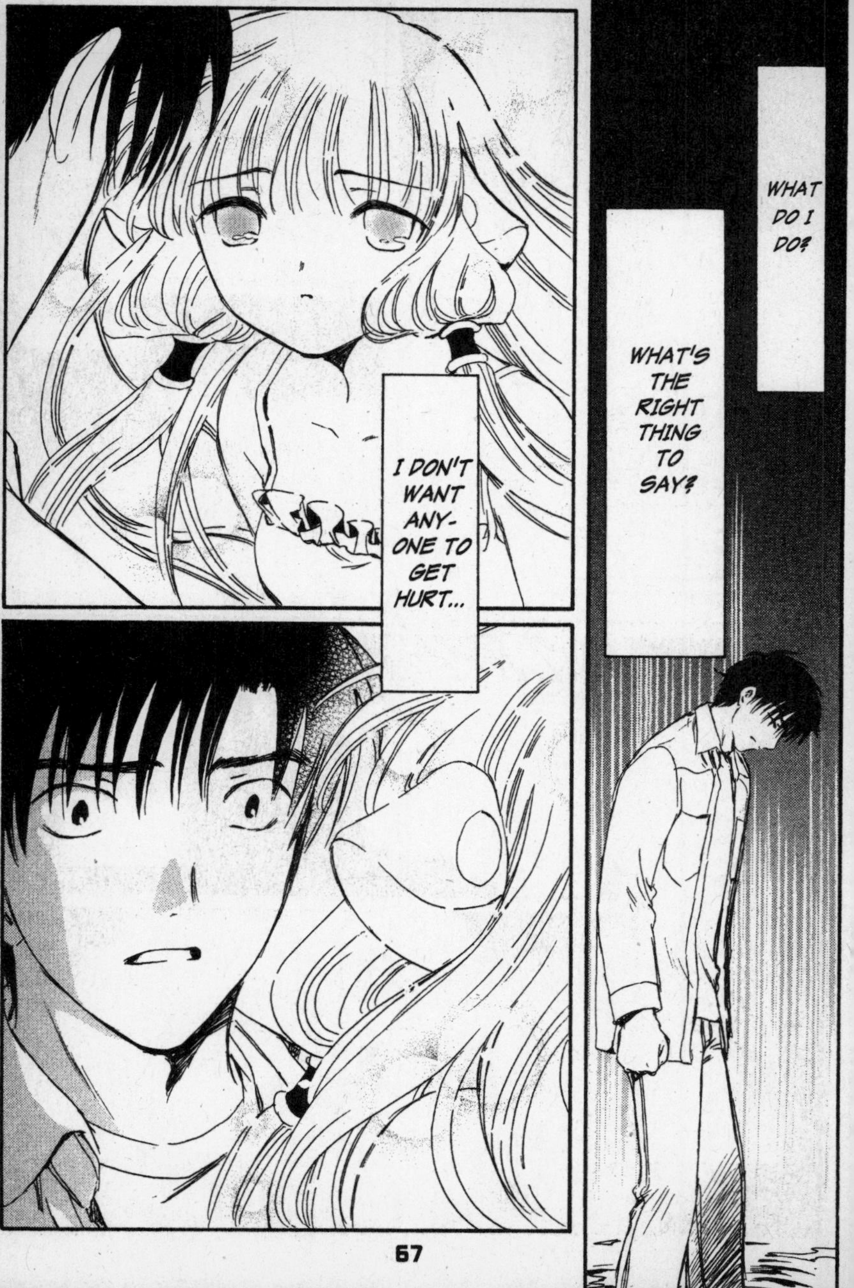
WHAT DO I DO?
WHAT'S THE RIGHT THING TO SAY?
I DON'T WANT ANY-ONE TO GET HURT...

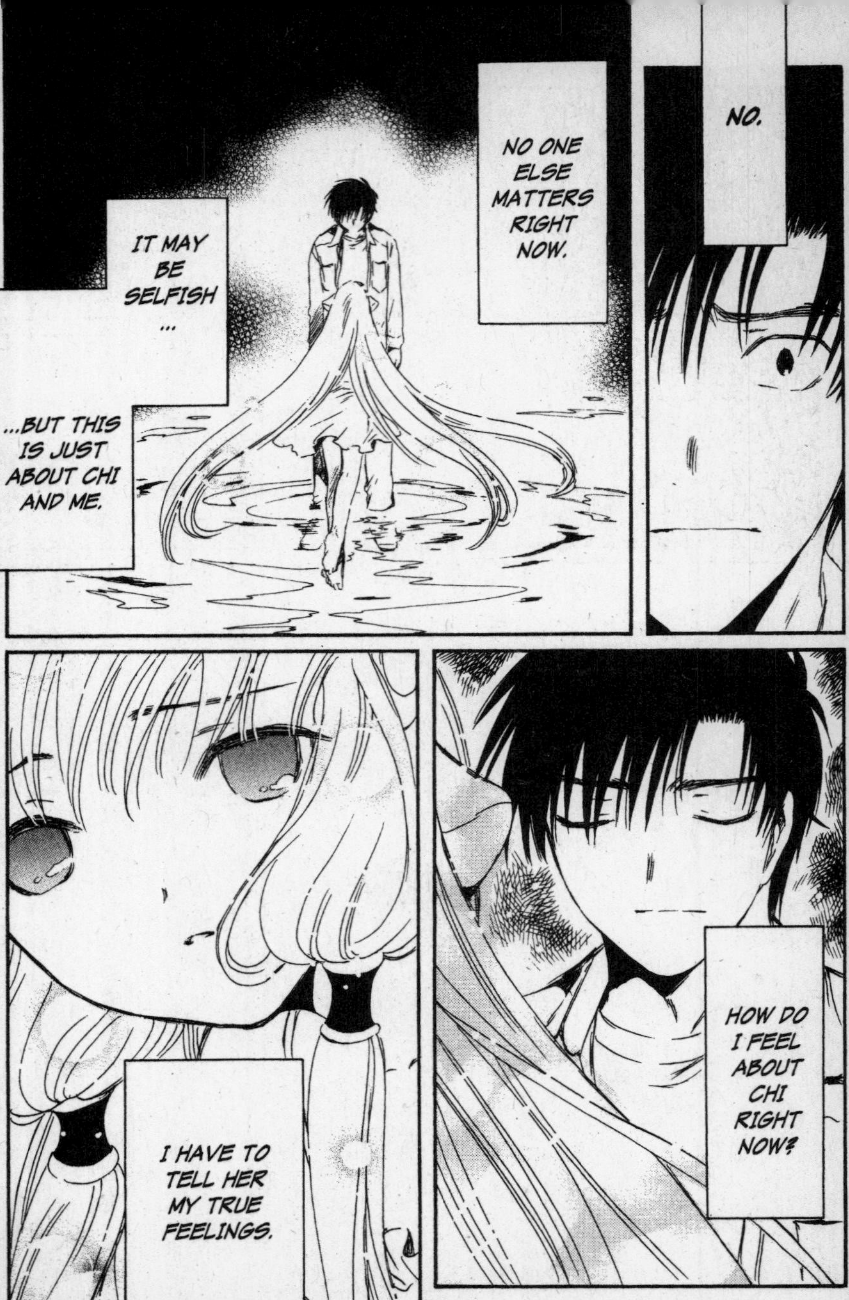
NO.
NO ONE ELSE MATTERS RIGHT NOW.
IT MAY BE SELFISH ...
...BUT THIS IS JUST ABOUT CHI AND ME.
HOW DO I FEEL ABOUT CHI RIGHT NOW?
I HAVE TO TELL HER MY TRUE FEELINGS.

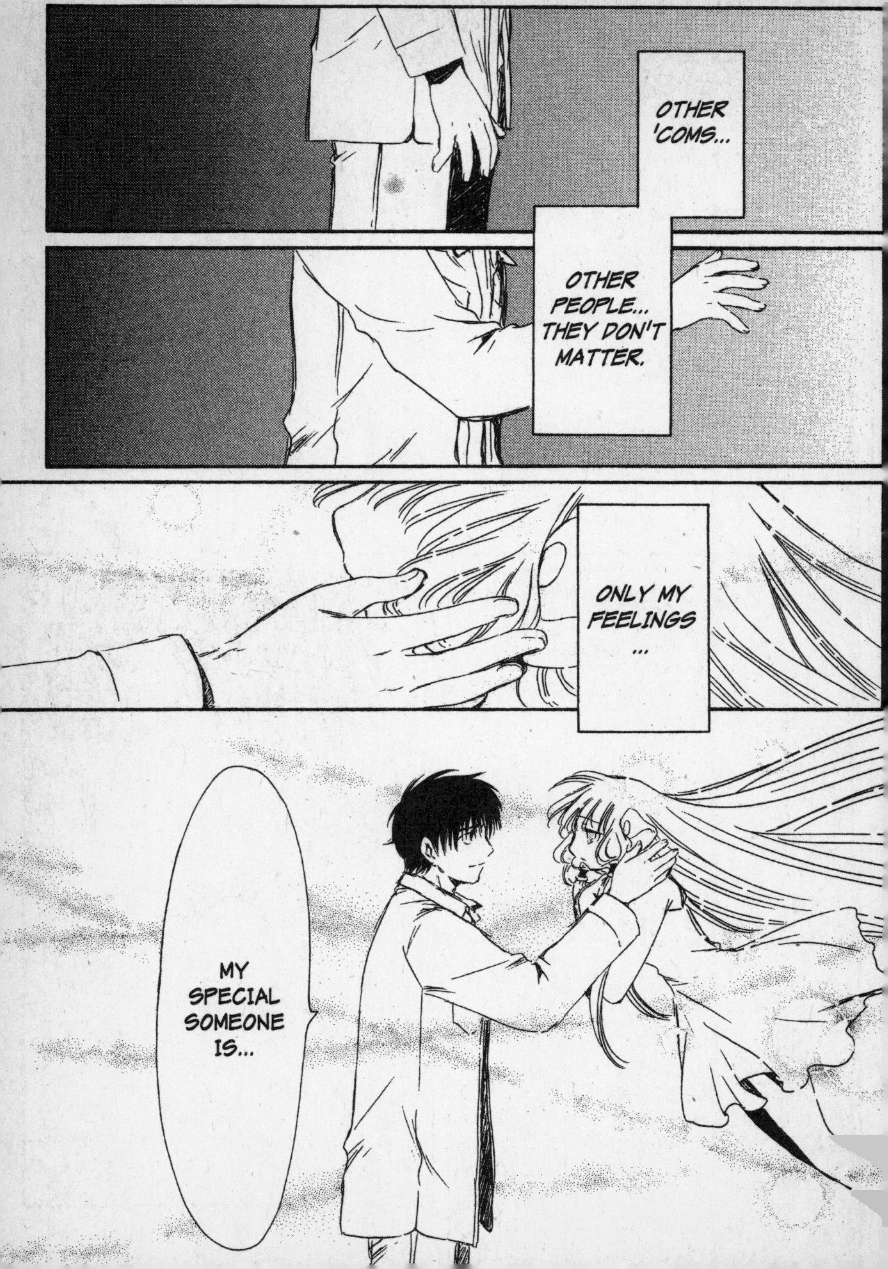
OTHER 'COMS...
OTHER PEOPLE... THEY DON'T MATTER.
ONLY MY FEELINGS ...
MY SPECIAL SOMEONE IS...

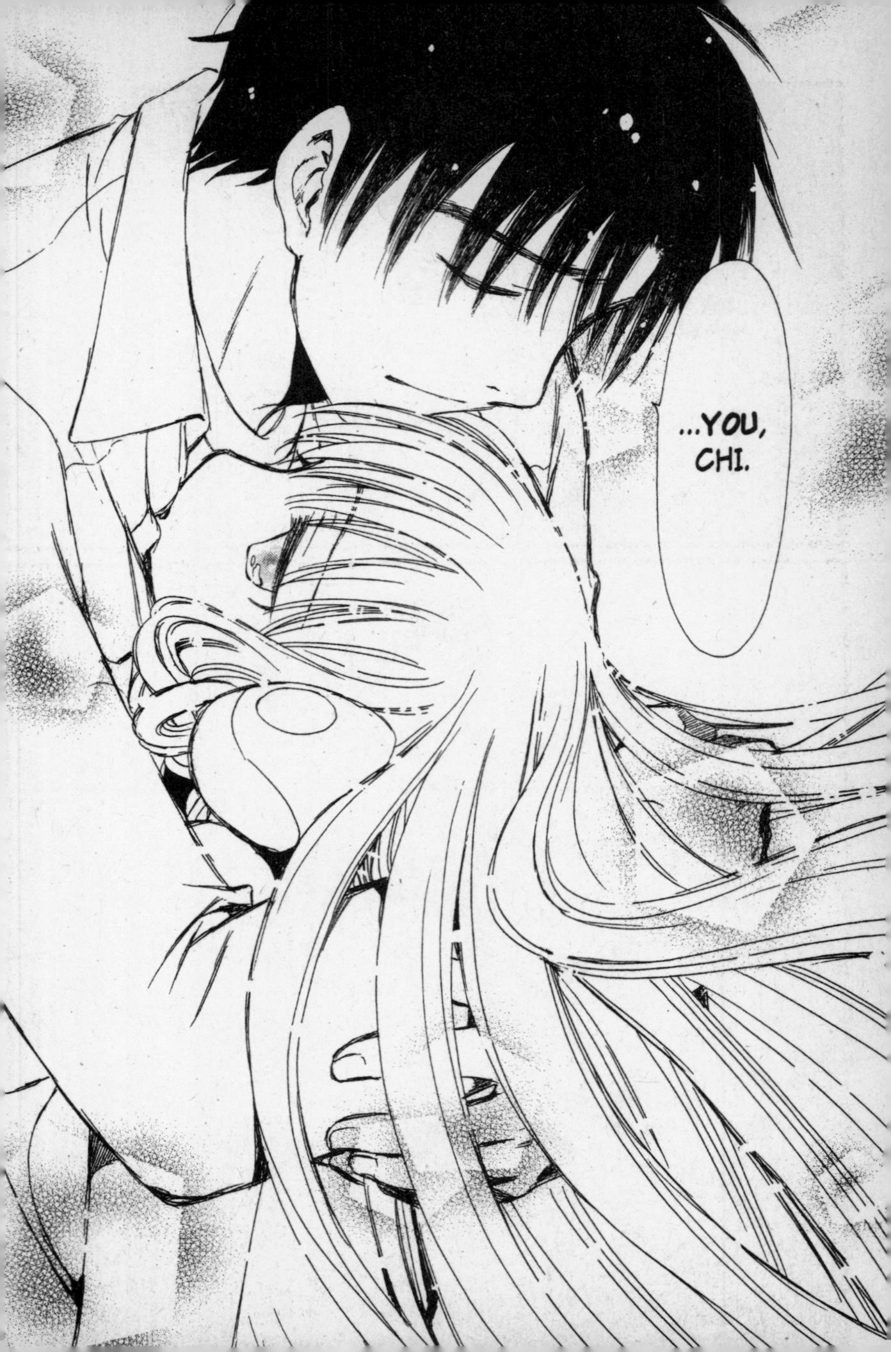
...YOU, CHI.

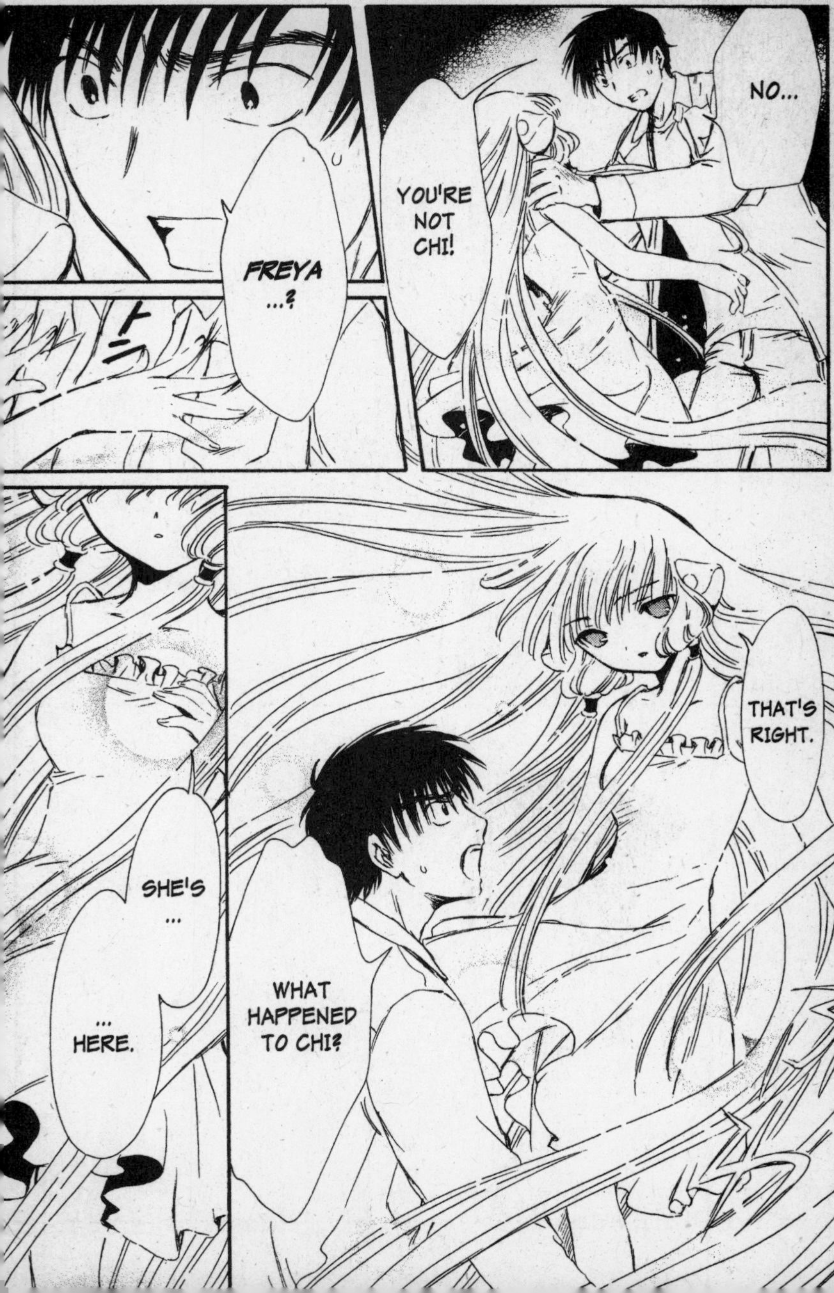
NO...
YOU'RE NOT CHI!
FREYA ...?
THAT'S RIGHT.
WHAT HAPPENED TO CHI?
SHE'S ...
... HERE.

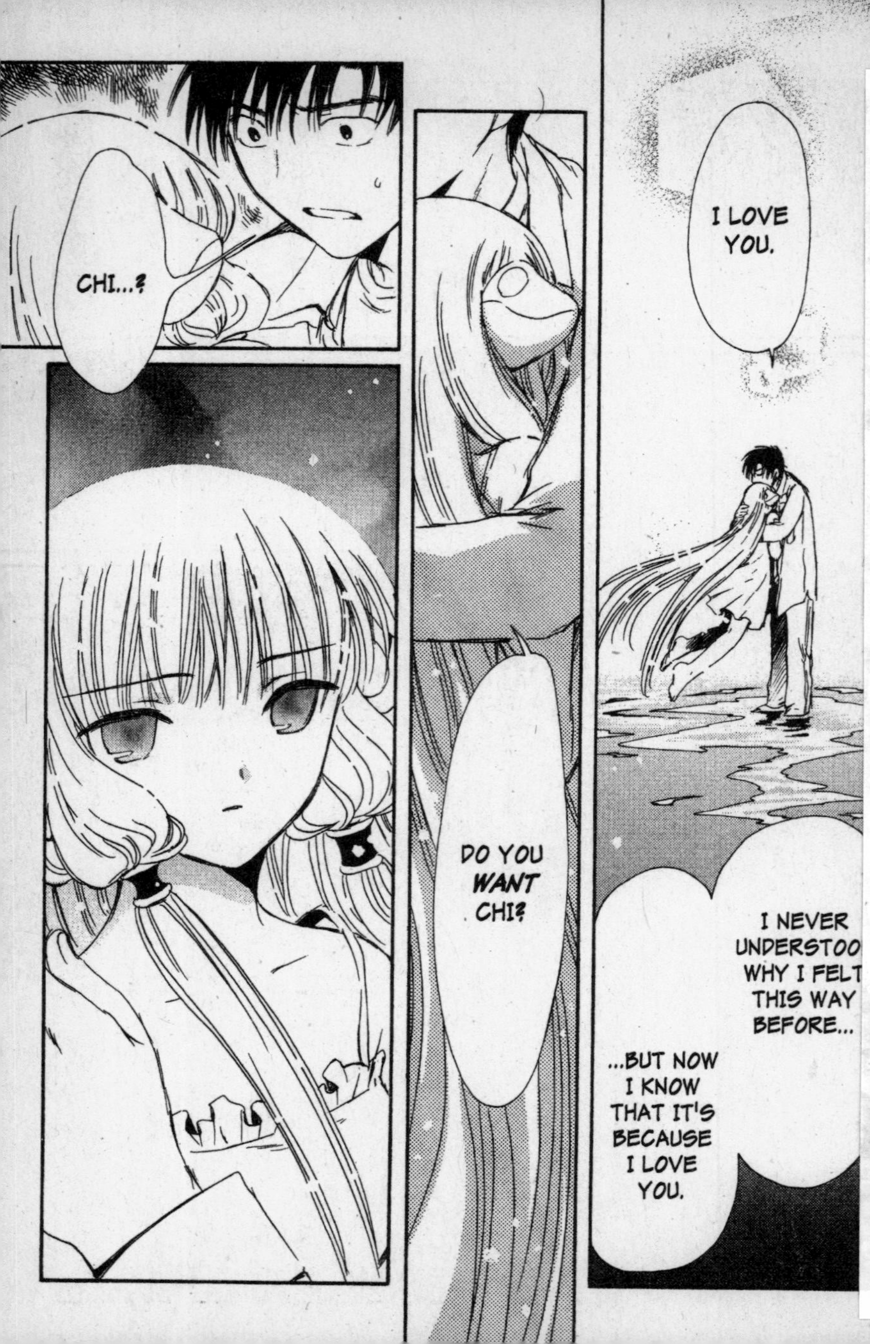
I LOVE YOU.
I NEVER UNDERSTOO WHY I FELT THIS WAY BEFORE...
...BUT NOW I KNOW THAT IT'S BECAUSE I LOVE YOU.
DO YOU *WANT* CHI?
CHI...?

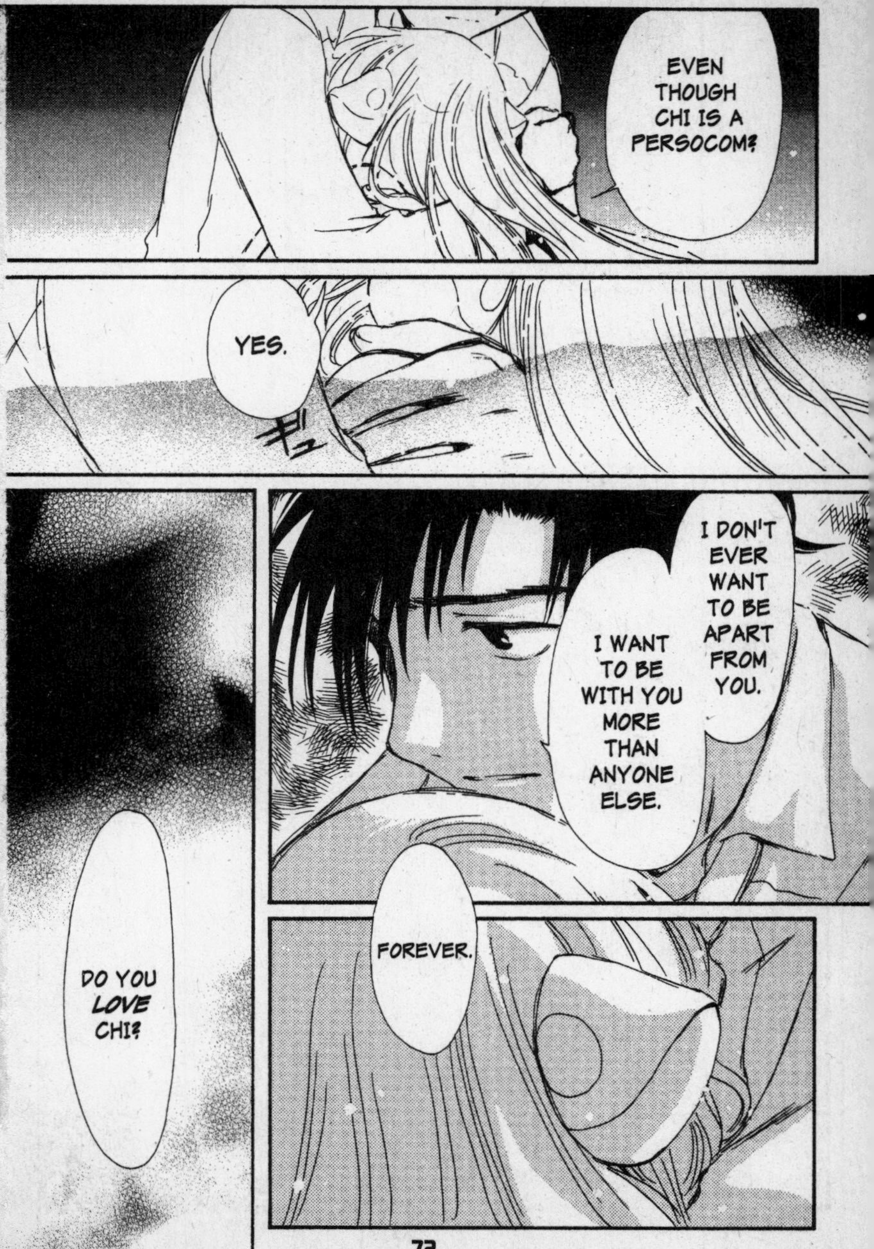
EVEN THOUGH CHI IS A PERSOCOM?
YES.
I DON'T EVER WANT TO BE APART FROM YOU.
I WANT TO BE WITH YOU MORE THAN ANYONE ELSE.
FOREVER.
DO YOU *LOVE* CHI?

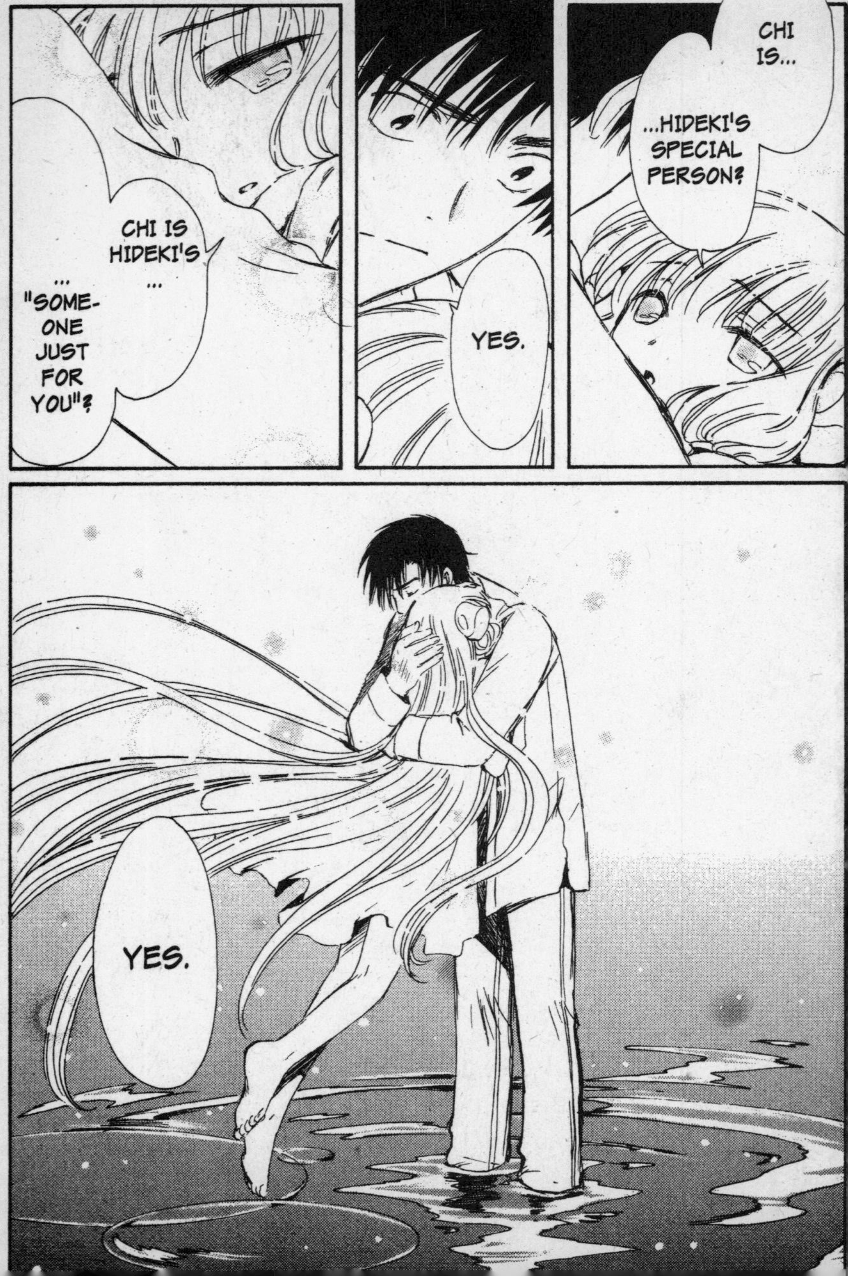
CHI IS... ...HIDEKI'S SPECIAL PERSON?
YES.
CHI IS HIDEKI'S ... ... "SOME-ONE JUST FOR YOU"?
YES.

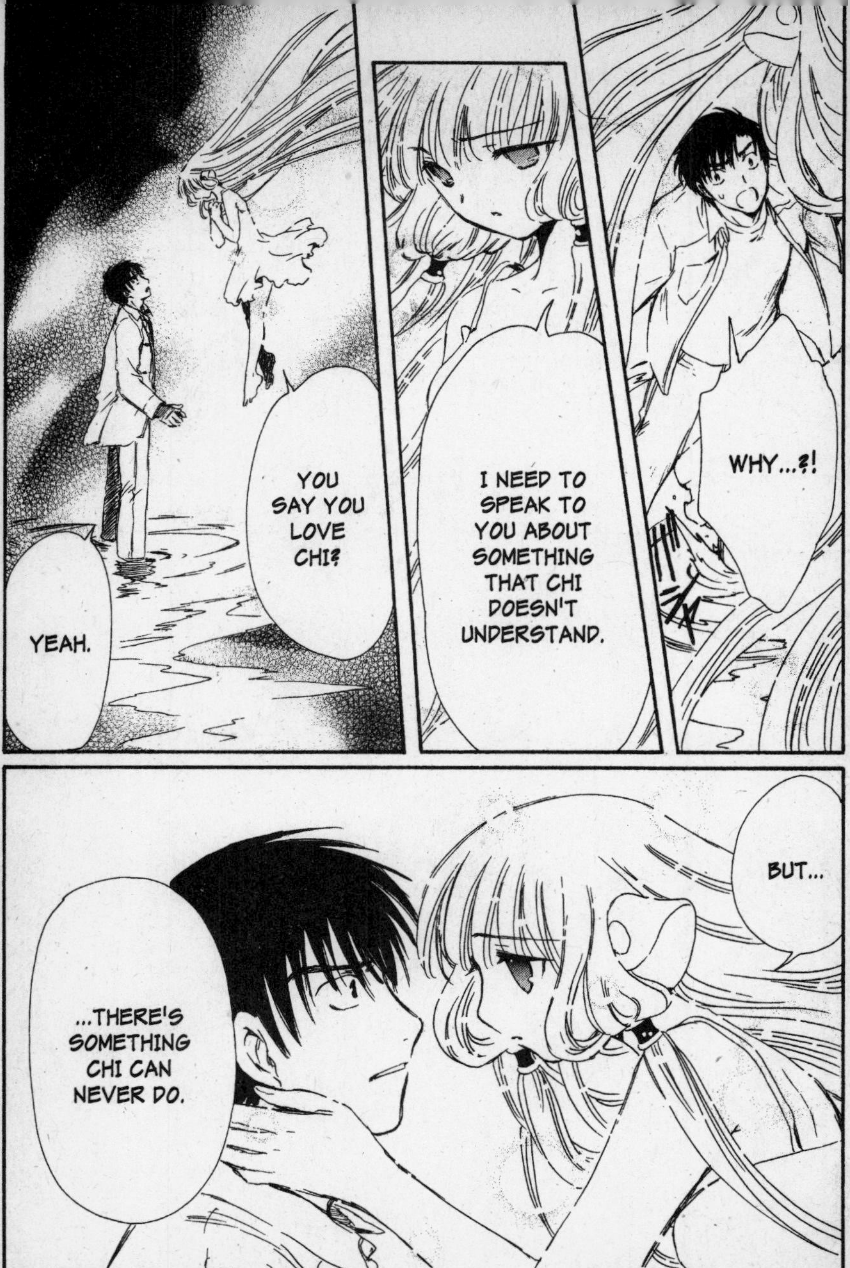
WHY...?!
I NEED TO SPEAK TO YOU ABOUT SOMETHING THAT CHI DOESN'T UNDERSTAND.
YOU SAY YOU LOVE CHI?
YEAH.
BUT...
...THERE'S SOMETHING CHI CAN NEVER DO.

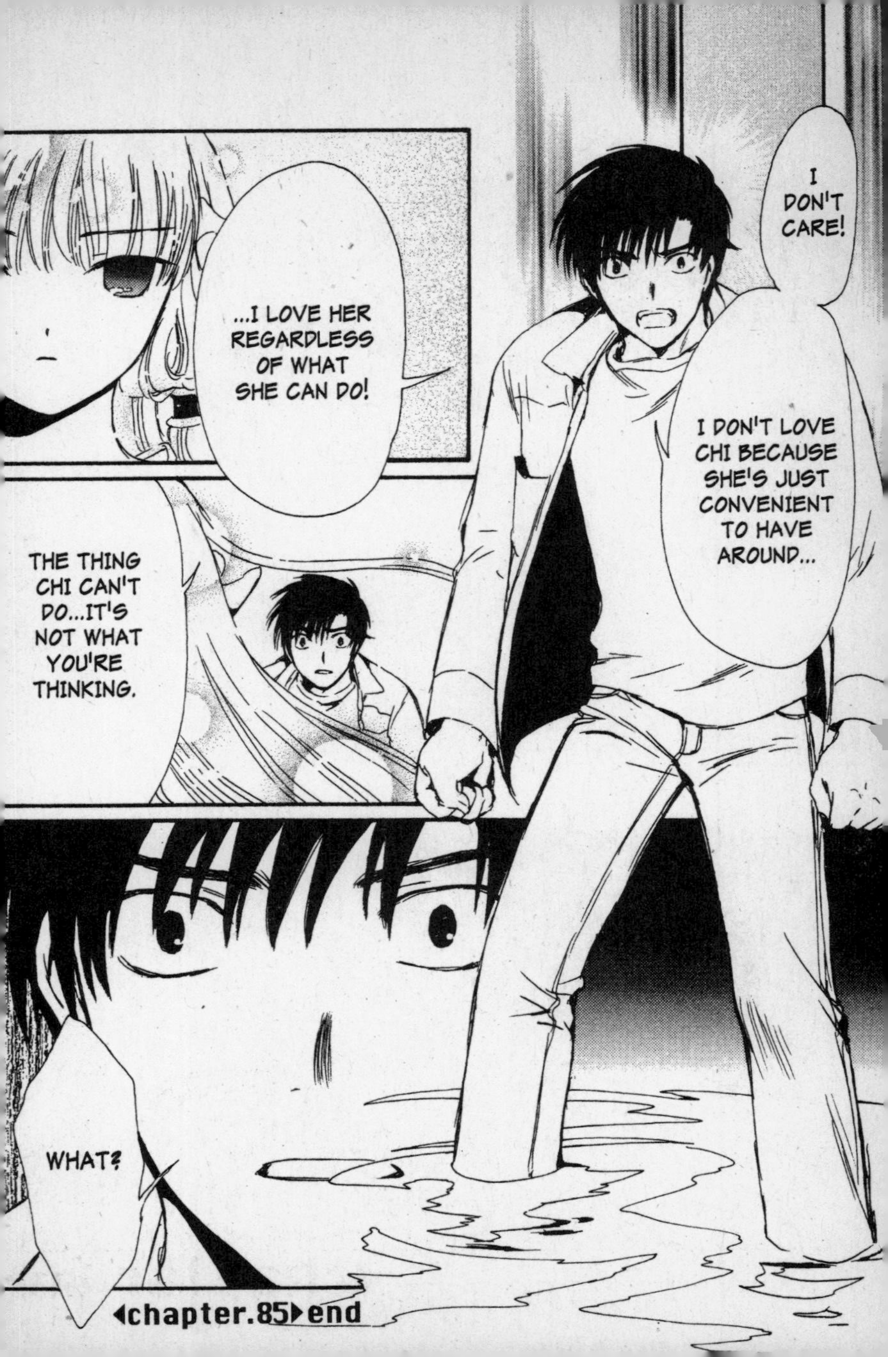
I DON'T CARE!
I DON'T LOVE CHI BECAUSE SHE'S JUST CONVENIENT TO HAVE AROUND...
...I LOVE HER REGARDLESS OF WHAT SHE CAN DO!
THE THING CHI CAN'T DO...IT'S NOT WHAT YOU'RE THINKING.
WHAT?
◂chapter.85▸ end

ちょびっツ
Chobits

◀chapter.86▶

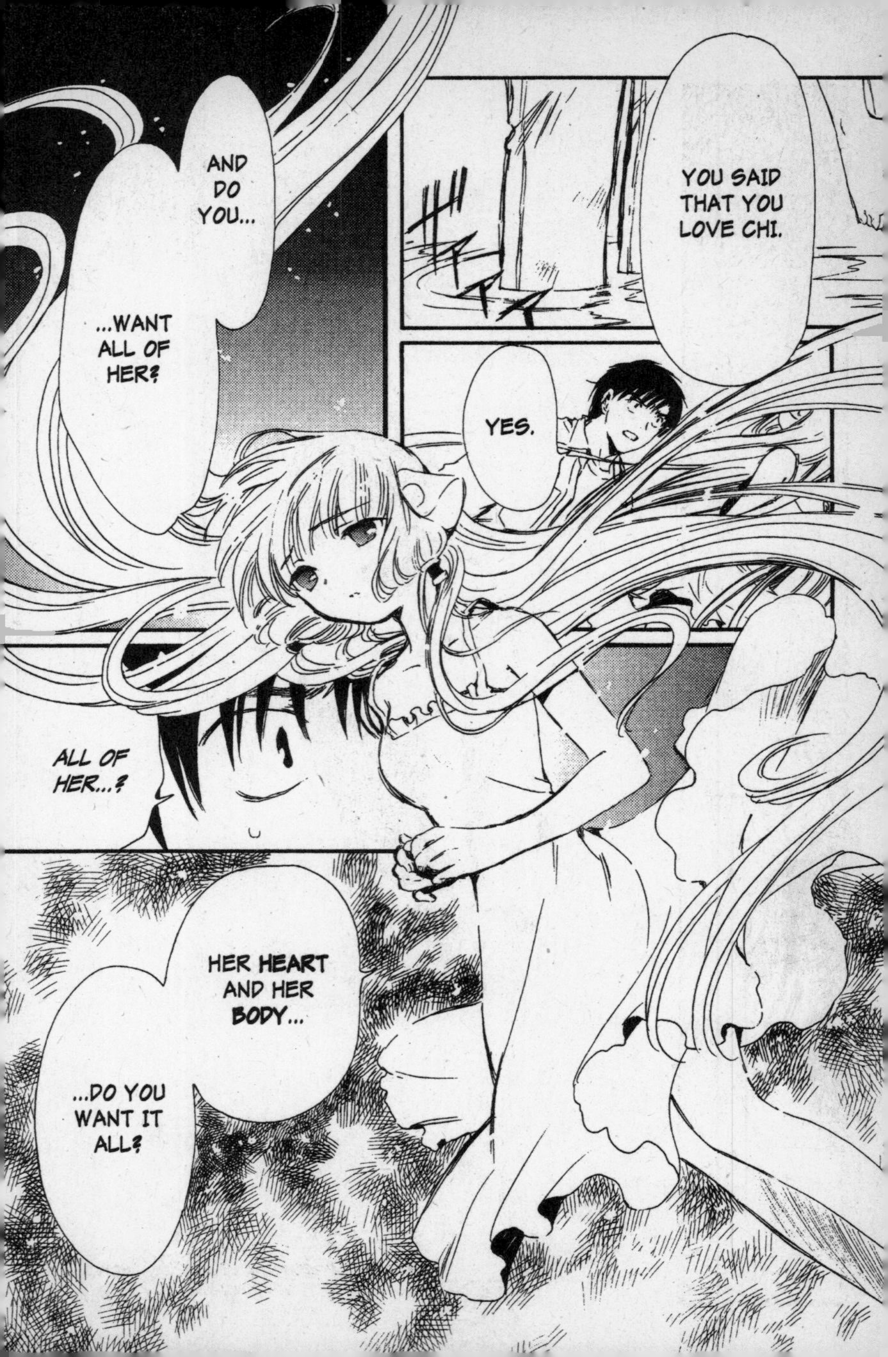
YOU SAID THAT YOU LOVE CHI.
YES.
AND DO YOU...
...WANT ALL OF HER?
ALL OF HER...?
HER HEART AND HER BODY...
...DO YOU WANT IT ALL?

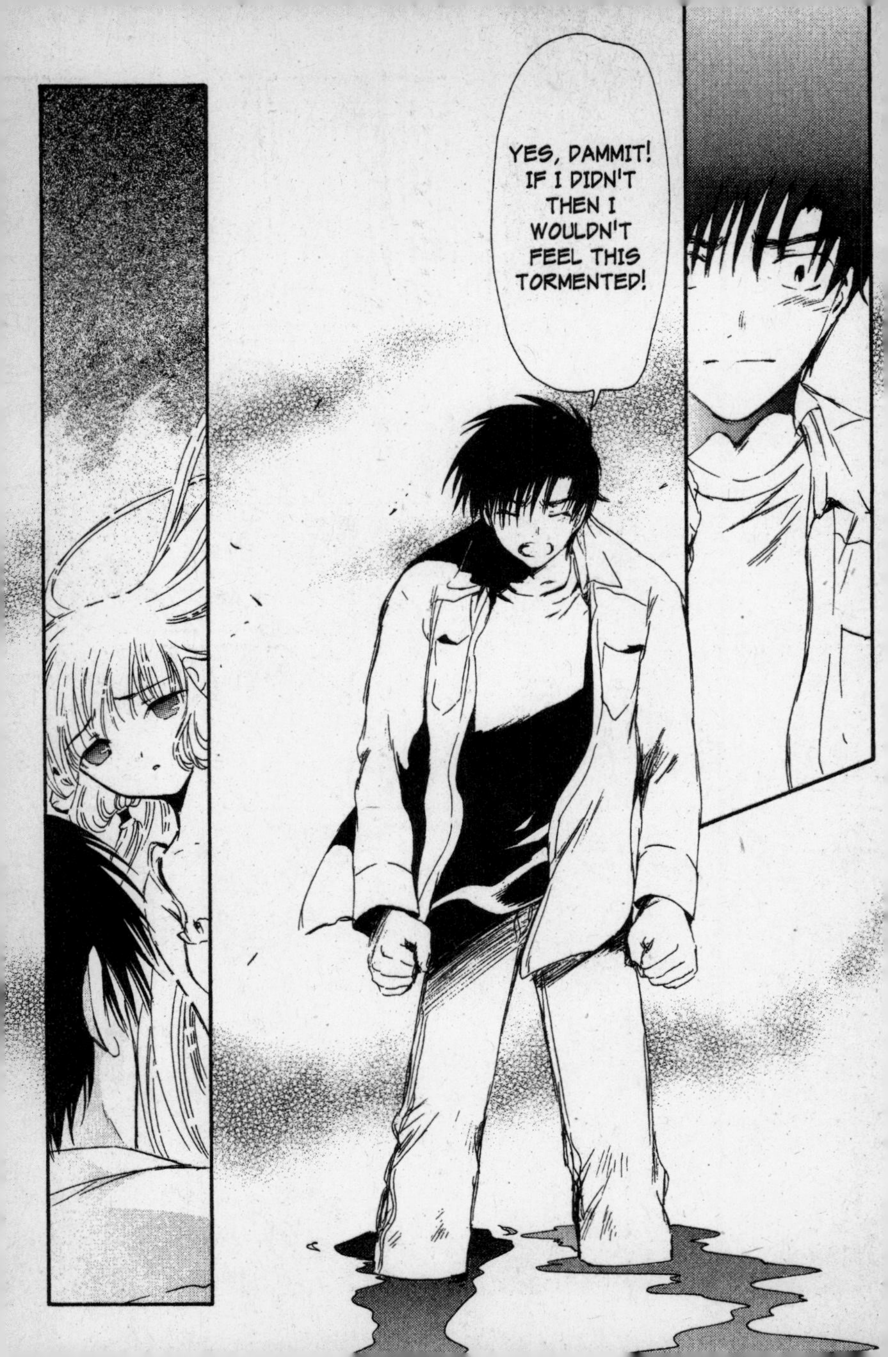
YES, DAMMIT! IF I DIDN'T THEN I WOULDN'T FEEL THIS TORMENTED!

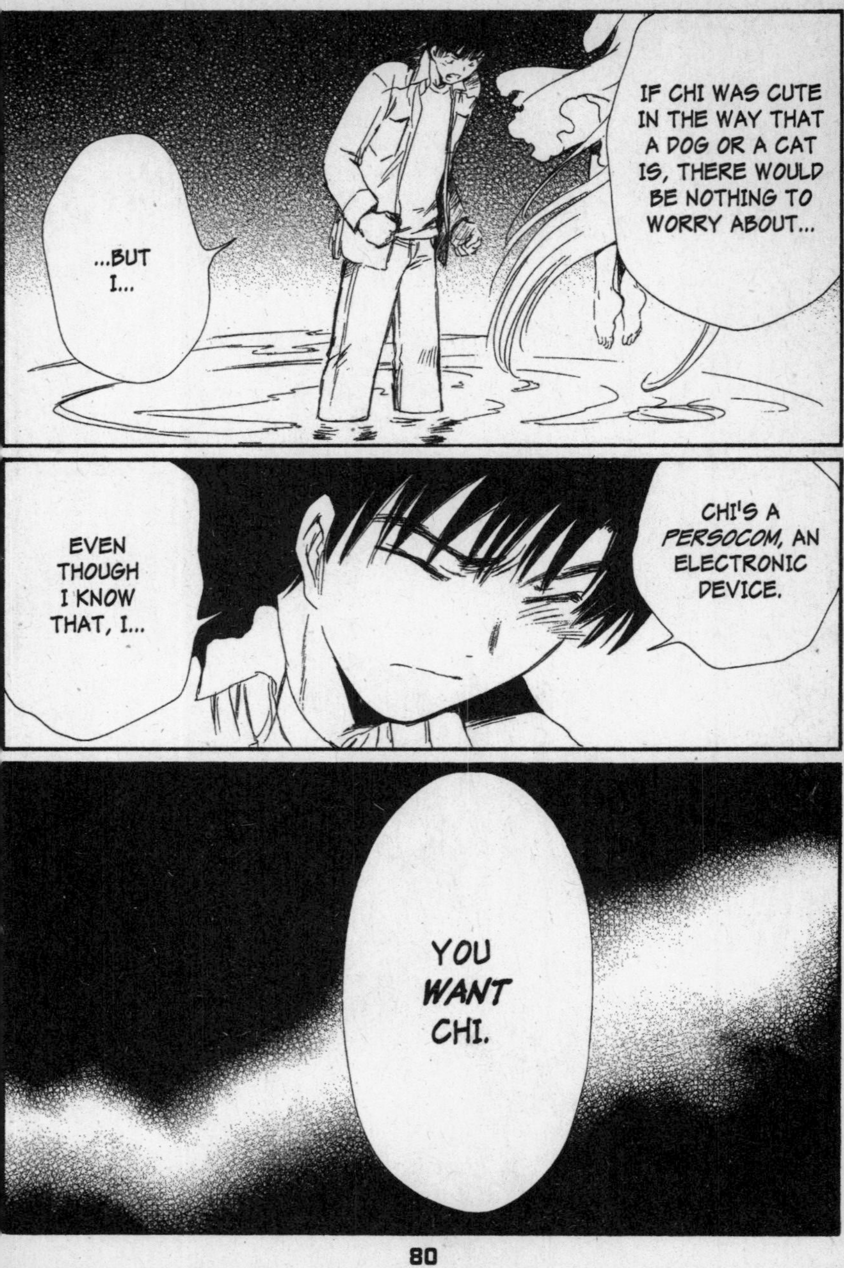
IF CHI WAS CUTE IN THE WAY THAT A DOG OR A CAT IS, THERE WOULD BE NOTHING TO WORRY ABOUT...
...BUT I...
CHI'S A *PERSOCOM*, AN ELECTRONIC DEVICE.
EVEN THOUGH I KNOW THAT, I...
YOU *WANT* CHI.

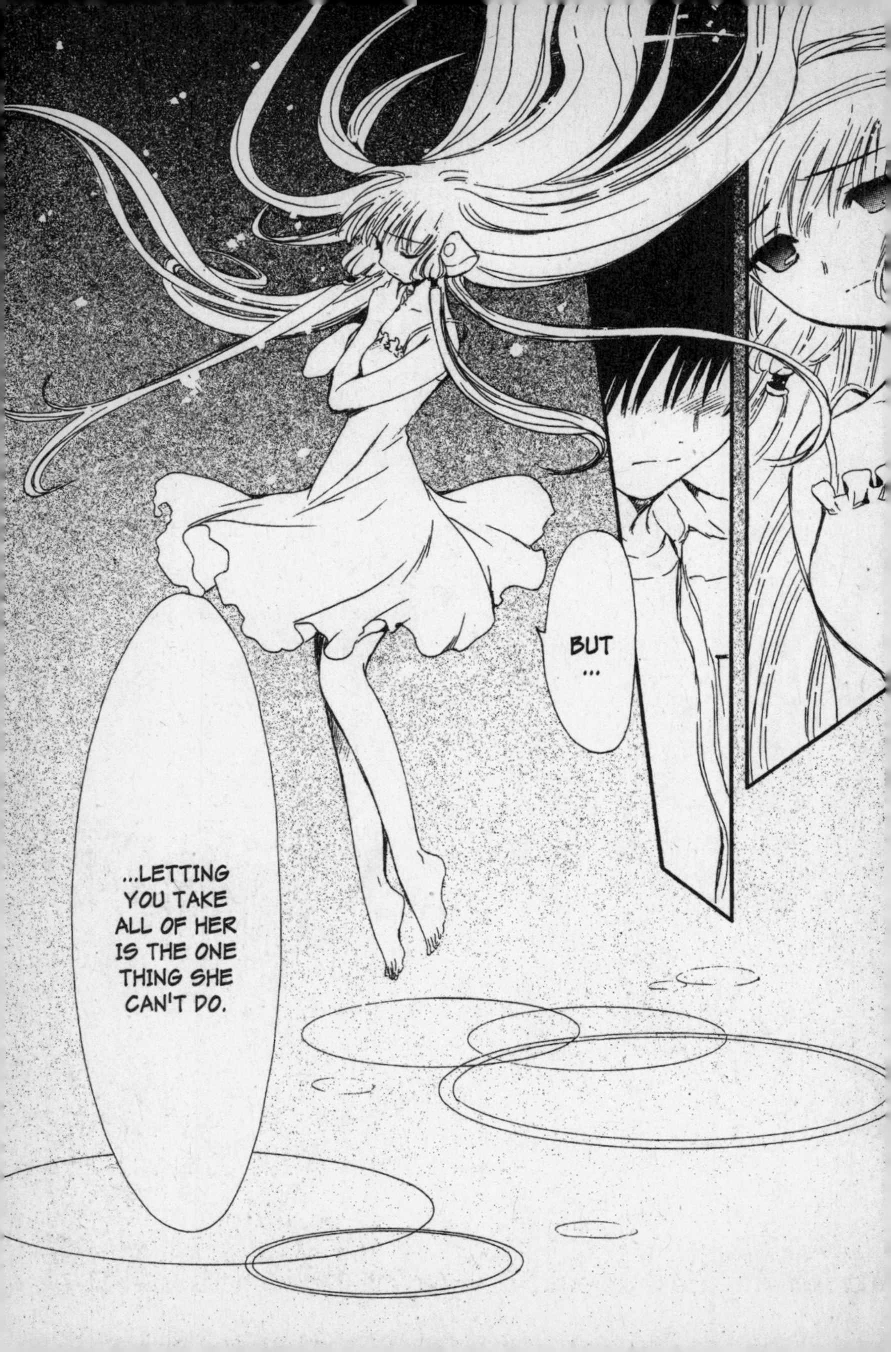
BUT ...
...LETTING YOU TAKE ALL OF HER IS THE ONE THING SHE CAN'T DO.

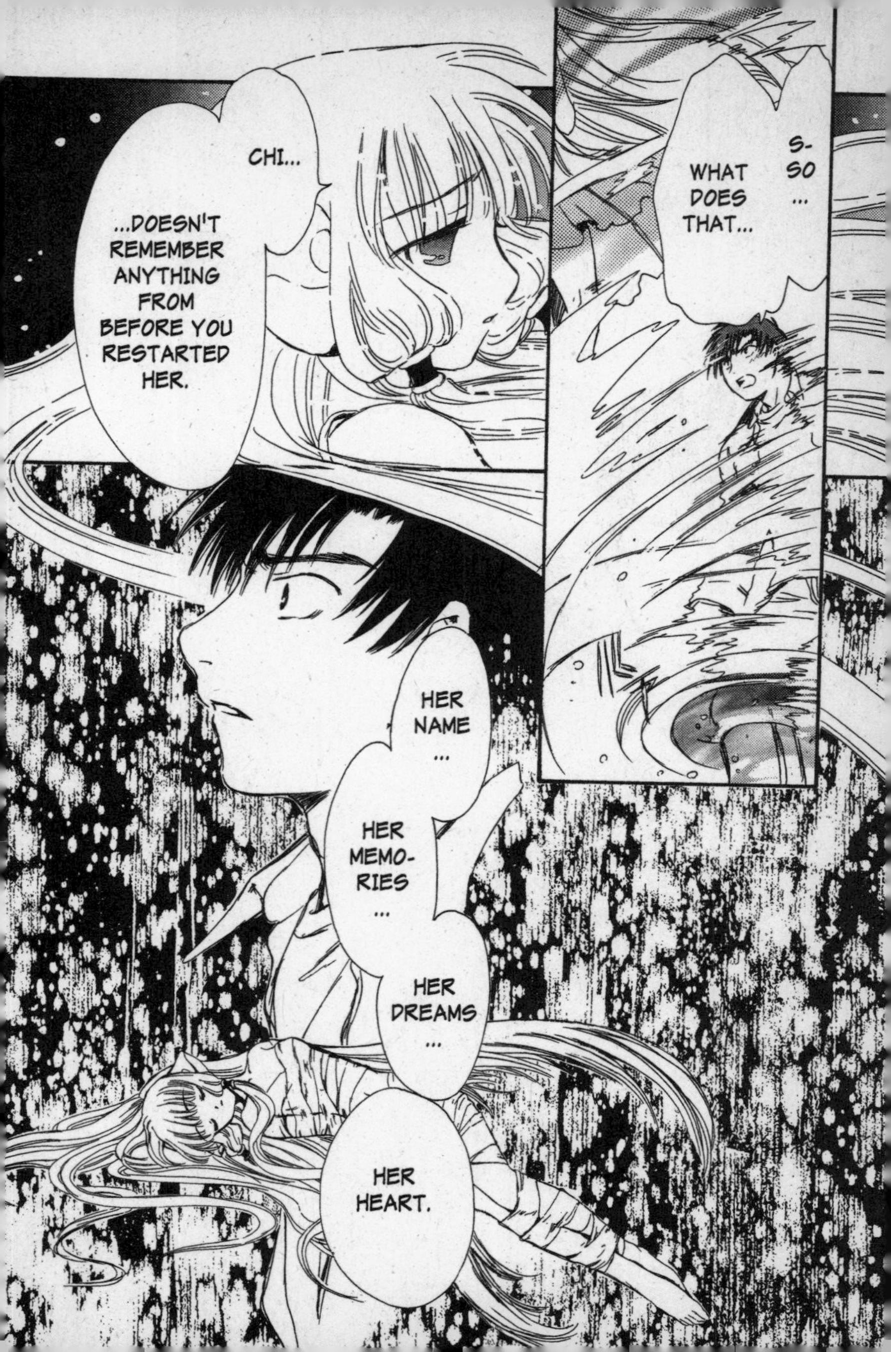
S-SO...
WHAT DOES THAT...
CHI...
...DOESN'T REMEMBER ANYTHING FROM BEFORE YOU RESTARTED HER.
HER NAME...
HER MEMORIES...
HER DREAMS...
HER HEART.

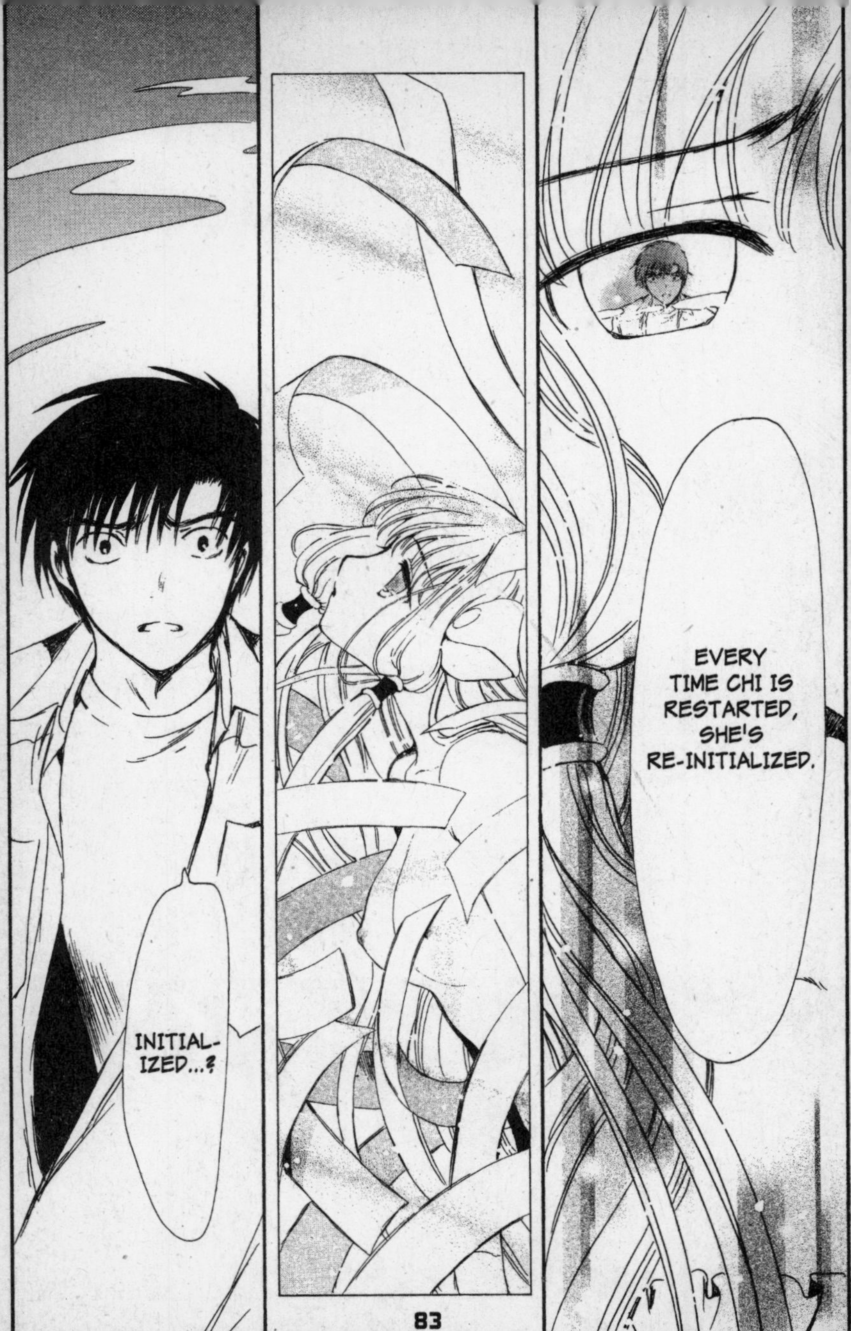
EVERY TIME CHI IS RESTARTED, SHE'S RE-INITIALIZED.
INITIAL-IZED...?

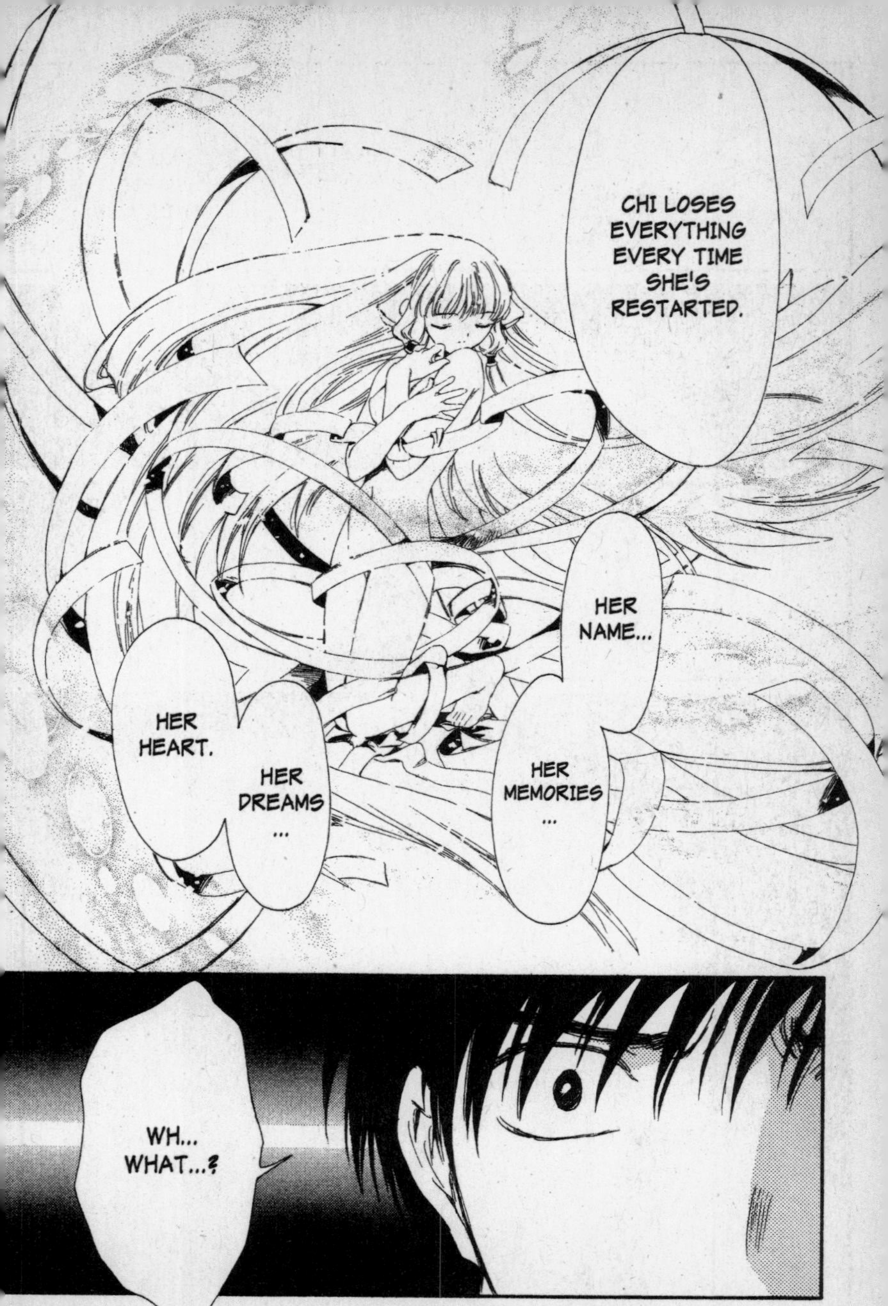
CHI LOSES EVERYTHING EVERY TIME SHE'S RESTARTED.
HER NAME...
HER MEMORIES...
HER DREAMS...
HER HEART.
WH... WHAT...?

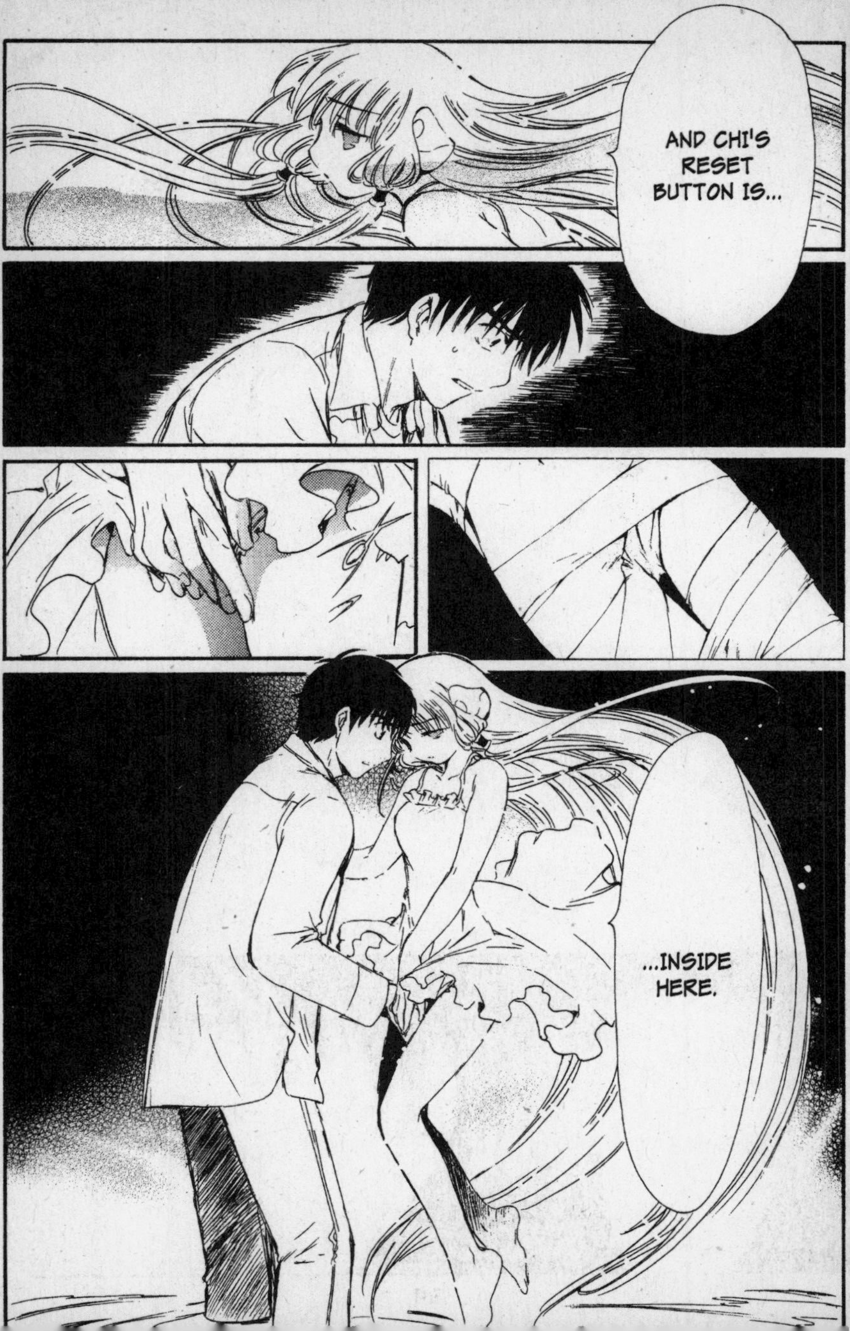

AND CHI'S RESET BUTTON IS...
...INSIDE HERE.

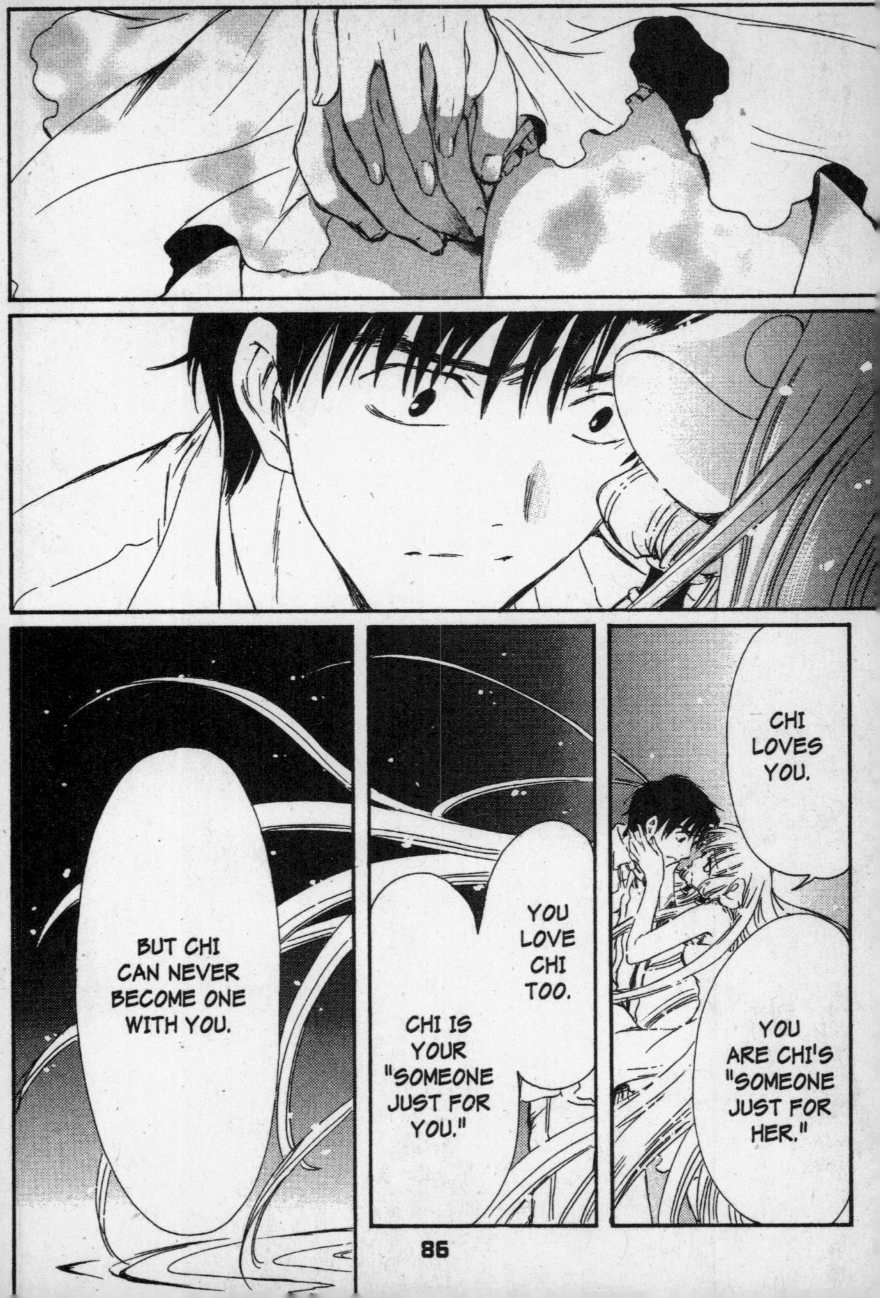
CHI LOVES YOU.
YOU ARE CHI'S "SOMEONE JUST FOR HER."
YOU LOVE CHI TOO.
CHI IS YOUR "SOMEONE JUST FOR YOU."
BUT CHI CAN NEVER BECOME ONE WITH YOU.

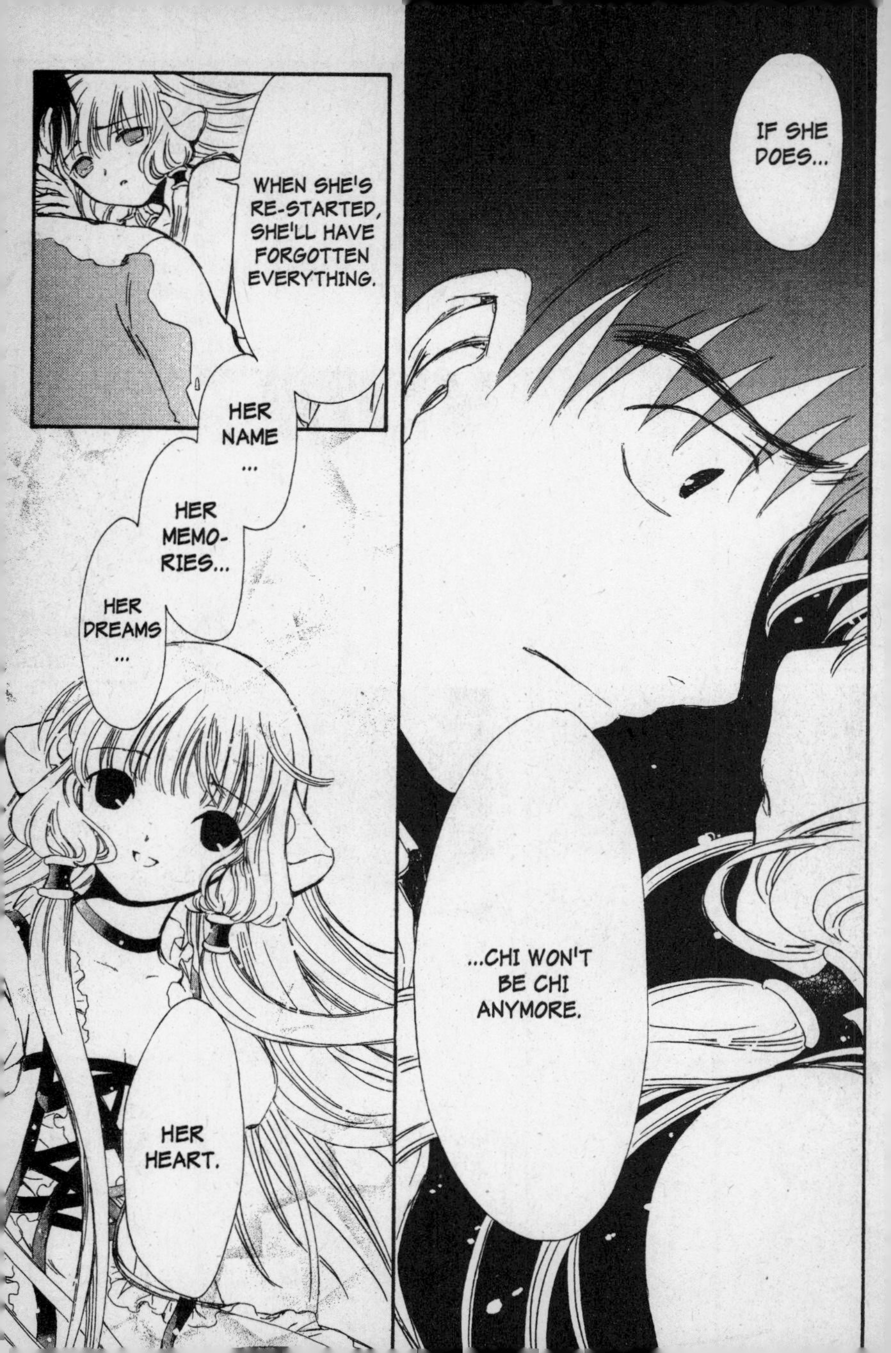
WHEN SHE'S RE-STARTED, SHE'LL HAVE FORGOTTEN EVERYTHING.
HER NAME ...
HER MEMORIES...
HER DREAMS ...
HER HEART.
IF SHE DOES...
...CHI WON'T BE CHI ANYMORE.

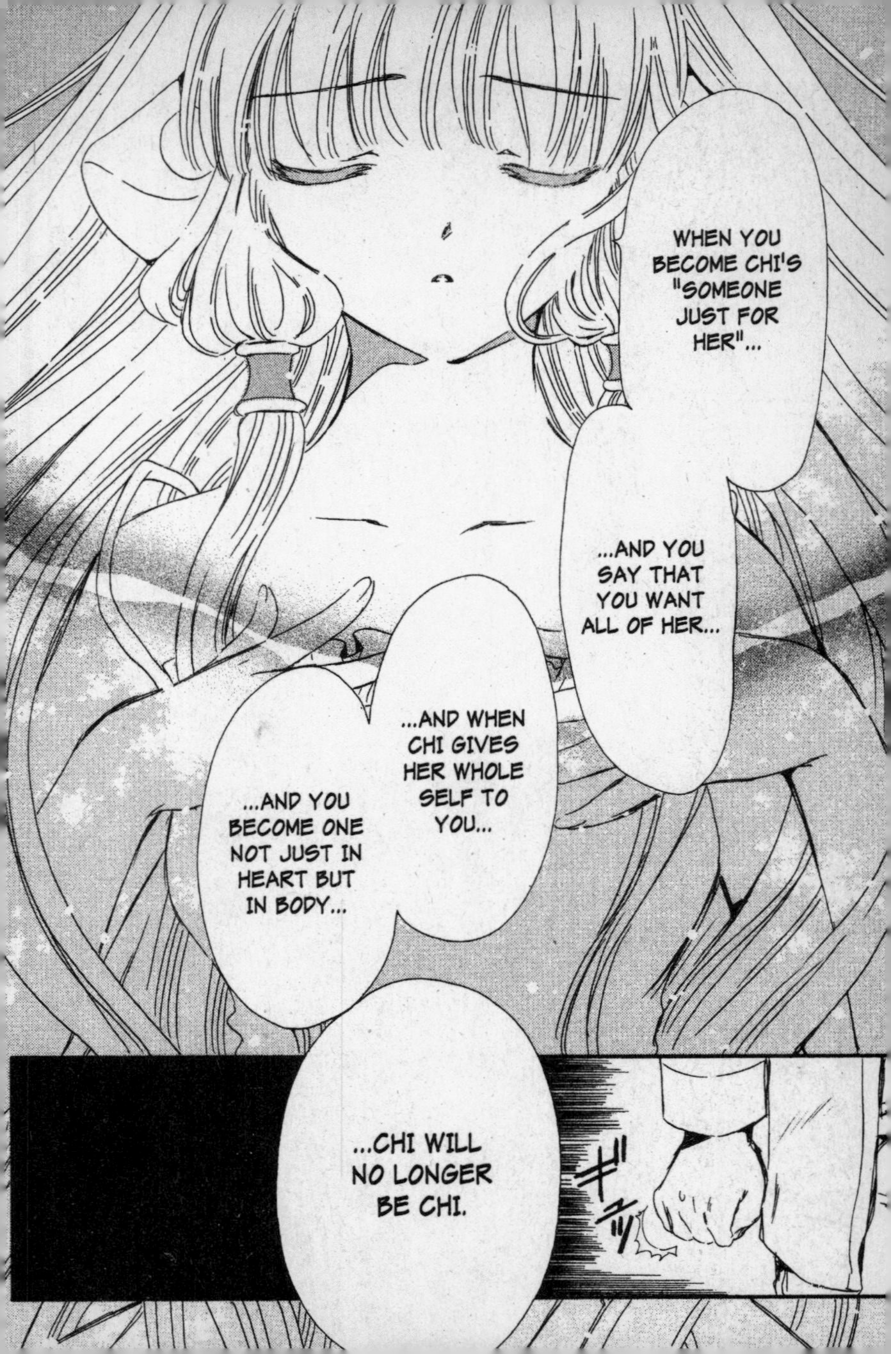
WHEN YOU BECOME CHI'S "SOMEONE JUST FOR HER"...
...AND YOU SAY THAT YOU WANT ALL OF HER...
...AND WHEN CHI GIVES HER WHOLE SELF TO YOU...
...AND YOU BECOME ONE NOT JUST IN HEART BUT IN BODY...
...CHI WILL NO LONGER BE CHI.

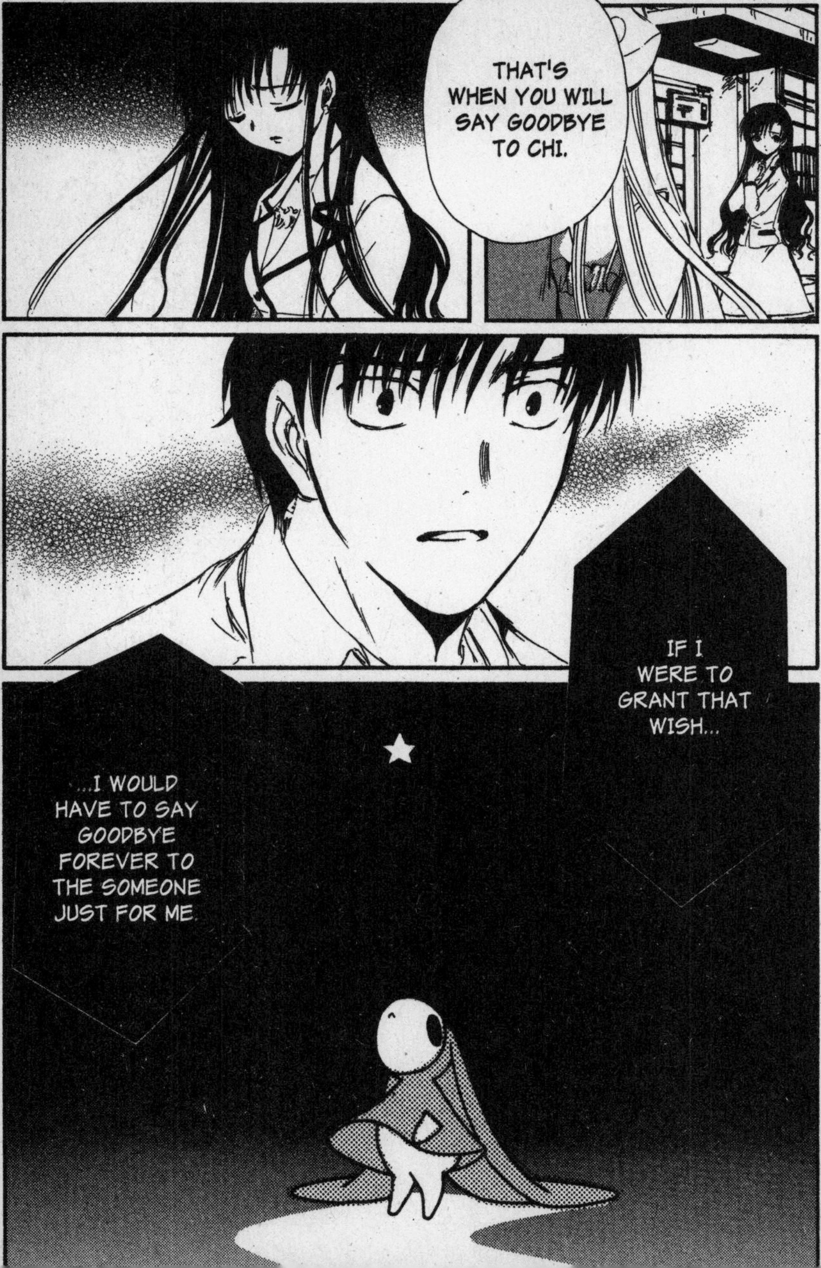
THAT'S WHEN YOU WILL SAY GOODBYE TO CHI.
IF I WERE TO GRANT THAT WISH...
...I WOULD HAVE TO SAY GOODBYE FOREVER TO THE SOMEONE JUST FOR ME.

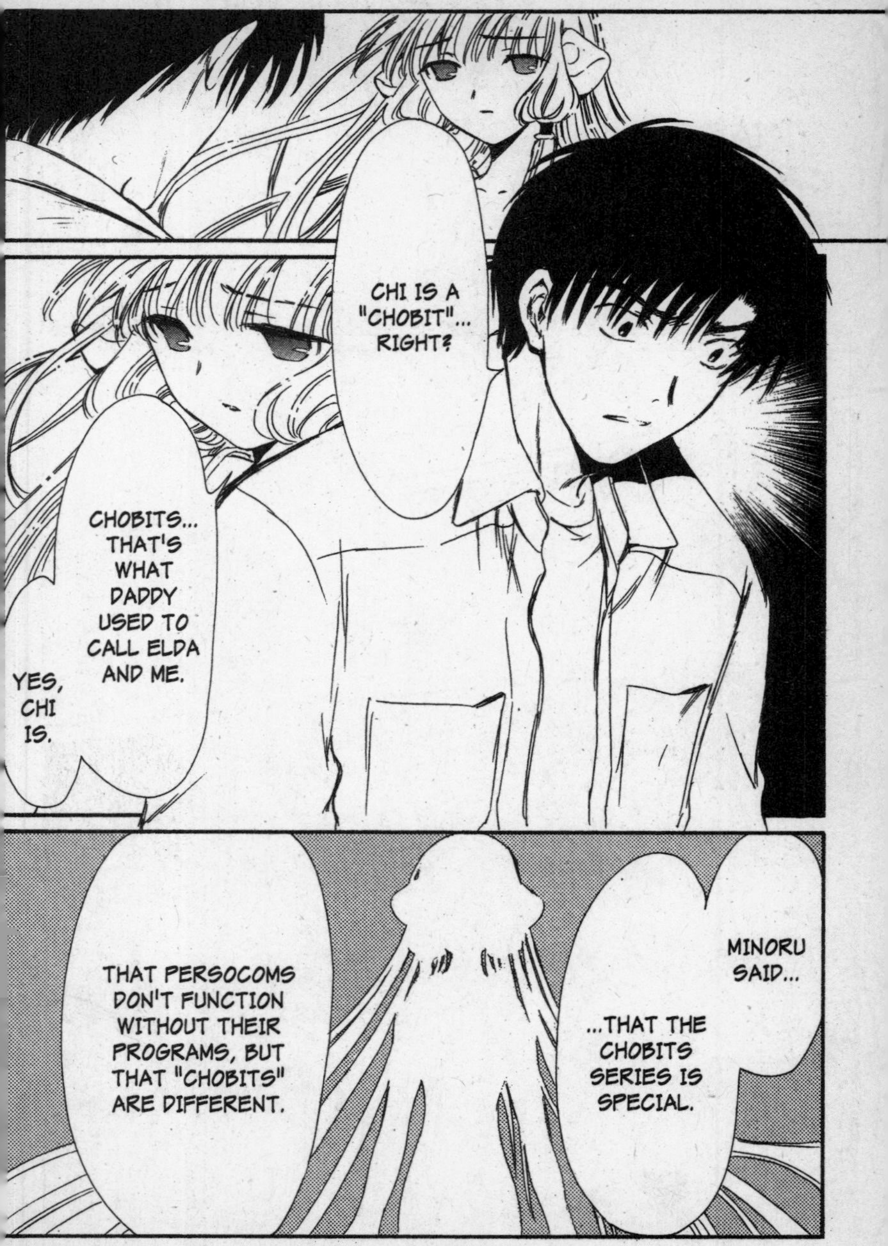
CHI IS A "CHOBIT"... RIGHT?
CHOBITS... THAT'S WHAT DADDY USED TO CALL ELDA AND ME.
YES, CHI IS.
MINORU SAID...
...THAT THE CHOBITS SERIES IS SPECIAL.
THAT PERSOCOMS DON'T FUNCTION WITHOUT THEIR PROGRAMS, BUT THAT "CHOBITS" ARE DIFFERENT.

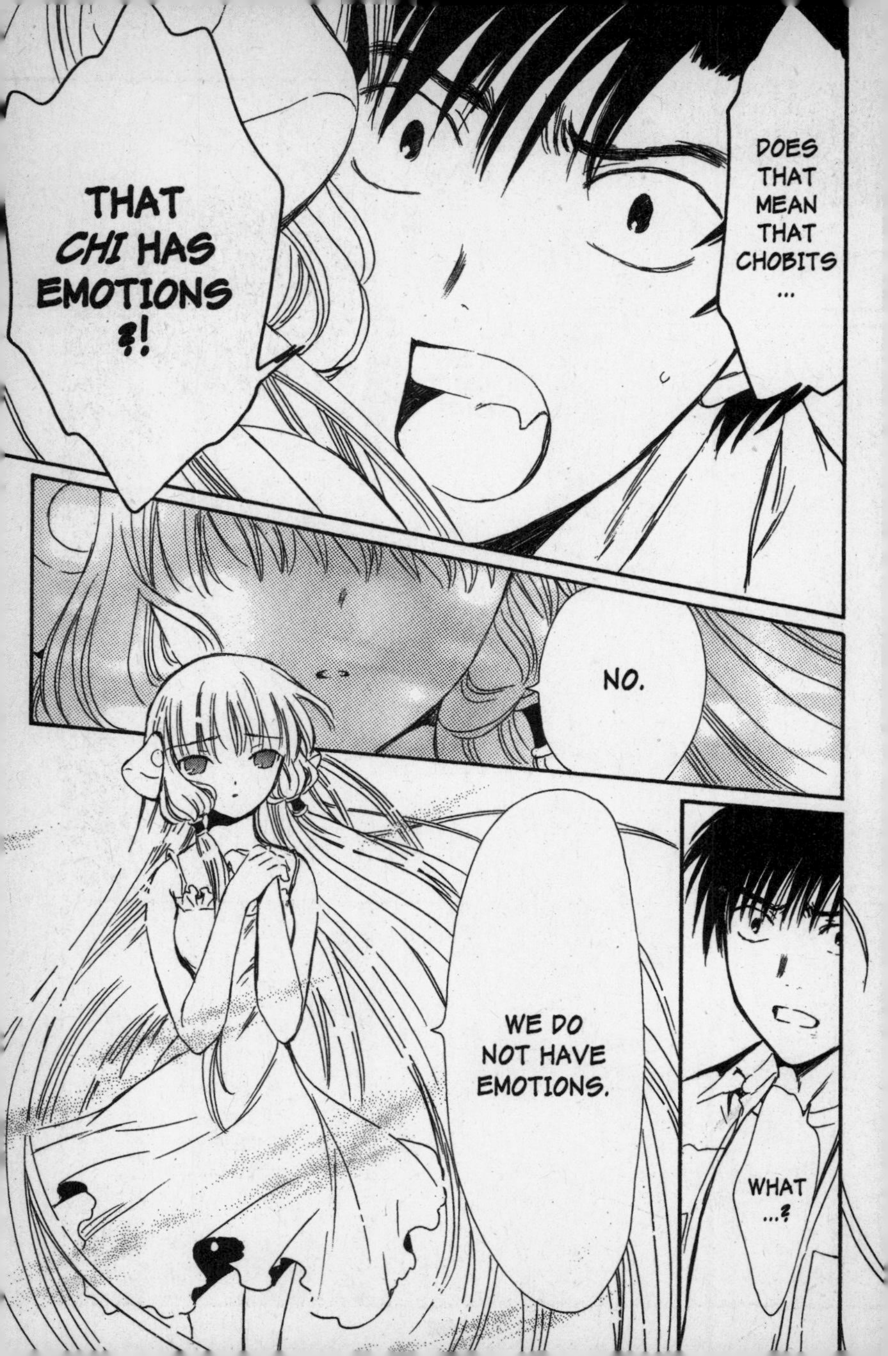
DOES THAT MEAN THAT CHOBITS ...
THAT *CHI* HAS EMOTIONS ?!
NO.
WHAT ...?
WE DO NOT HAVE EMOTIONS.

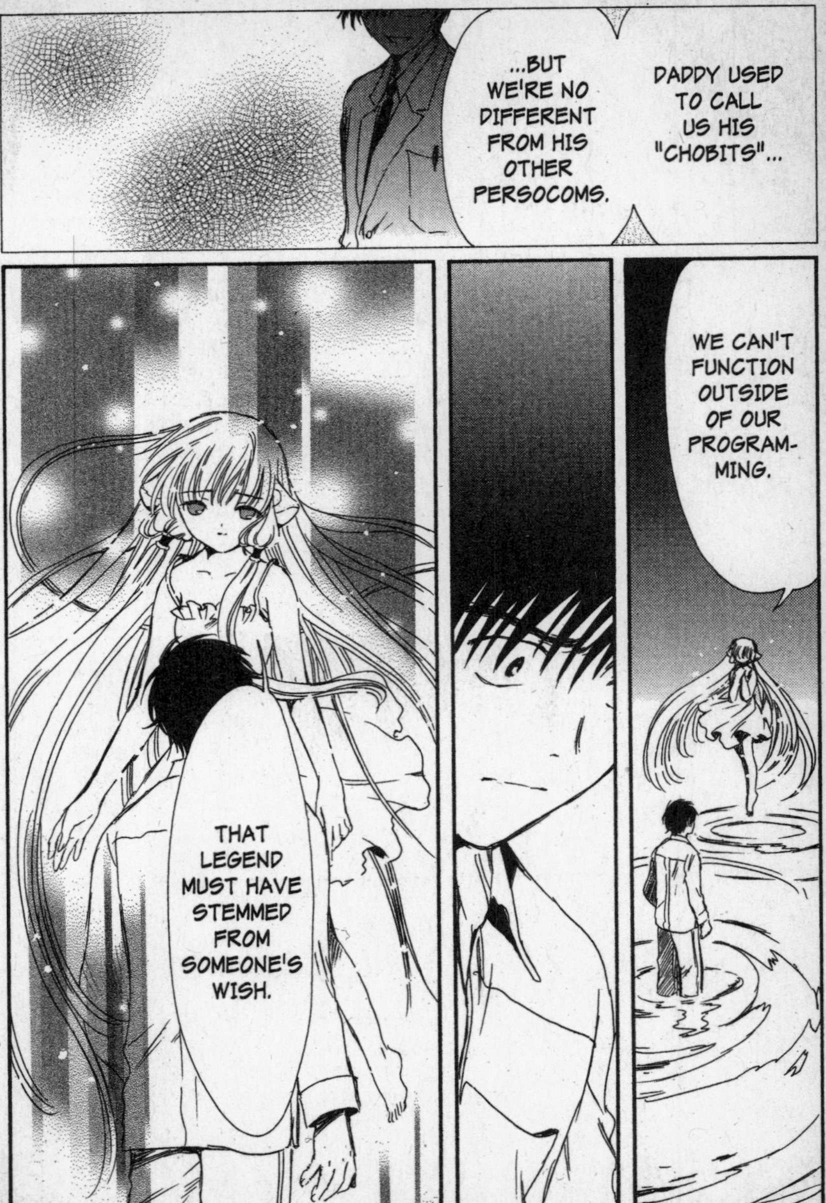
DADDY USED TO CALL US HIS "CHOBITS"...
...BUT WE'RE NO DIFFERENT FROM HIS OTHER PERSOCOMS.
WE CAN'T FUNCTION OUTSIDE OF OUR PROGRAM-MING.
THAT LEGEND MUST HAVE STEMMED FROM SOMEONE'S WISH.

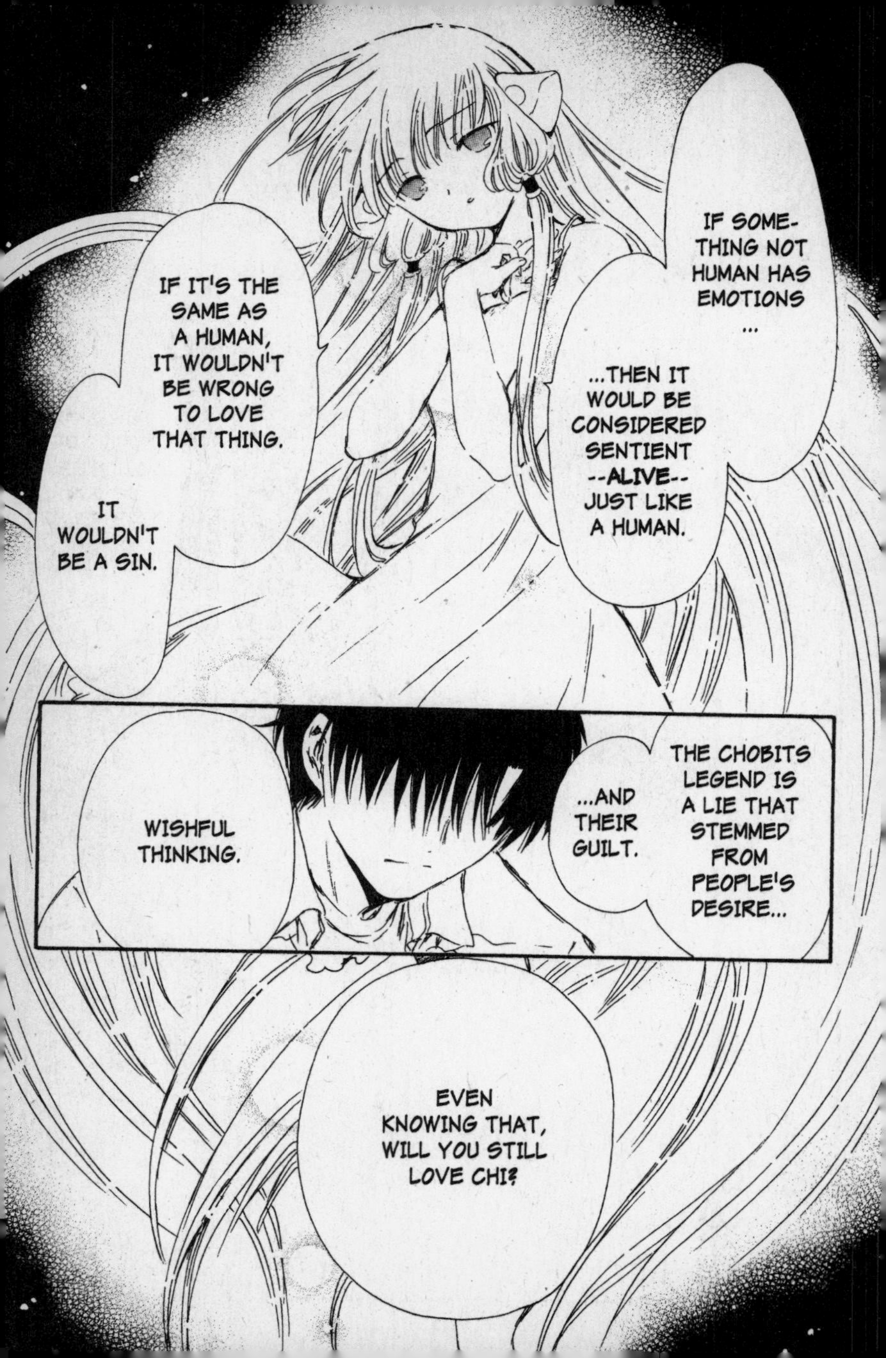
IF SOME-THING NOT HUMAN HAS EMOTIONS ...
...THEN IT WOULD BE CONSIDERED SENTIENT --ALIVE-- JUST LIKE A HUMAN.
IF IT'S THE SAME AS A HUMAN, IT WOULDN'T BE WRONG TO LOVE THAT THING.
IT WOULDN'T BE A SIN.
THE CHOBITS LEGEND IS A LIE THAT STEMMED FROM PEOPLE'S DESIRE...
...AND THEIR GUILT.
WISHFUL THINKING.
EVEN KNOWING THAT, WILL YOU STILL LOVE CHI?

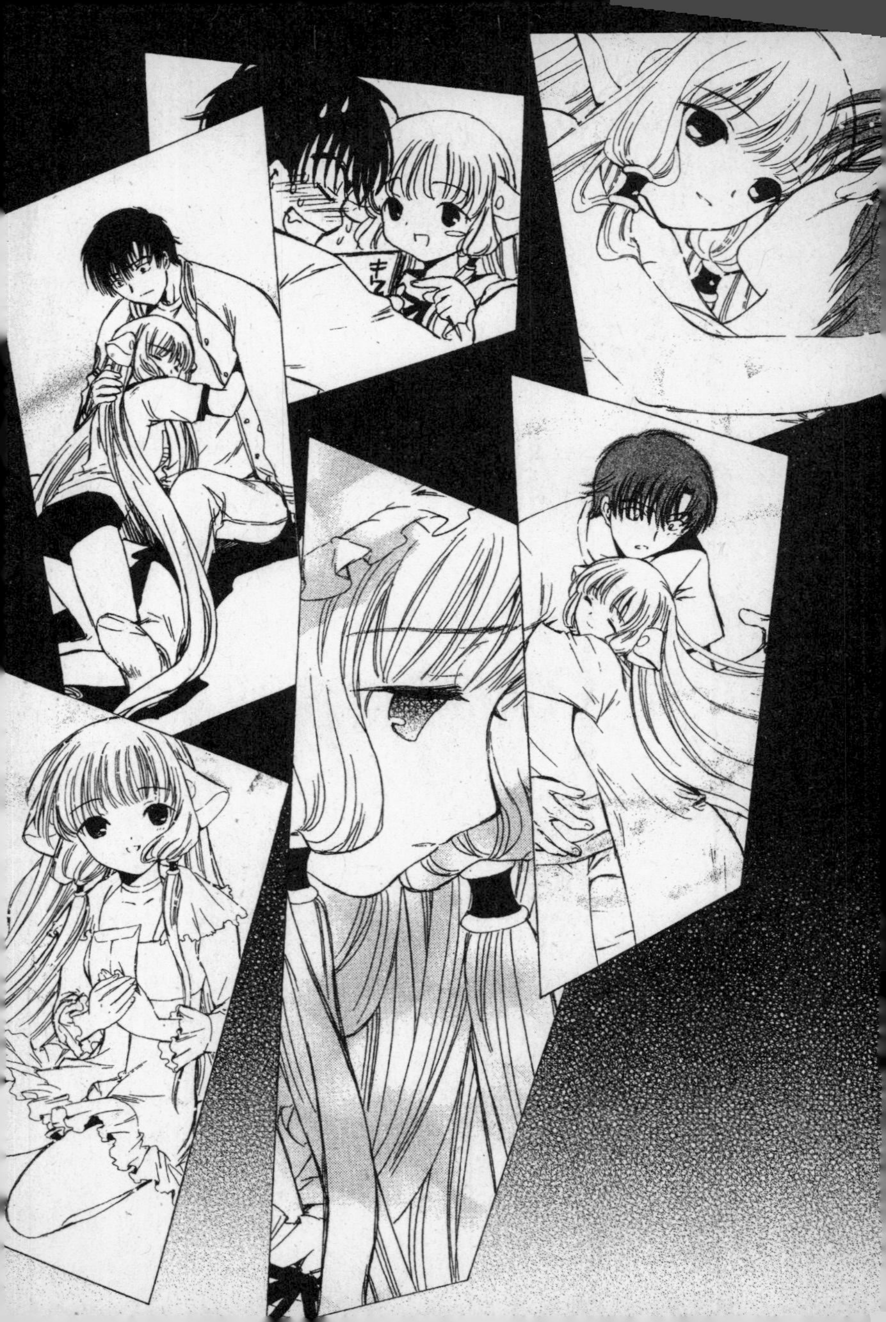

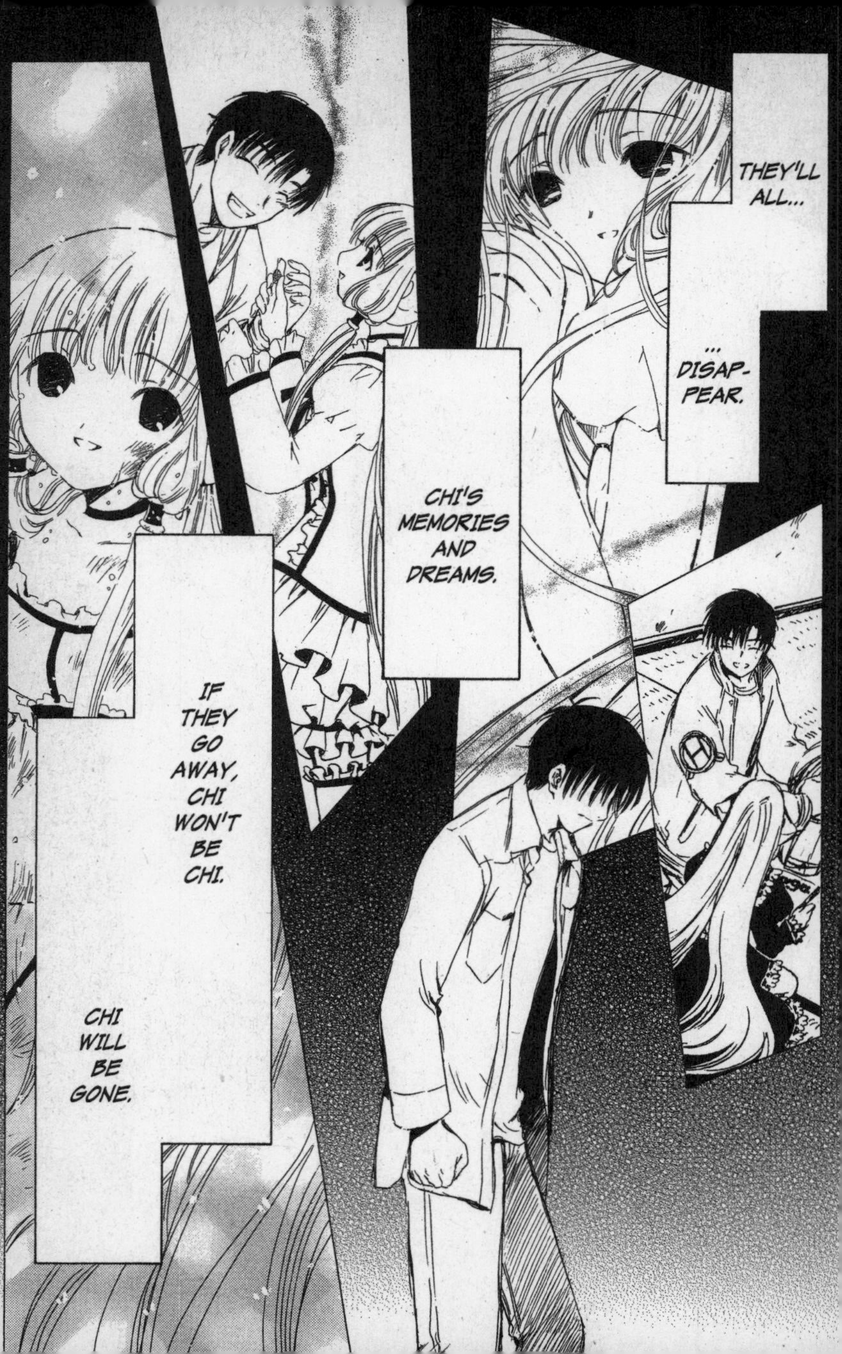
THEY'LL ALL...
...DISAP-PEAR.
CHI'S MEMORIES AND DREAMS.
IF THEY GO AWAY, CHI WON'T BE CHI.
CHI WILL BE GONE.

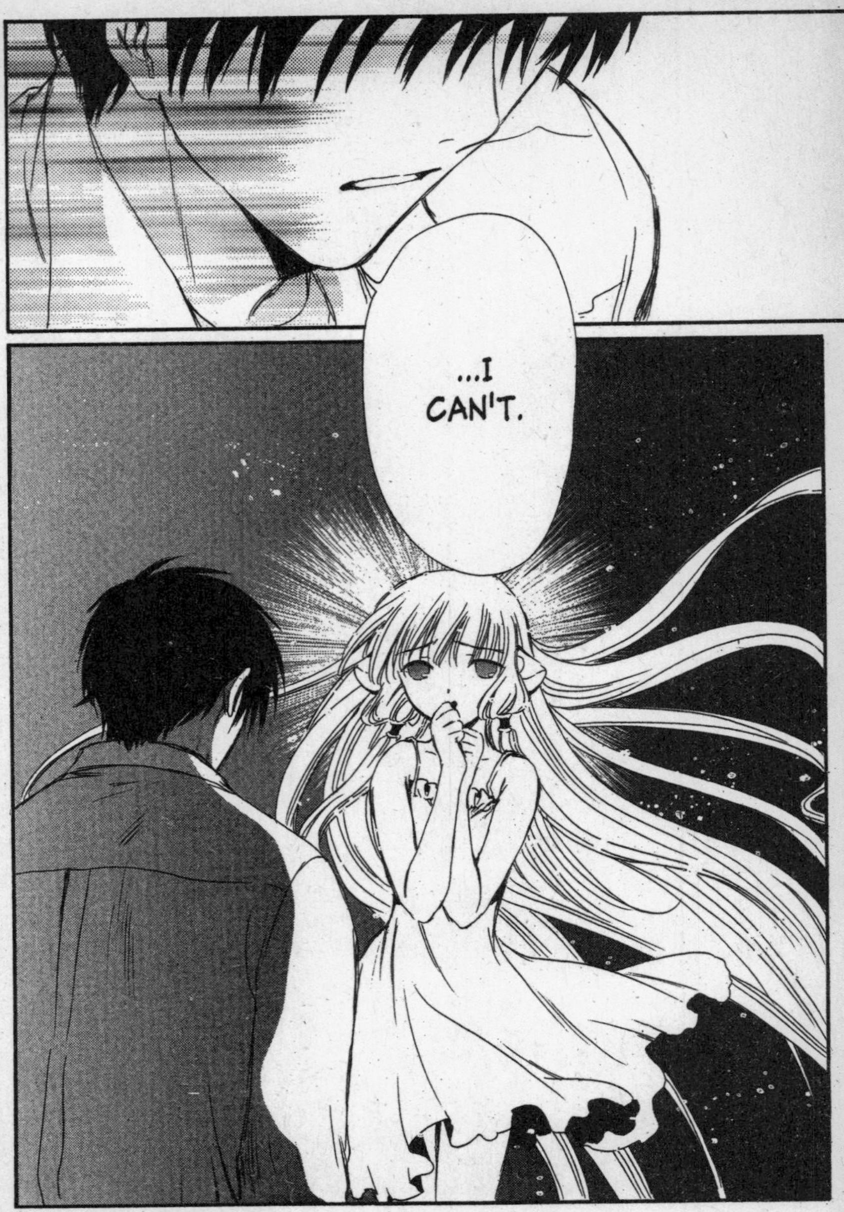
...I
CAN'T.

◀chapter.86▶end

ちょびっツ
Chobits

◀chapter.87▶

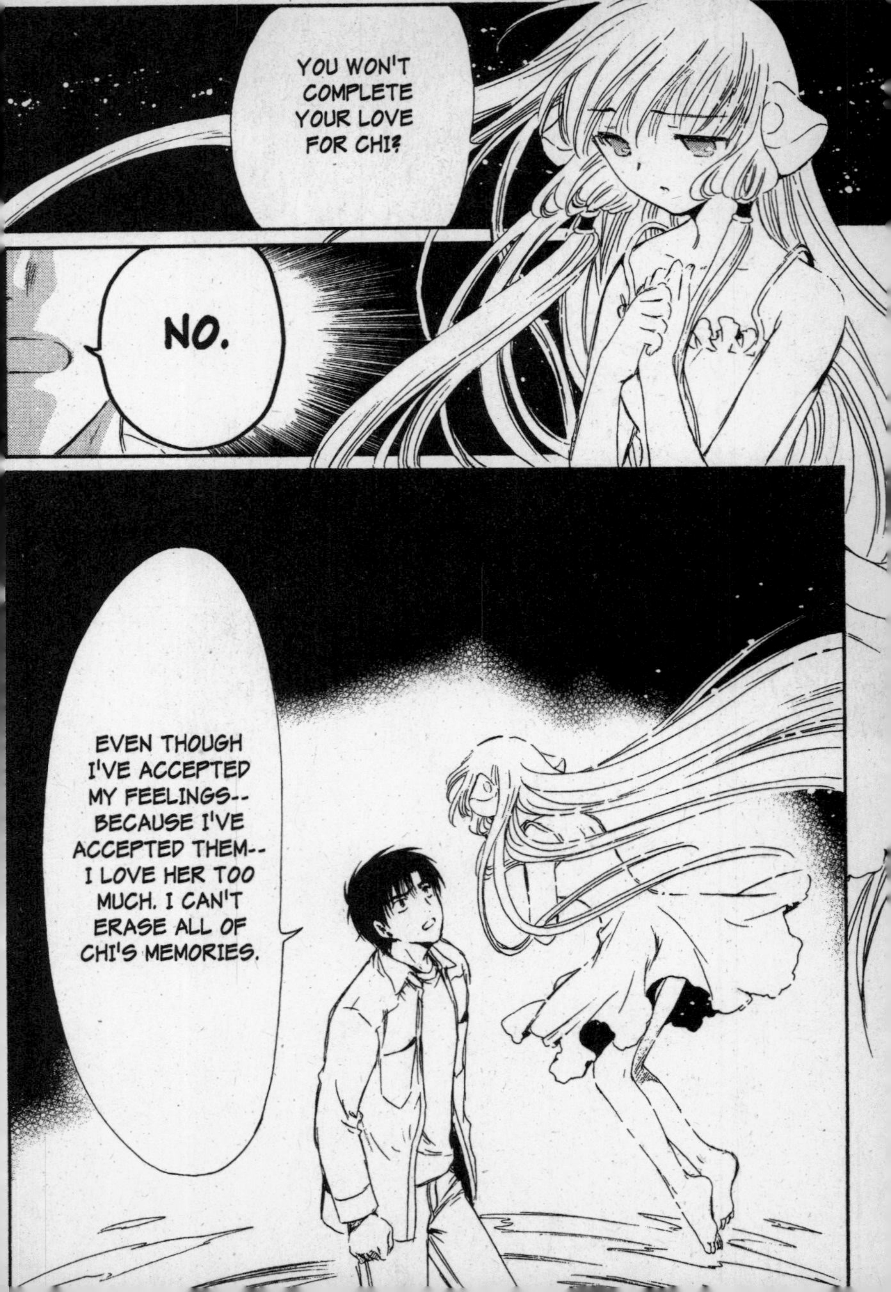
YOU WON'T COMPLETE YOUR LOVE FOR CHI?
NO.
EVEN THOUGH I'VE ACCEPTED MY FEELINGS-- BECAUSE I'VE ACCEPTED THEM-- I LOVE HER TOO MUCH. I CAN'T ERASE ALL OF CHI'S MEMORIES.

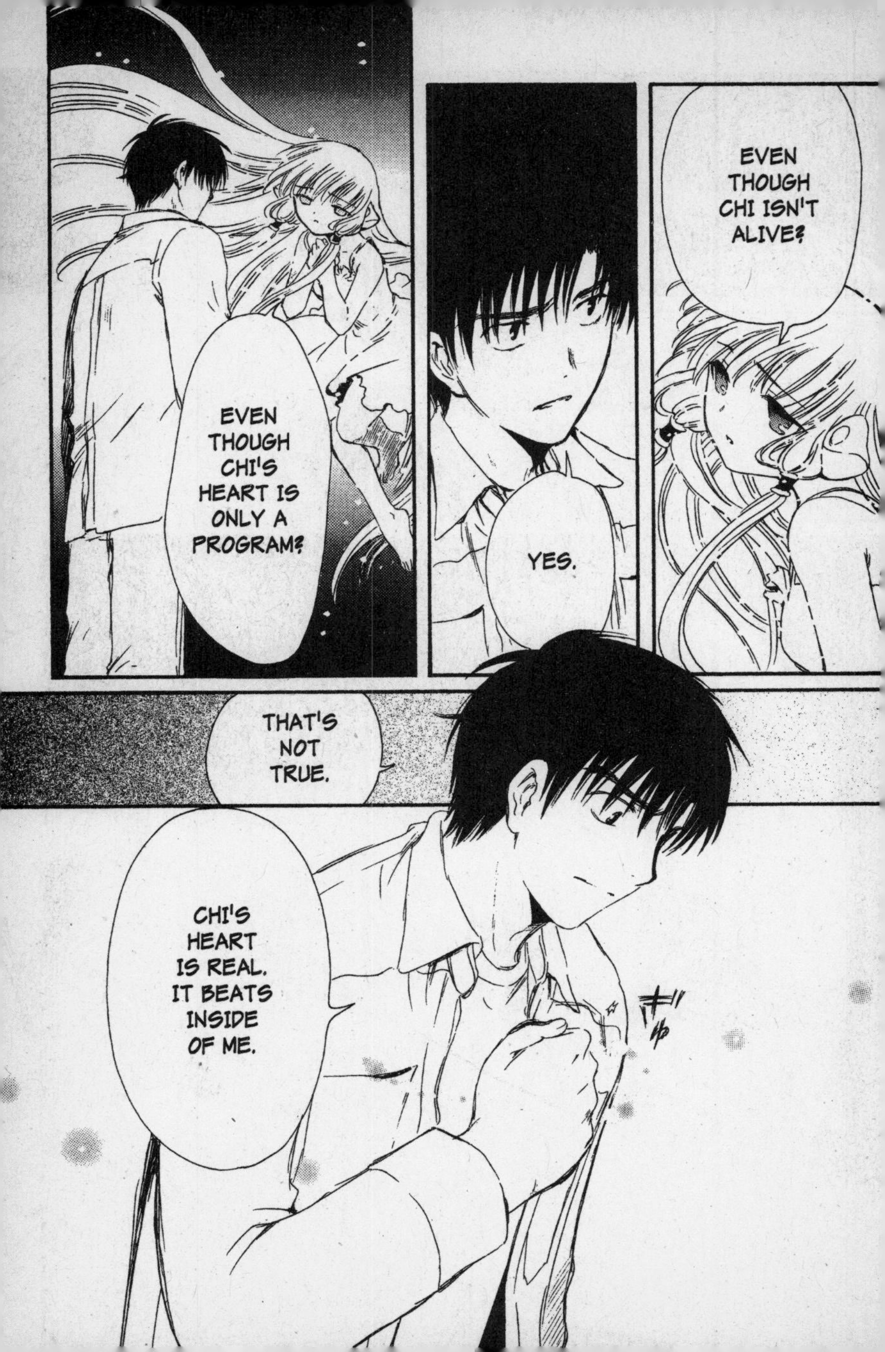
EVEN THOUGH CHI ISN'T ALIVE?
YES.
EVEN THOUGH CHI'S HEART IS ONLY A PROGRAM?
THAT'S NOT TRUE.
CHI'S HEART IS REAL. IT BEATS INSIDE OF ME.

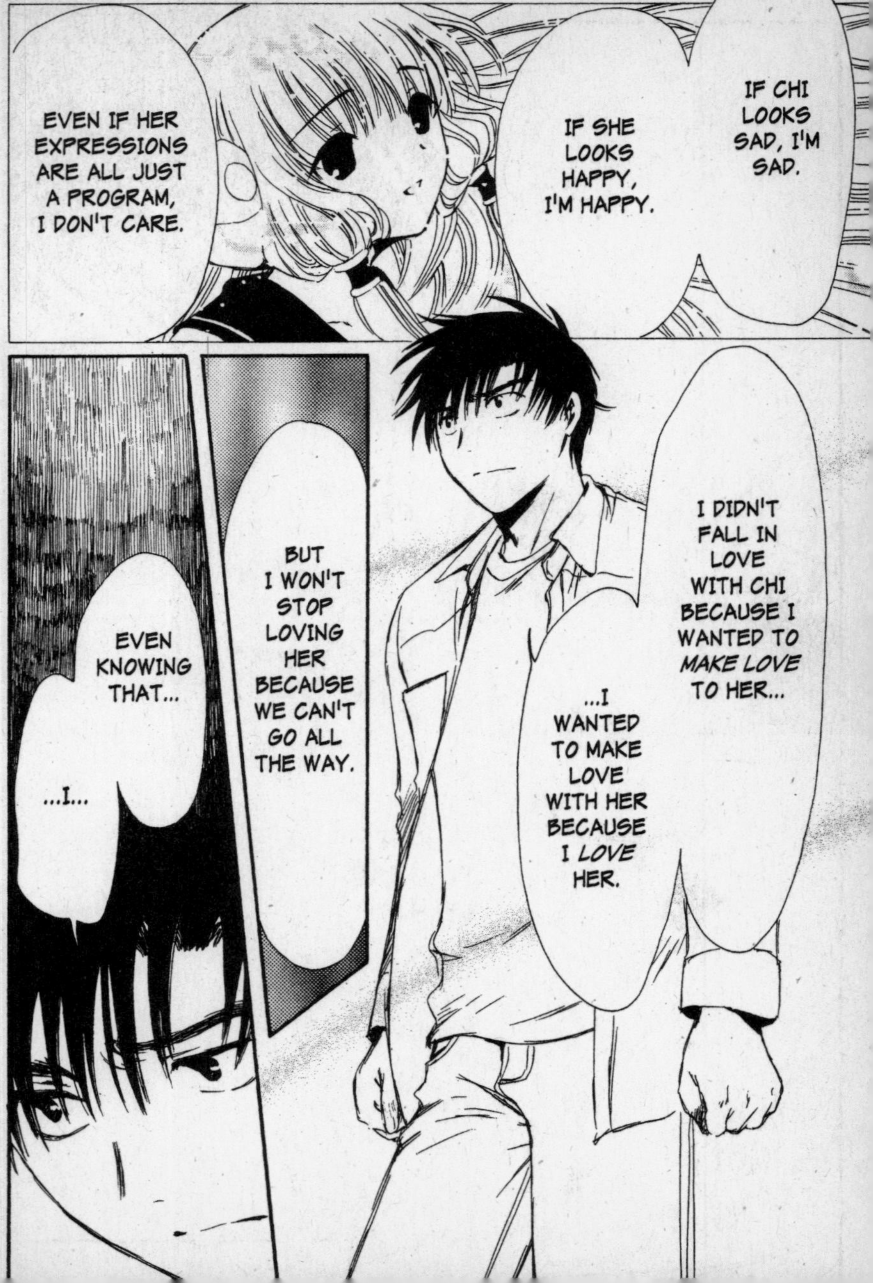
IF CHI LOOKS SAD, I'M SAD.
IF SHE LOOKS HAPPY, I'M HAPPY.
EVEN IF HER EXPRESSIONS ARE ALL JUST A PROGRAM, I DON'T CARE.
I DIDN'T FALL IN LOVE WITH CHI BECAUSE I WANTED TO *MAKE LOVE* TO HER...
...I WANTED TO MAKE LOVE WITH HER BECAUSE I *LOVE* HER.
BUT I WON'T STOP LOVING HER BECAUSE WE CAN'T GO ALL THE WAY.
EVEN KNOWING THAT...
...I...

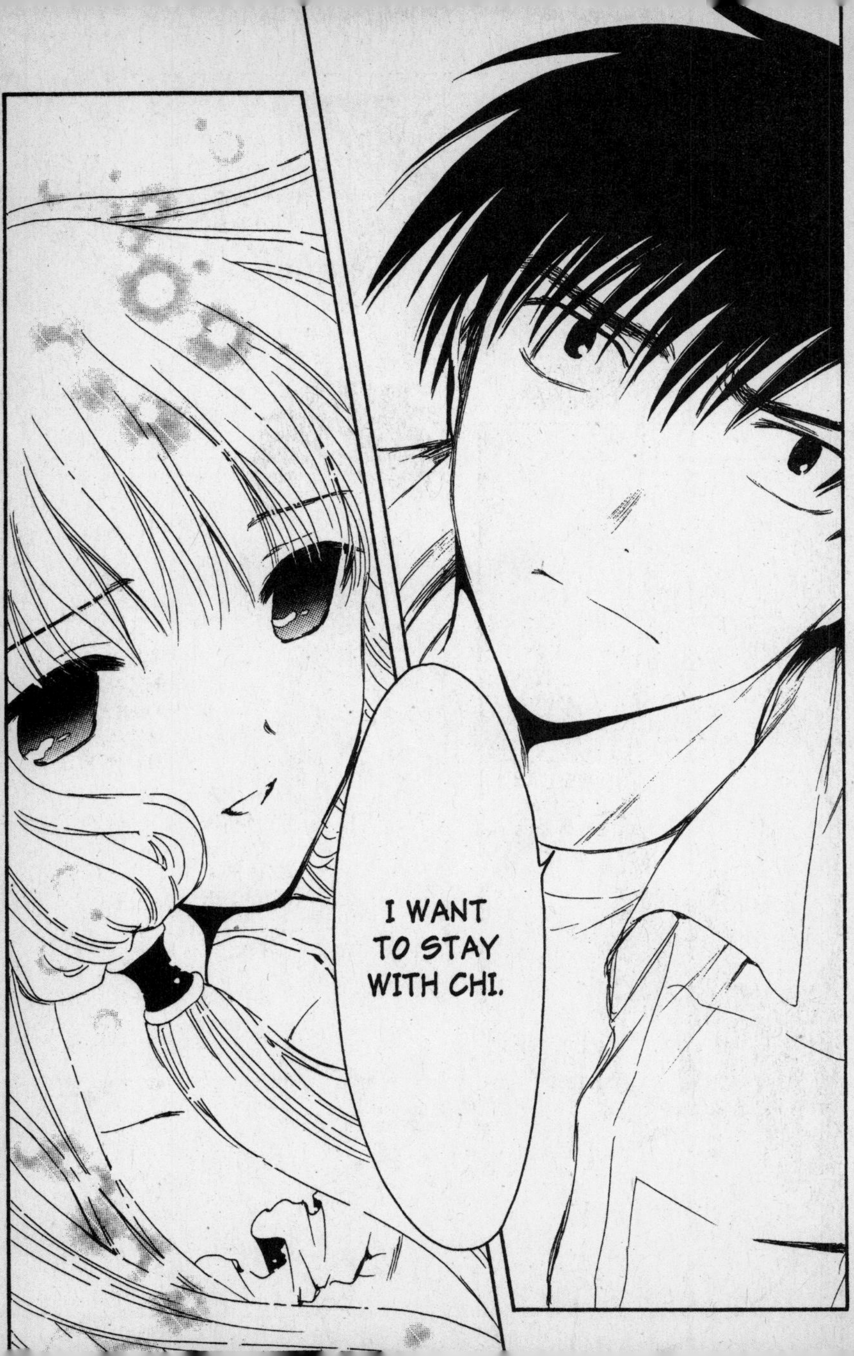
I WANT TO STAY WITH CHI.

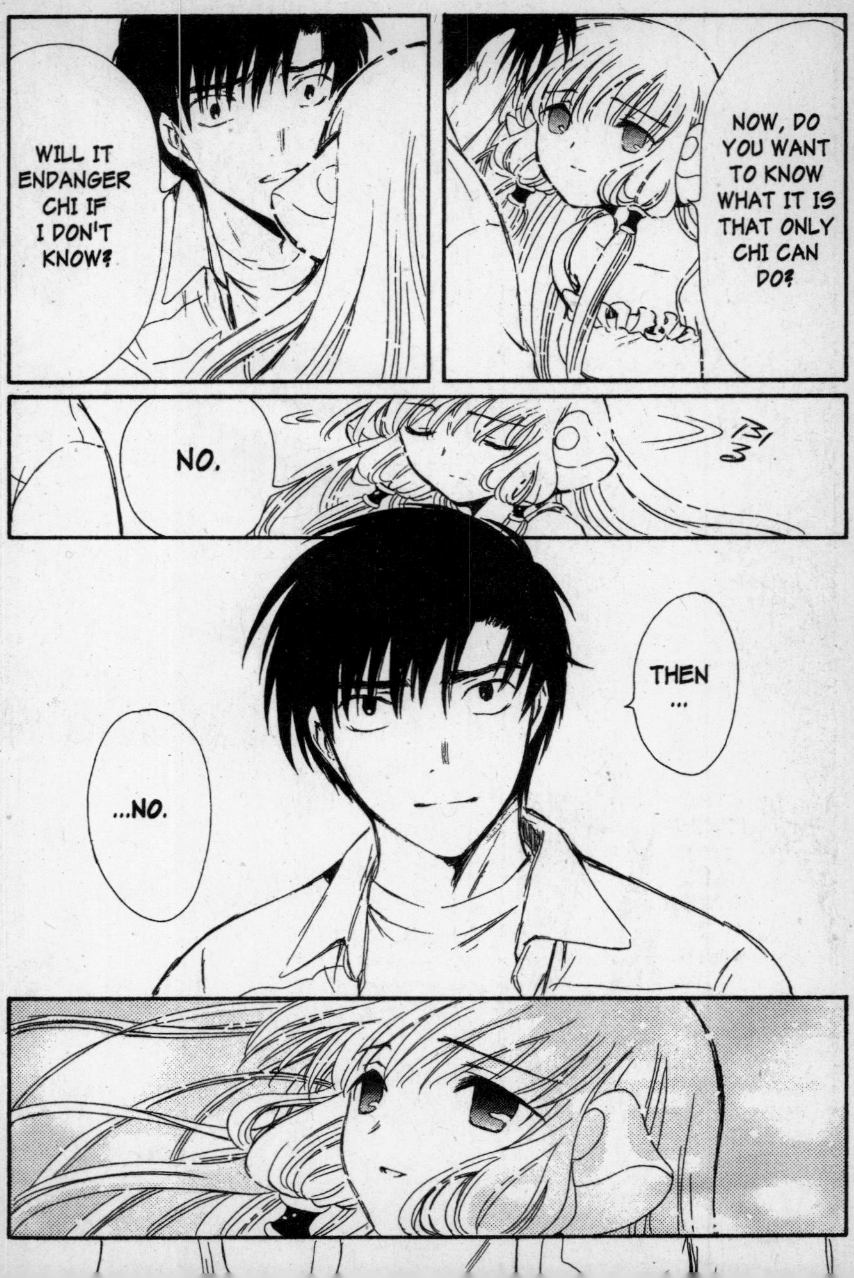
NOW, DO YOU WANT TO KNOW WHAT IT IS THAT ONLY CHI CAN DO?
WILL IT ENDANGER CHI IF I DON'T KNOW?
NO.
THEN ...
...NO.

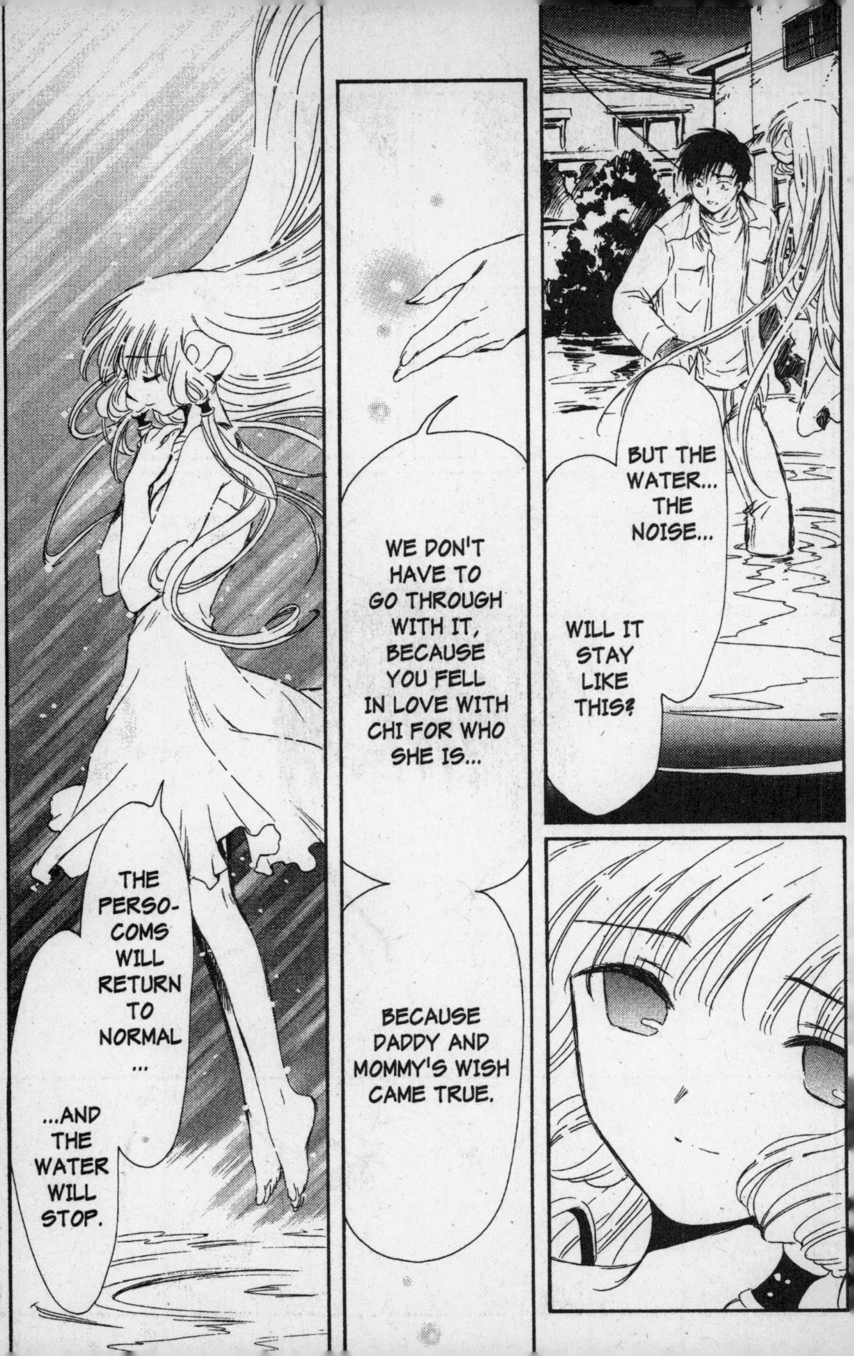
BUT THE WATER... THE NOISE...
WILL IT STAY LIKE THIS?
WE DON'T HAVE TO GO THROUGH WITH IT, BECAUSE YOU FELL IN LOVE WITH CHI FOR WHO SHE IS...
BECAUSE DADDY AND MOMMY'S WISH CAME TRUE.
THE PERSO-COMS WILL RETURN TO NORMAL ...
...AND THE WATER WILL STOP.

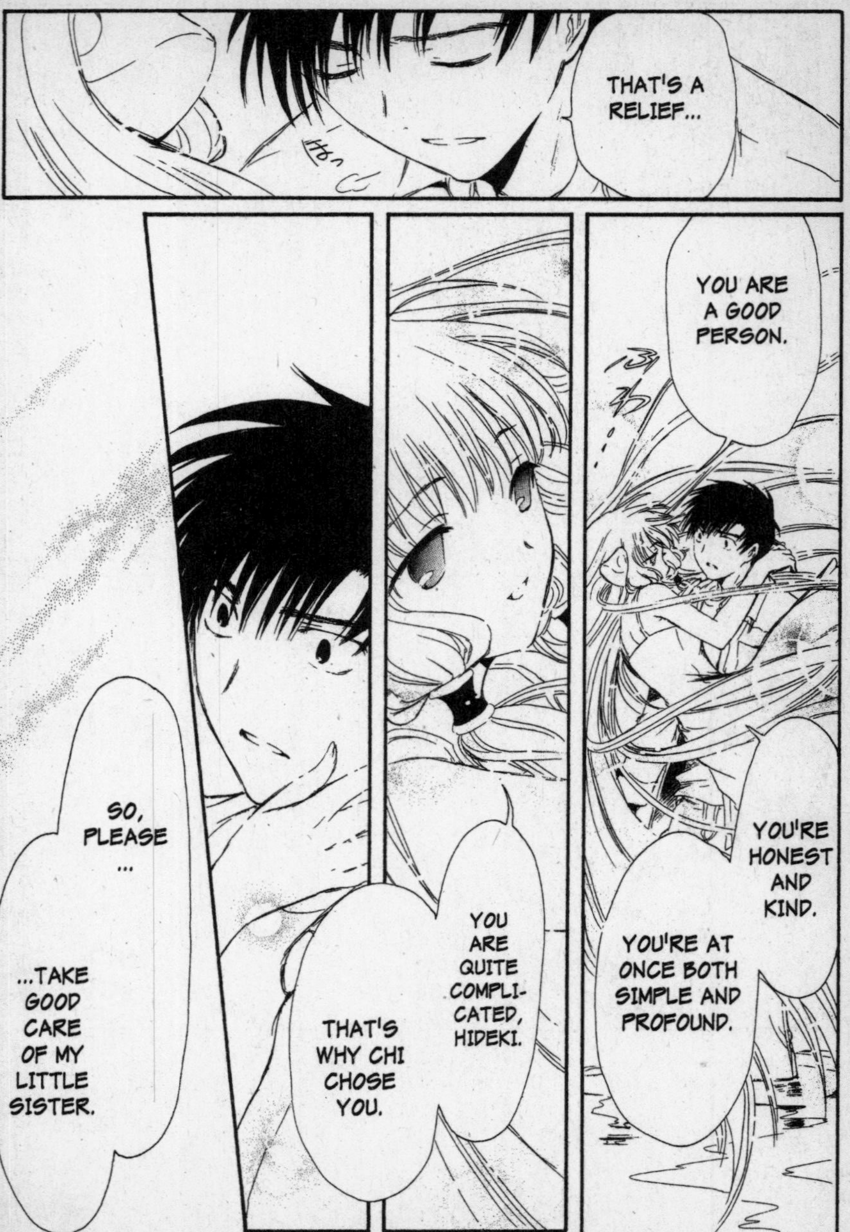
THAT'S A RELIEF...
YOU ARE A GOOD PERSON.
YOU'RE HONEST AND KIND.
YOU'RE AT ONCE BOTH SIMPLE AND PROFOUND.
YOU ARE QUITE COMPLICATED, HIDEKI.
THAT'S WHY CHI CHOSE YOU.
SO, PLEASE ...
...TAKE GOOD CARE OF MY LITTLE SISTER.

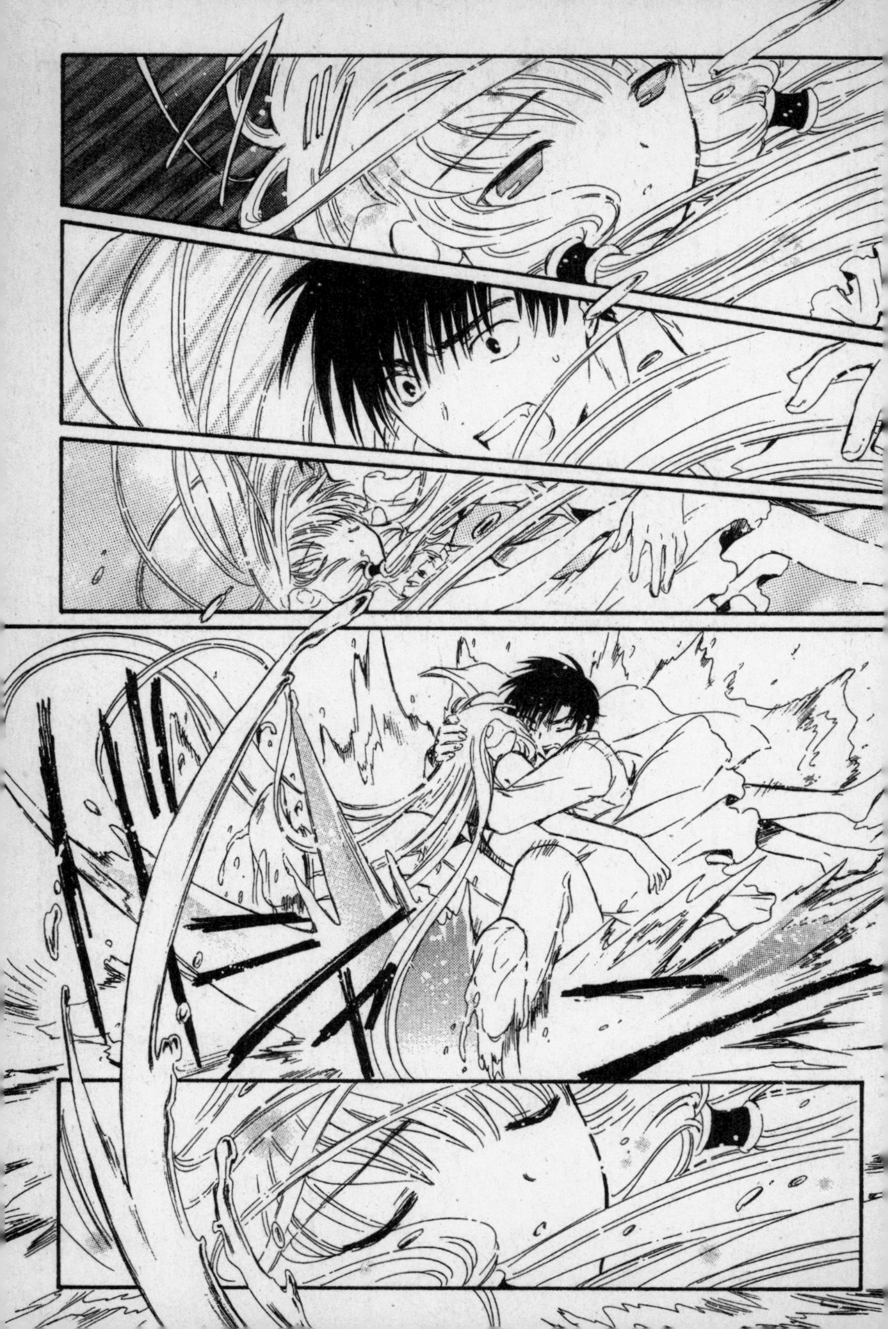

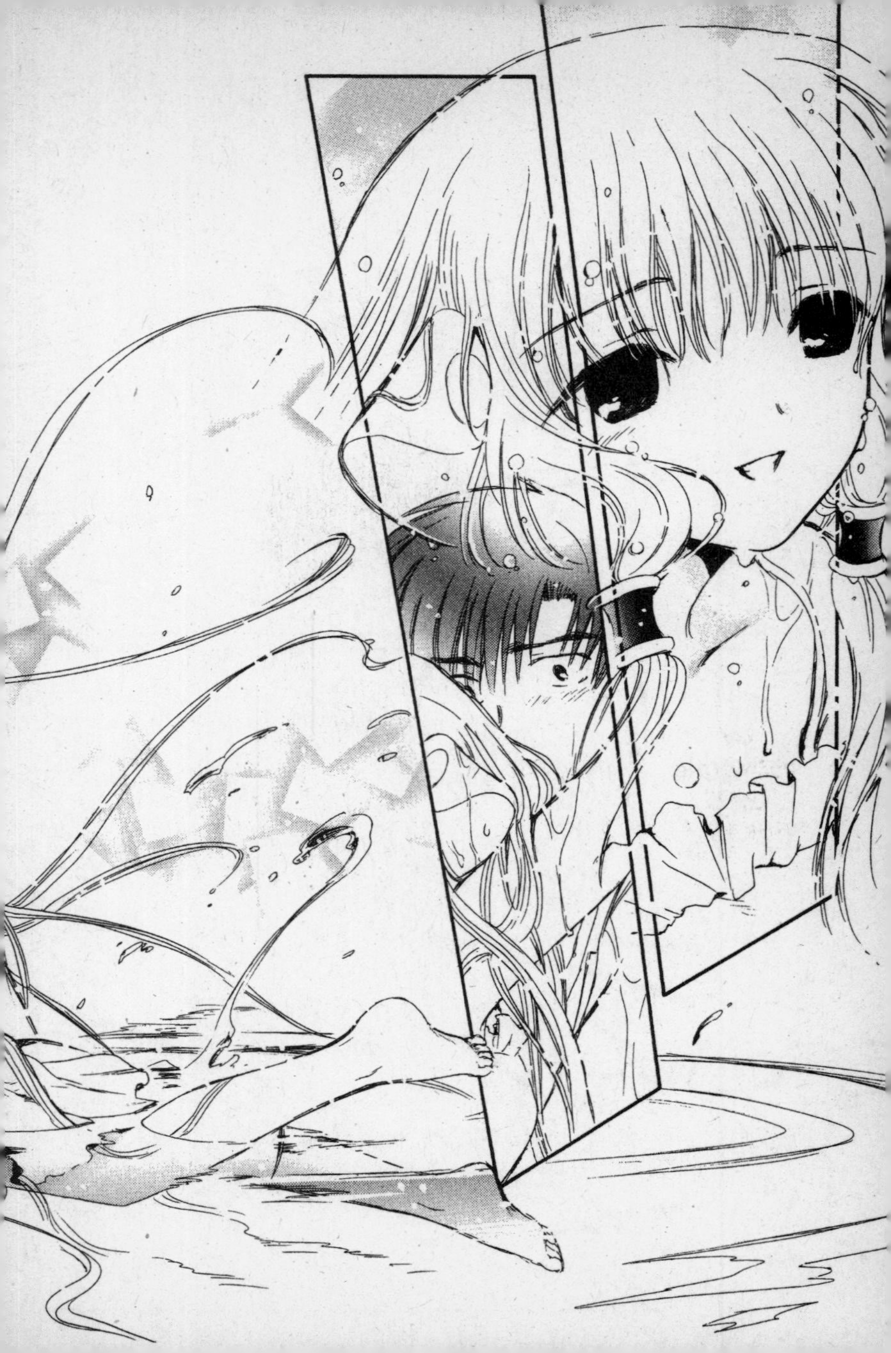

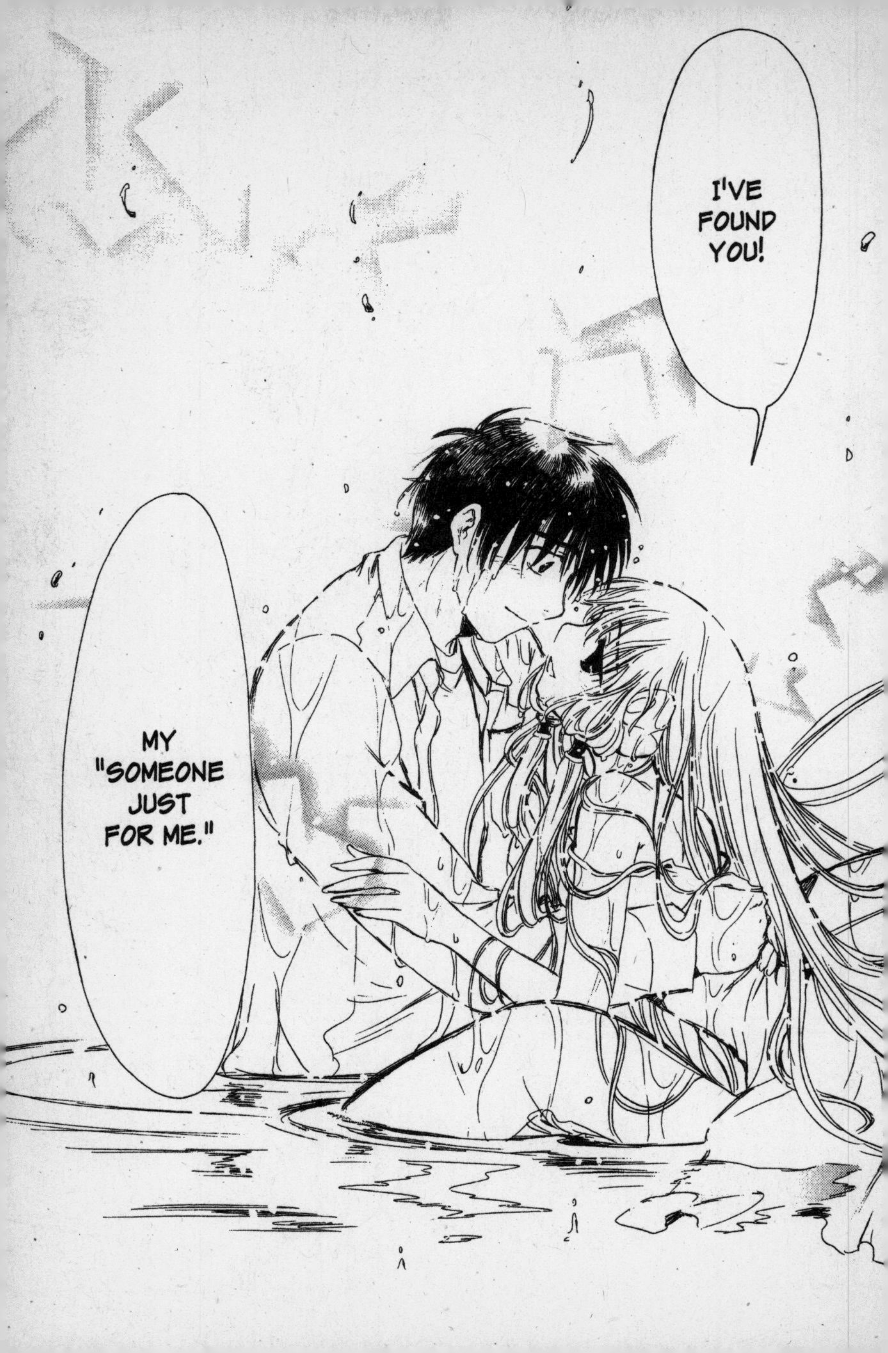
I'VE FOUND YOU!
MY "SOMEONE JUST FOR ME."

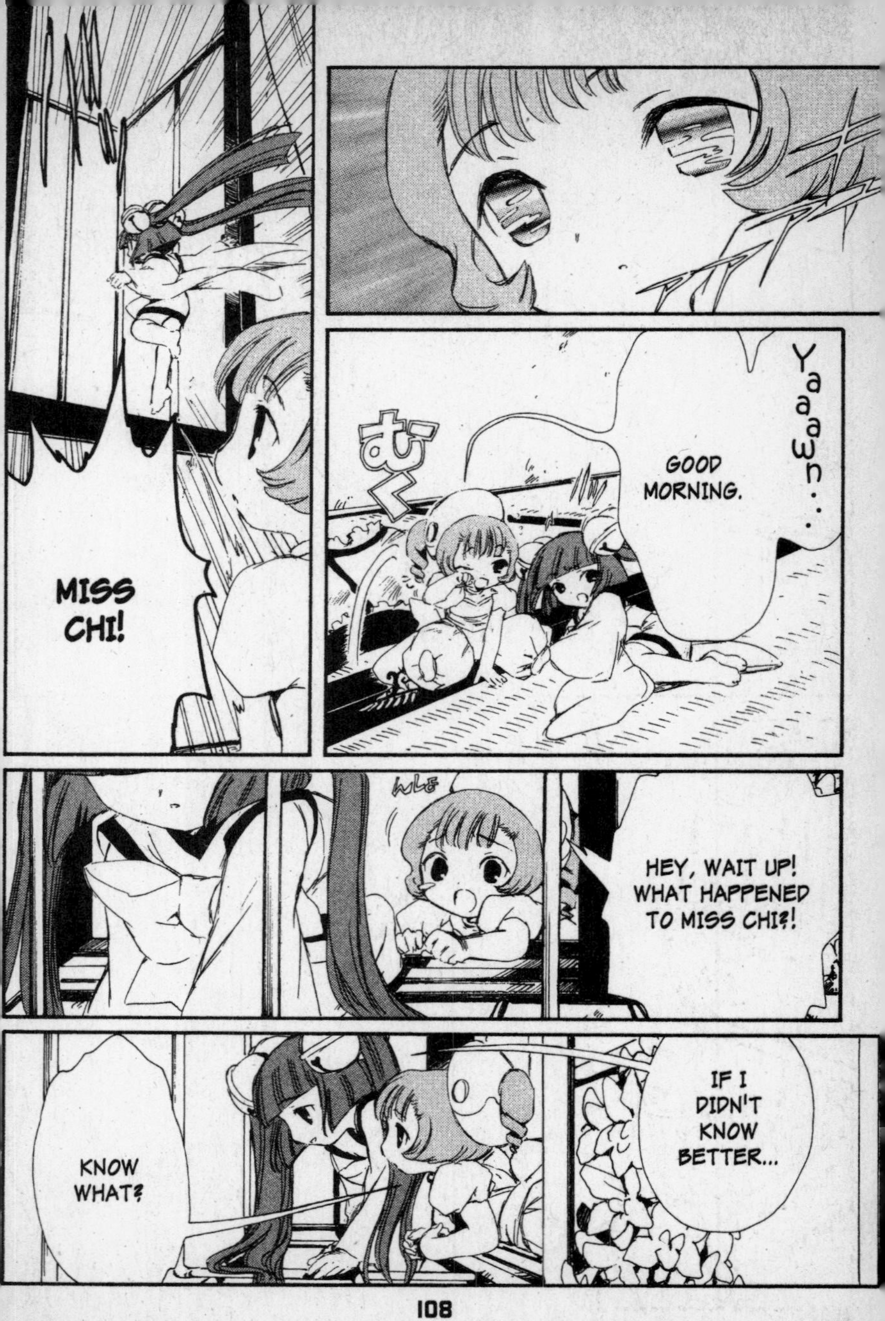
Yaaawn...
GOOD MORNING.
むく
MISS CHI!
HEY, WAIT UP! WHAT HAPPENED TO MISS CHI?!
IF I DIDN'T KNOW BETTER...
KNOW WHAT?

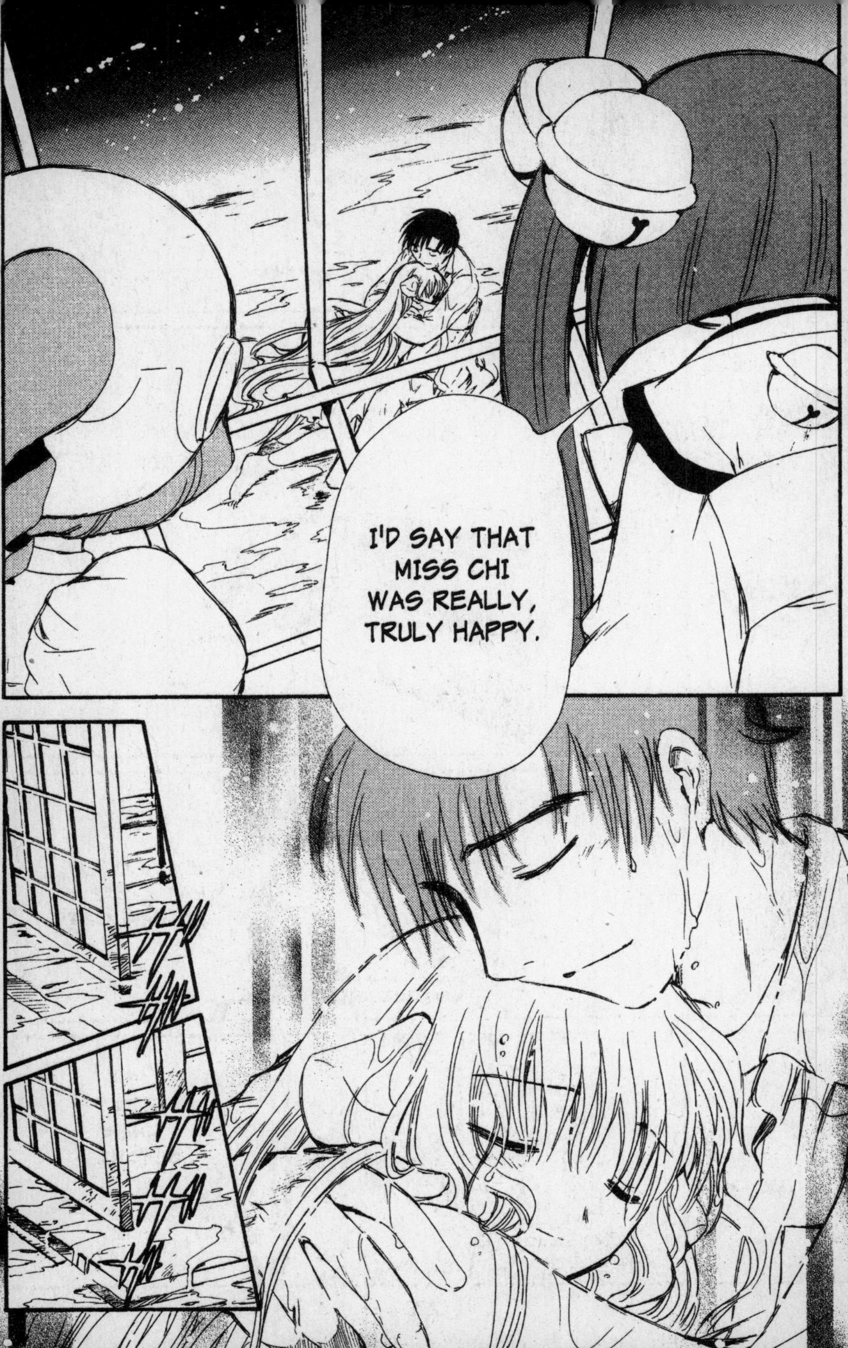
I'D SAY THAT MISS CHI WAS REALLY, TRULY HAPPY.

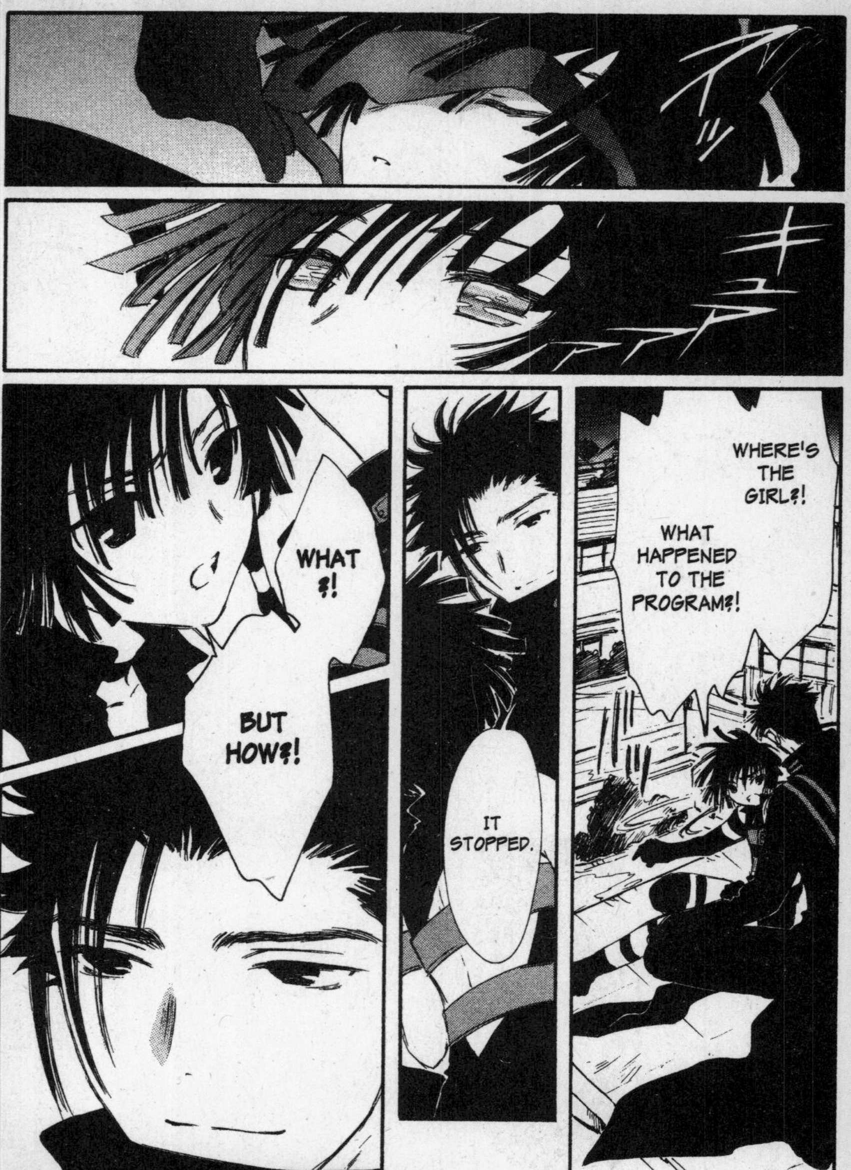
WHERE'S THE GIRL?!
WHAT HAPPENED TO THE PROGRAM?!
IT STOPPED.
WHAT?!
BUT HOW?!

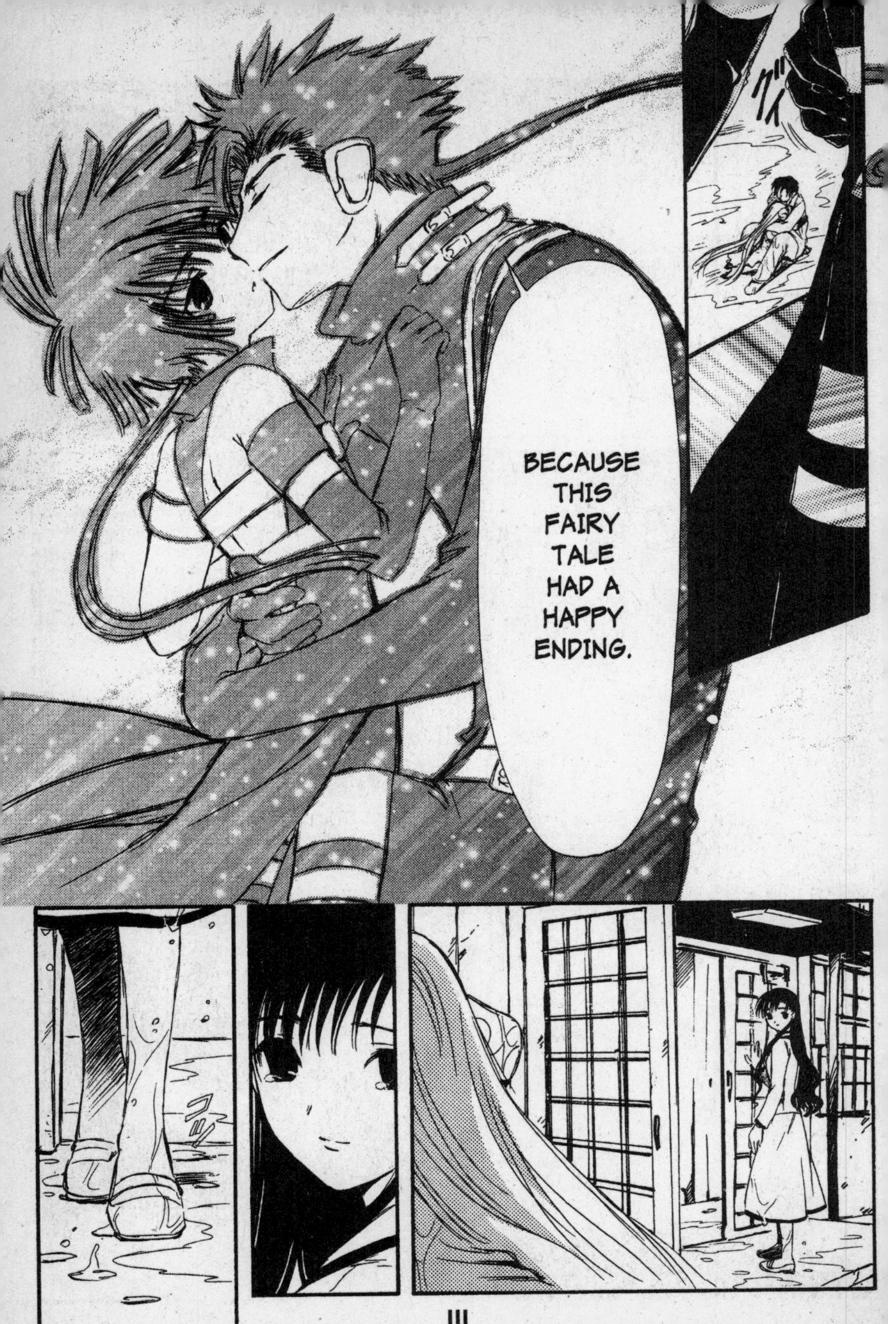
BECAUSE THIS FAIRY TALE HAD A HAPPY ENDING.

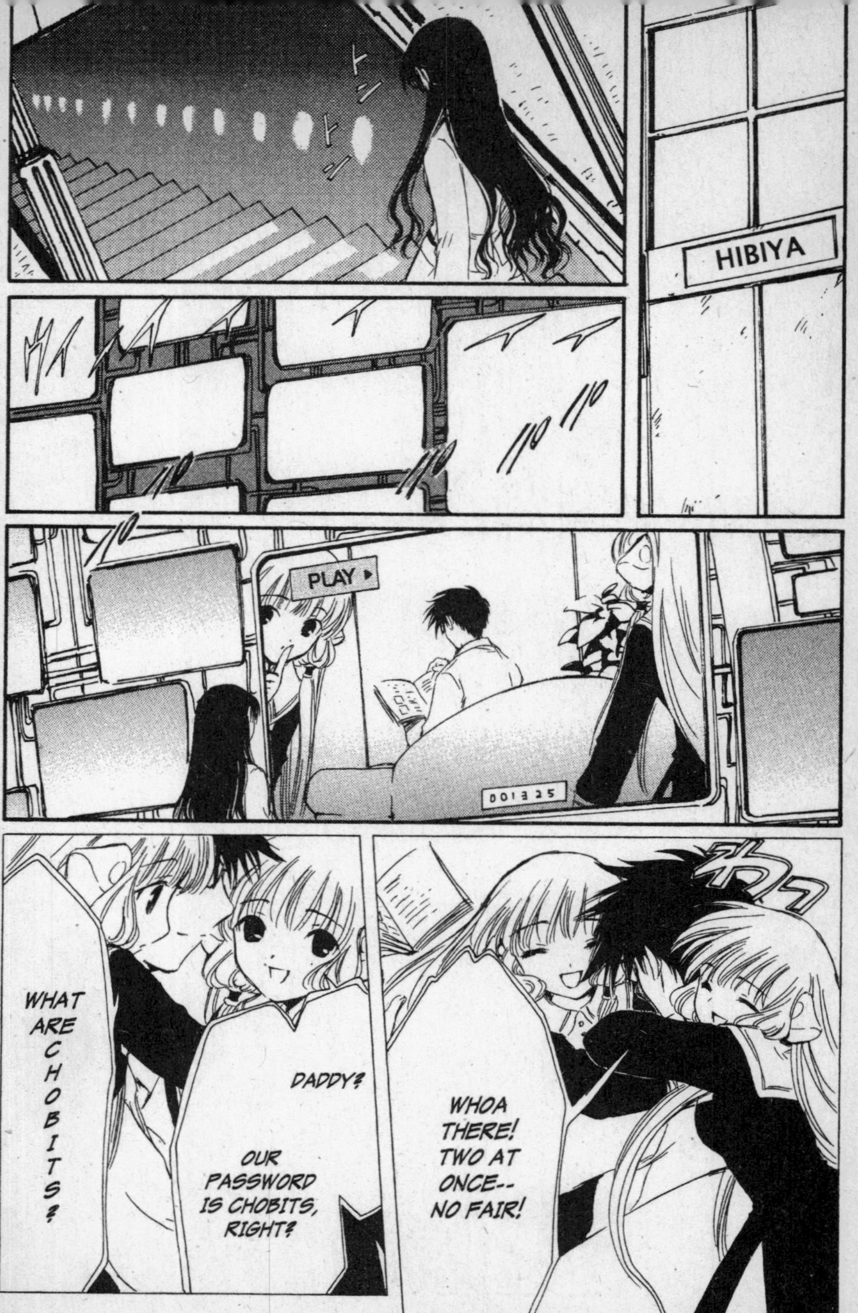
HIBIYA
PLAY ▶
001325
WHOA THERE! TWO AT ONCE-- NO FAIR!
DADDY?
OUR PASSWORD IS CHOBITS, RIGHT?
WHAT ARE CHOBITS?

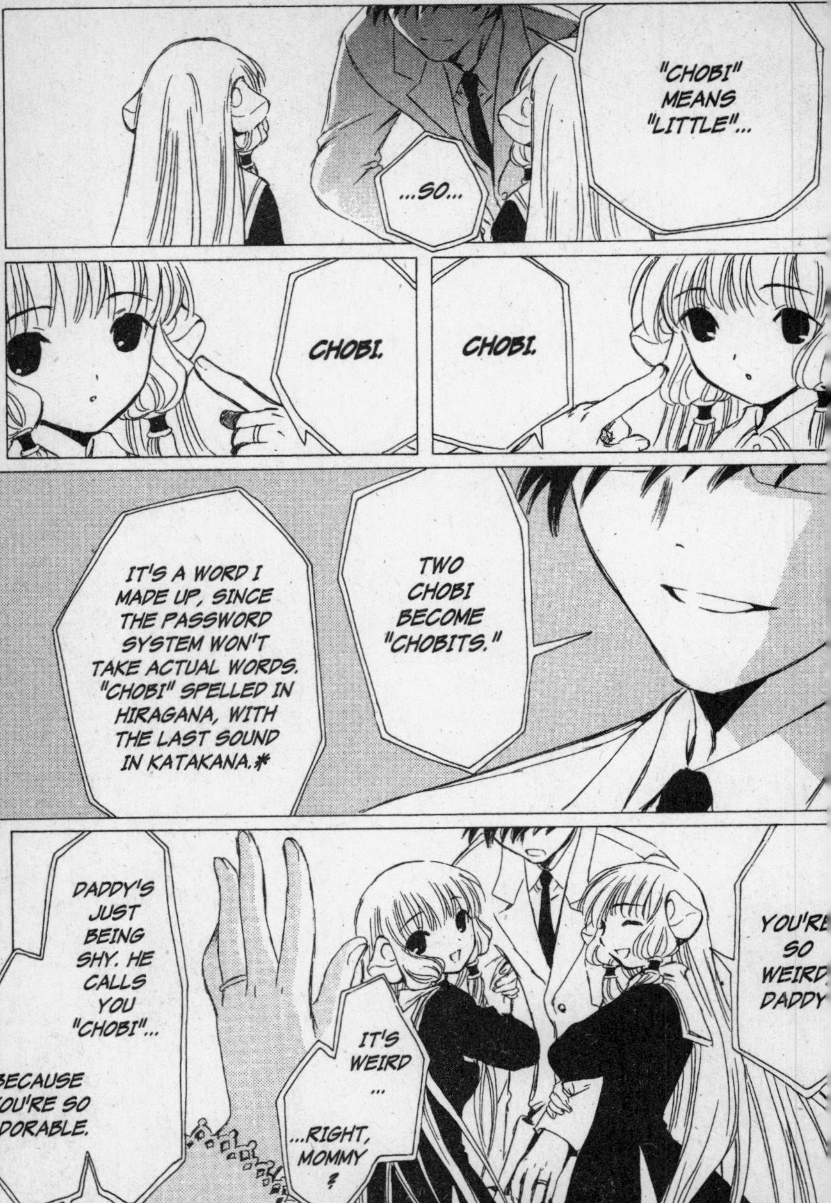
"CHOBI" MEANS "LITTLE"...
...SO...
CHOBI.
CHOBI.
TWO CHOBI BECOME "CHOBITS."
IT'S A WORD I MADE UP, SINCE THE PASSWORD SYSTEM WON'T TAKE ACTUAL WORDS. "CHOBI" SPELLED IN HIRAGANA, WITH THE LAST SOUND IN KATAKANA.*
YOU'RE SO WEIRD, DADDY
DADDY'S JUST BEING SHY. HE CALLS YOU "CHOBI"...
BECAUSE YOU'RE SO ADORABLE.
IT'S WEIRD ...
...RIGHT, MOMMY?

*Hiragana and Katakana are the two phonetic Japanese alphabets. They sound identical, but in writing, Hiragana is used for native Japanese words and Katakana is used for foreign words.

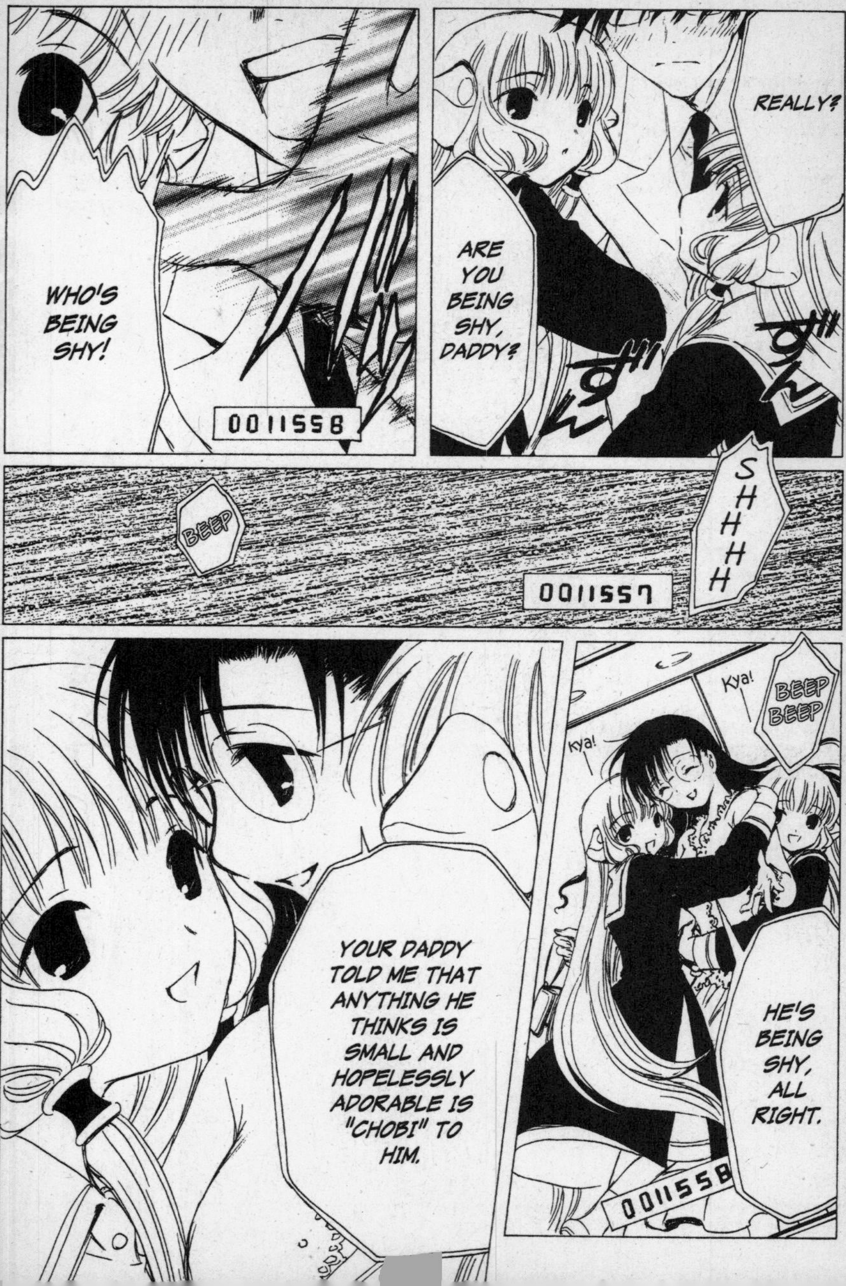
REALLY?
ARE YOU BEING SHY, DADDY?
WHO'S BEING SHY!
0011558
SHHHH
0011557
BEEP
BEEP BEEP
Kya!
Kya!
HE'S BEING SHY, ALL RIGHT.
0011558
YOUR DADDY TOLD ME THAT ANYTHING HE THINKS IS SMALL AND HOPELESSLY ADORABLE IS "CHOBI" TO HIM.

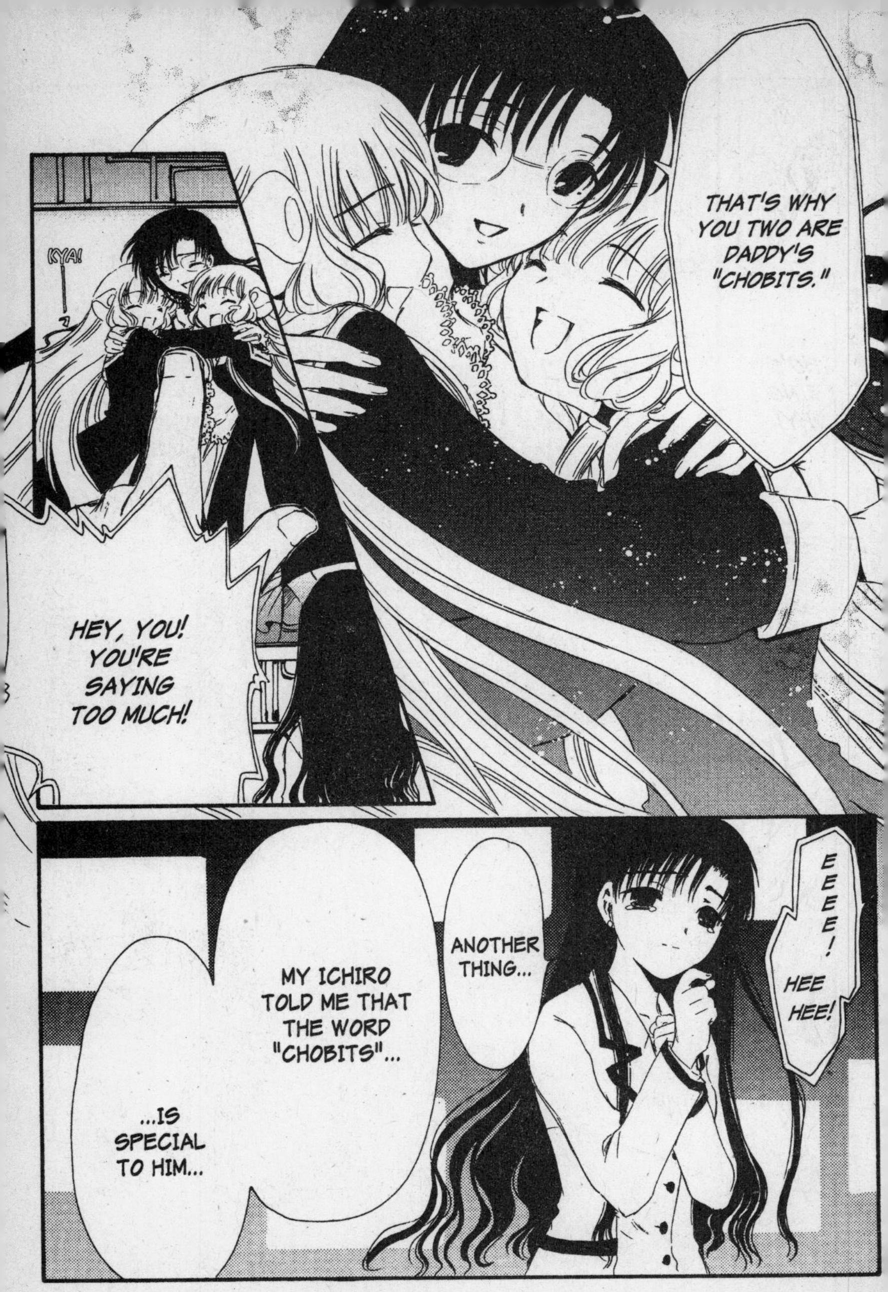

THAT'S WHY YOU TWO ARE DADDY'S "CHOBITS."
KYA!
HEY, YOU! YOU'RE SAYING TOO MUCH!
EEEE! HEE HEE!
ANOTHER THING...
MY ICHIRO TOLD ME THAT THE WORD "CHOBITS"...
...IS SPECIAL TO HIM...

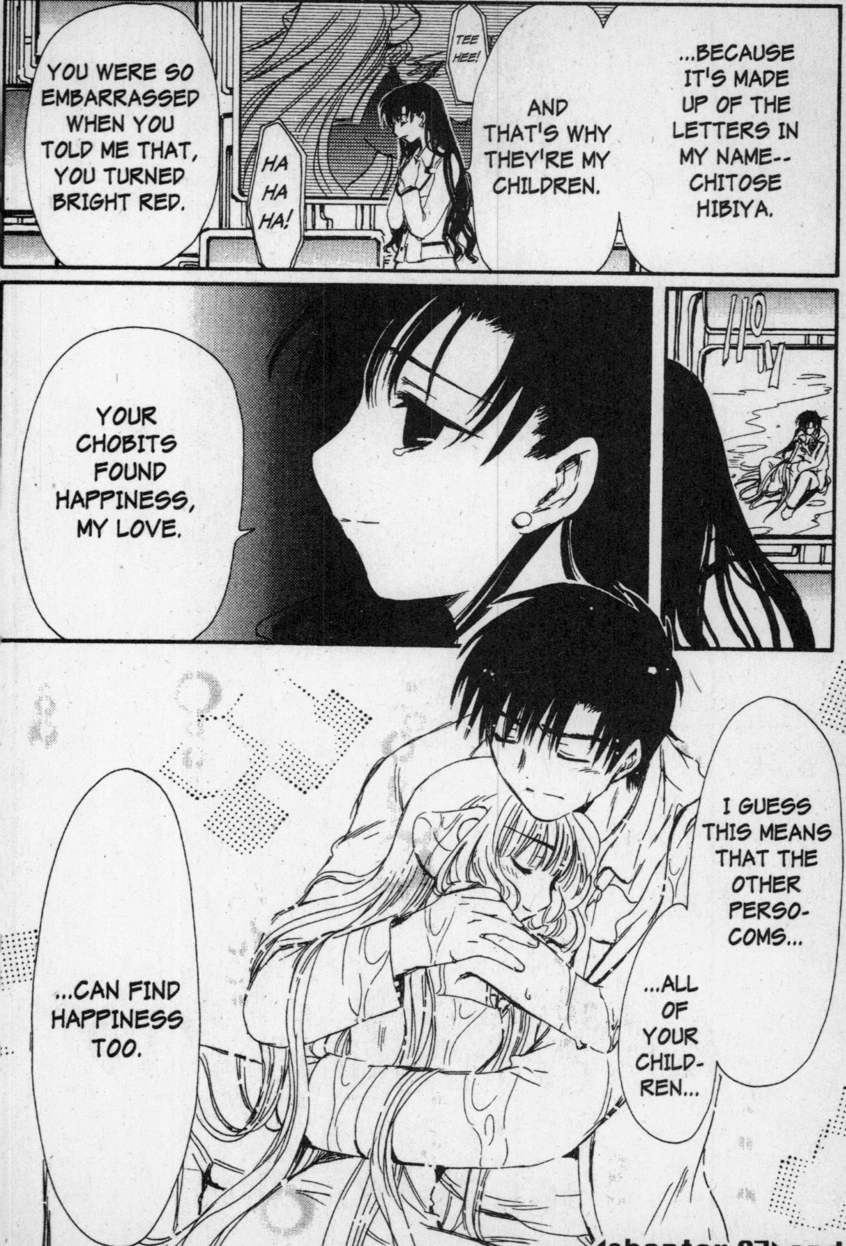
...BECAUSE IT'S MADE UP OF THE LETTERS IN MY NAME--CHITOSE HIBIYA.
AND THAT'S WHY THEY'RE MY CHILDREN.
TEE HEE!
HA HA HA!
YOU WERE SO EMBARRASSED WHEN YOU TOLD ME THAT, YOU TURNED BRIGHT RED.
YOUR CHOBITS FOUND HAPPINESS, MY LOVE.
I GUESS THIS MEANS THAT THE OTHER PERSO-COMS...
...ALL OF YOUR CHILD-REN...
...CAN FIND HAPPINESS TOO.

◀chapter.87▶ end

ちょびっツ
Chobits

◀chapter.88▶

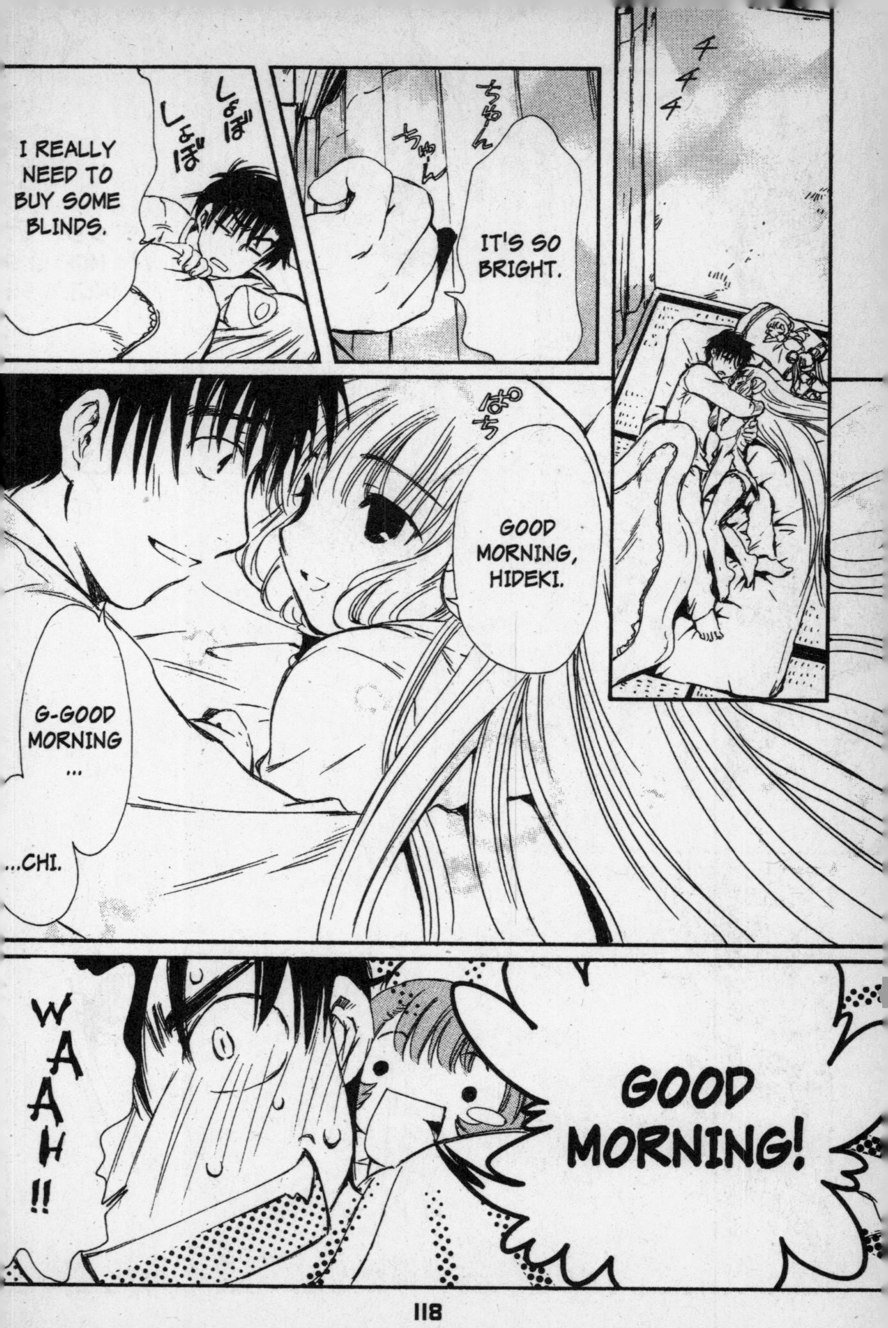
チチチ
ちゅん
ちゅん
IT'S SO BRIGHT.
しょぼ
しょぼ
I REALLY NEED TO BUY SOME BLINDS.
ぱち
GOOD MORNING, HIDEKI.
G-GOOD MORNING ...
...CHI.
GOOD MORNING!
WAAH!!

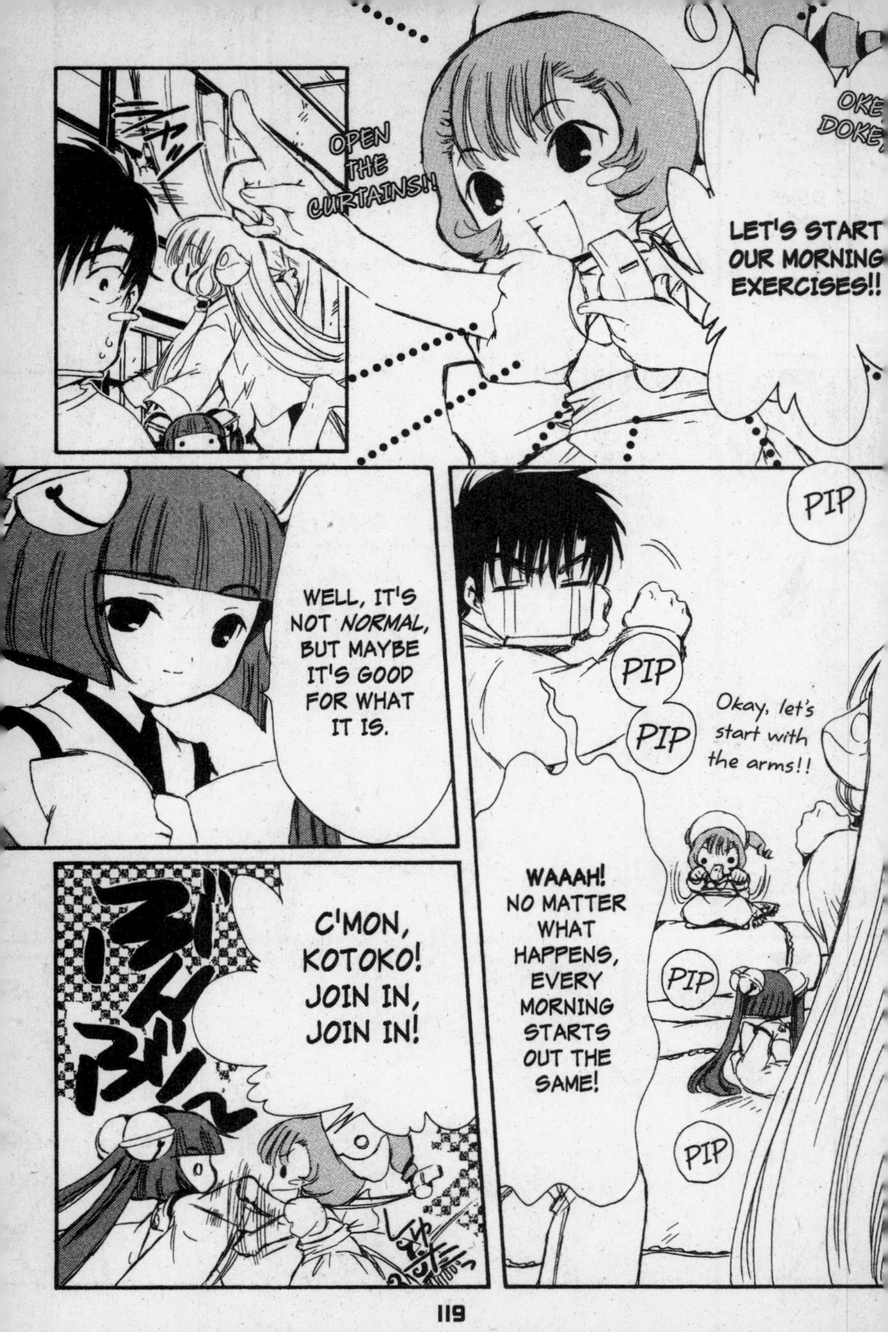
OKE DOKE,
LET'S START OUR MORNING EXERCISES!!
OPEN THE CURTAINS!!
PIP
PIP
PIP
Okay, let's start with the arms!!
PIP
PIP
WAAAH! NO MATTER WHAT HAPPENS, EVERY MORNING STARTS OUT THE SAME!
WELL, IT'S NOT *NORMAL*, BUT MAYBE IT'S GOOD FOR WHAT IT IS.
C'MON, KOTOKO! JOIN IN, JOIN IN!

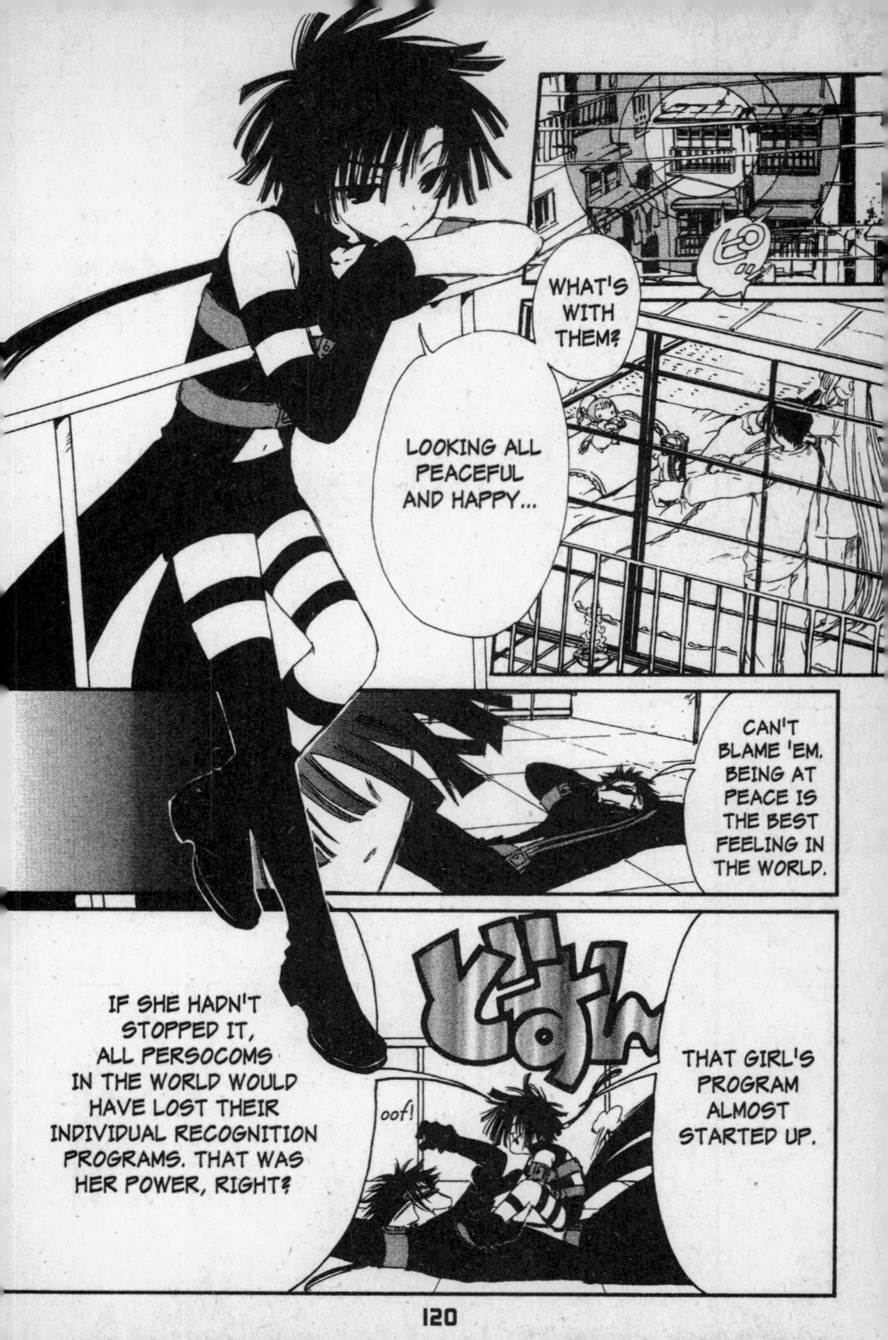
WHAT'S WITH THEM?
LOOKING ALL PEACEFUL AND HAPPY...
CAN'T BLAME 'EM. BEING AT PEACE IS THE BEST FEELING IN THE WORLD.
THAT GIRL'S PROGRAM ALMOST STARTED UP.
oof!
IF SHE HADN'T STOPPED IT, ALL PERSOCOMS IN THE WORLD WOULD HAVE LOST THEIR INDIVIDUAL RECOGNITION PROGRAMS. THAT WAS HER POWER, RIGHT?

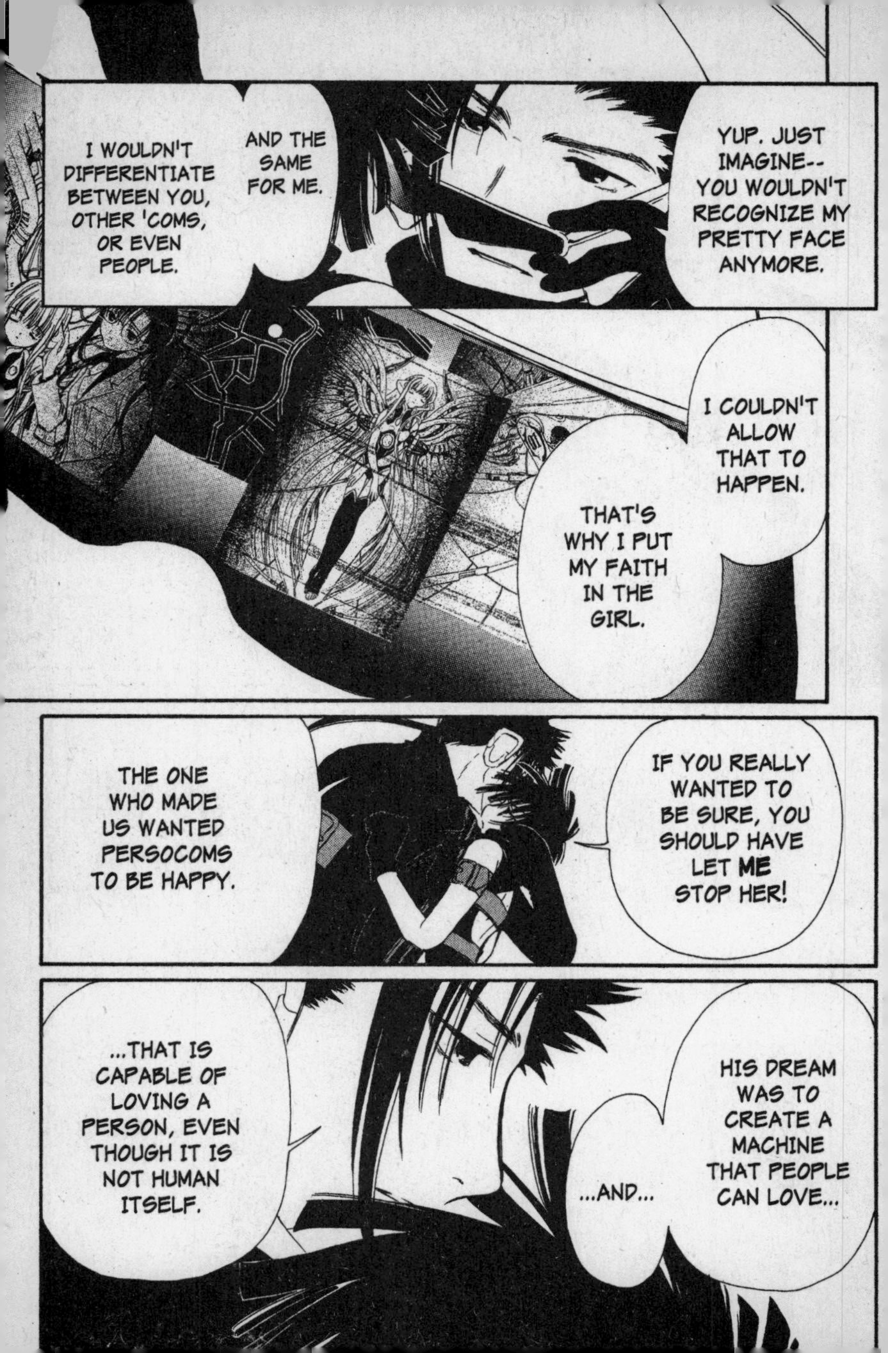
YUP. JUST IMAGINE-- YOU WOULDN'T RECOGNIZE MY PRETTY FACE ANYMORE.
AND THE SAME FOR ME.
I WOULDN'T DIFFERENTIATE BETWEEN YOU, OTHER 'COMS, OR EVEN PEOPLE.
I COULDN'T ALLOW THAT TO HAPPEN.
THAT'S WHY I PUT MY FAITH IN THE GIRL.
IF YOU REALLY WANTED TO BE SURE, YOU SHOULD HAVE LET **ME** STOP HER!
THE ONE WHO MADE US WANTED PERSOCOMS TO BE HAPPY.
HIS DREAM WAS TO CREATE A MACHINE THAT PEOPLE CAN LOVE...
...AND...
...THAT IS CAPABLE OF LOVING A PERSON, EVEN THOUGH IT IS NOT HUMAN ITSELF.

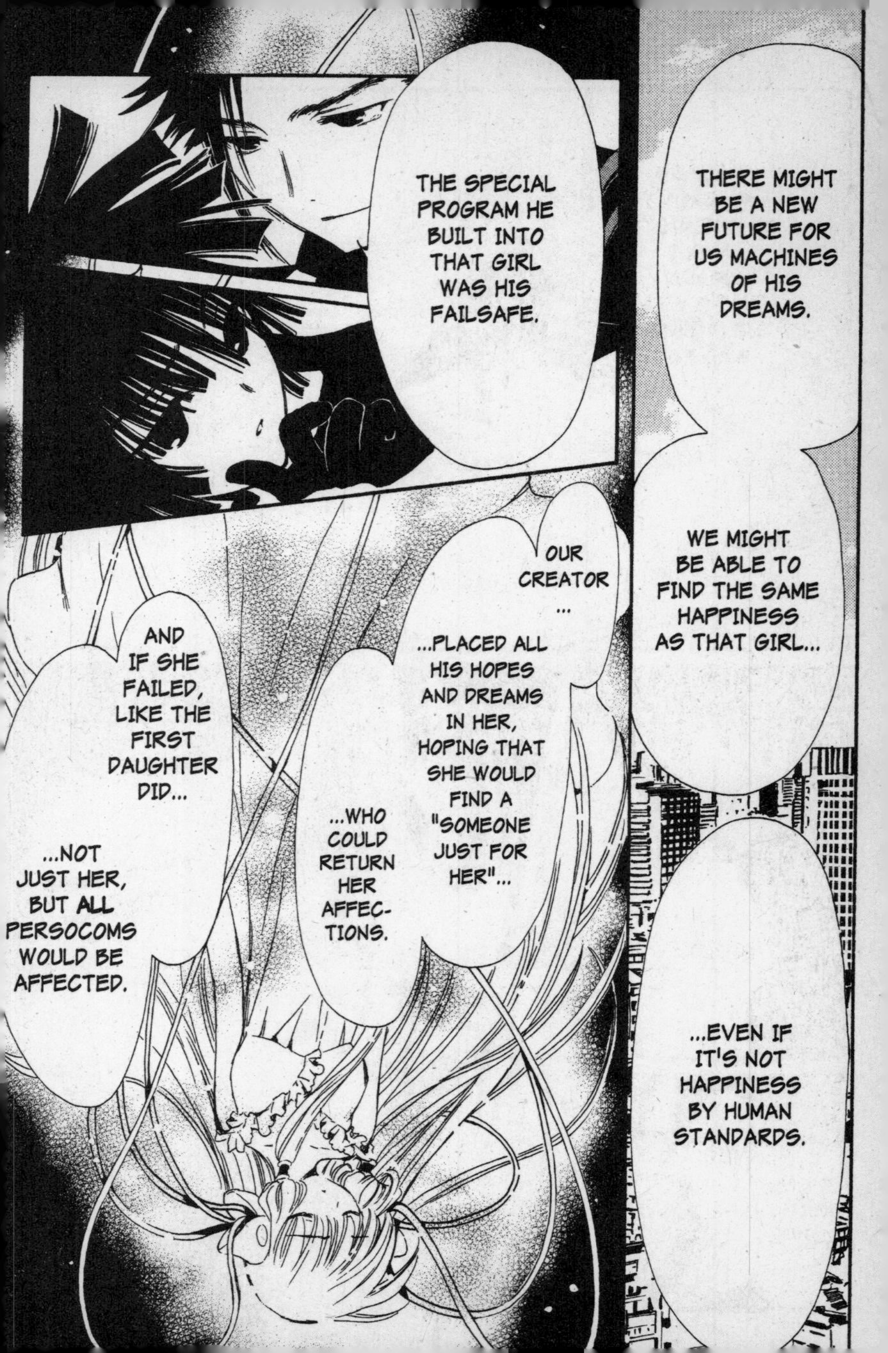
THERE MIGHT BE A NEW FUTURE FOR US MACHINES OF HIS DREAMS.
WE MIGHT BE ABLE TO FIND THE SAME HAPPINESS AS THAT GIRL...
...EVEN IF IT'S NOT HAPPINESS BY HUMAN STANDARDS.
THE SPECIAL PROGRAM HE BUILT INTO THAT GIRL WAS HIS FAILSAFE.
OUR CREATOR ...
...PLACED ALL HIS HOPES AND DREAMS IN HER, HOPING THAT SHE WOULD FIND A "SOMEONE JUST FOR HER"...
...WHO COULD RETURN HER AFFEC- TIONS.
AND IF SHE FAILED, LIKE THE FIRST DAUGHTER DID...
...NOT JUST HER, BUT ALL PERSOCOMS WOULD BE AFFECTED.

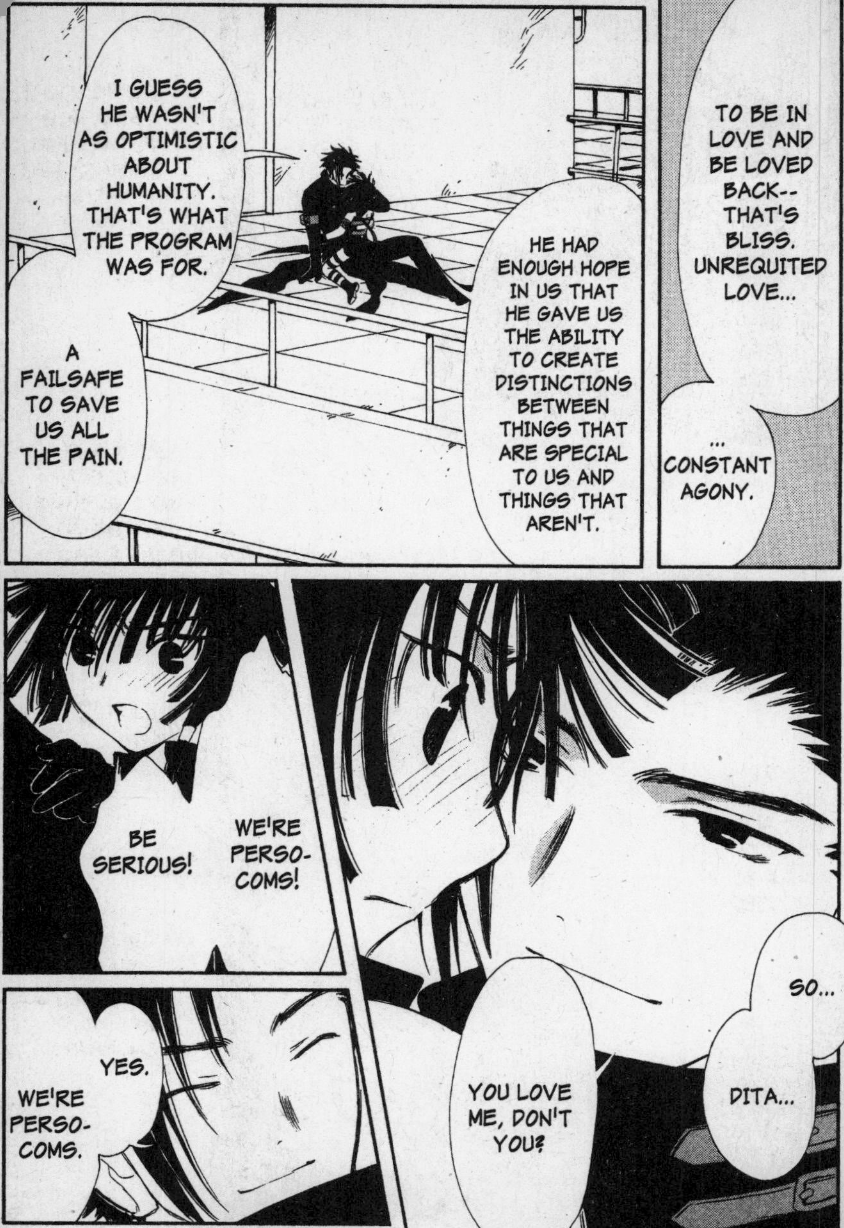
TO BE IN LOVE AND BE LOVED BACK--THAT'S BLISS. UNREQUITED LOVE...
... CONSTANT AGONY.
HE HAD ENOUGH HOPE IN US THAT HE GAVE US THE ABILITY TO CREATE DISTINCTIONS BETWEEN THINGS THAT ARE SPECIAL TO US AND THINGS THAT AREN'T.
I GUESS HE WASN'T AS OPTIMISTIC ABOUT HUMANITY. THAT'S WHAT THE PROGRAM WAS FOR.
A FAILSAFE TO SAVE US ALL THE PAIN.
SO...
DITA...
YOU LOVE ME, DON'T YOU?
WE'RE PERSO-COMS!
BE SERIOUS!
YES.
WE'RE PERSO-COMS.

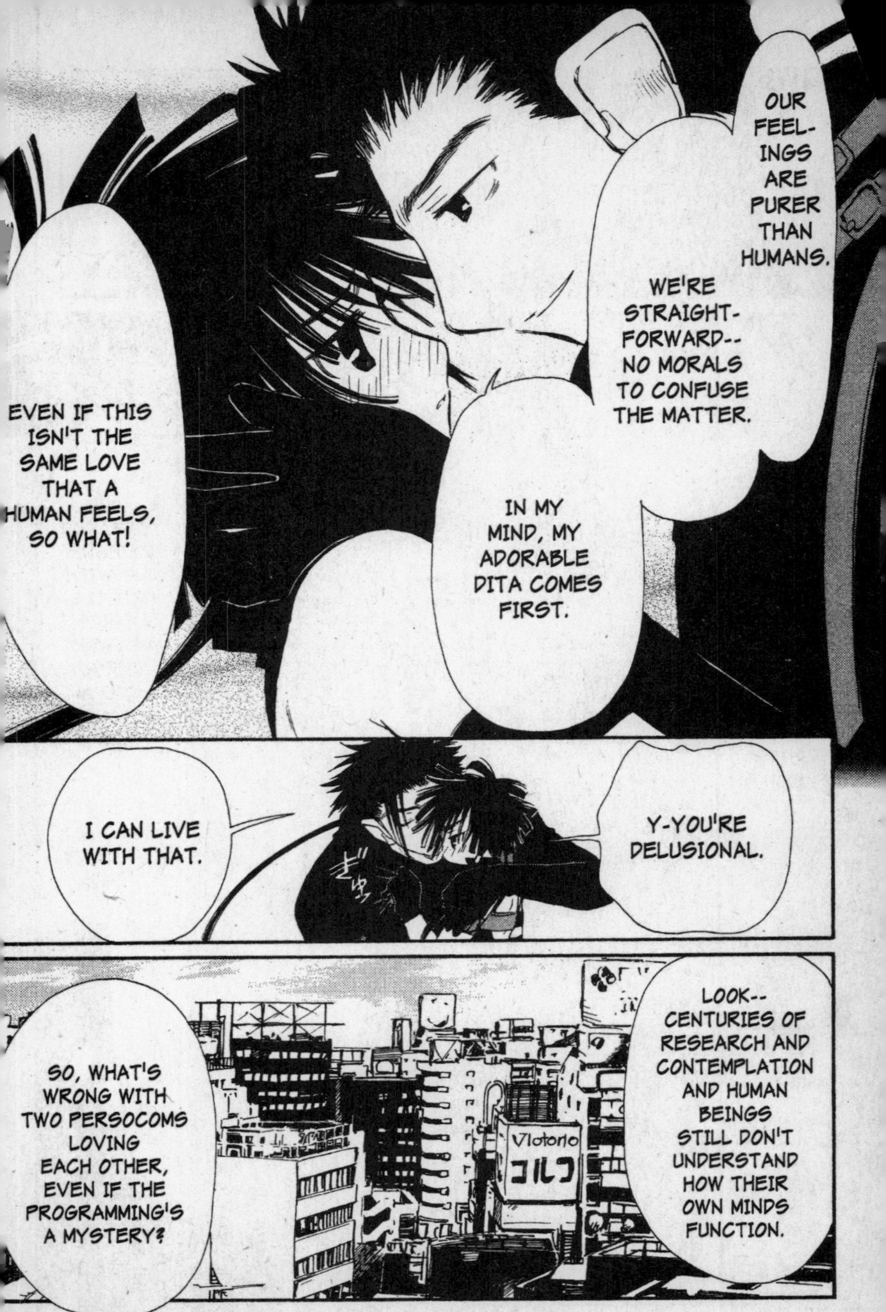
OUR FEEL-INGS ARE PURER THAN HUMANS.
WE'RE STRAIGHT-FORWARD-- NO MORALS TO CONFUSE THE MATTER.
IN MY MIND, MY ADORABLE DITA COMES FIRST.
EVEN IF THIS ISN'T THE SAME LOVE THAT A HUMAN FEELS, SO WHAT!
Y-YOU'RE DELUSIONAL.
I CAN LIVE WITH THAT.
LOOK-- CENTURIES OF RESEARCH AND CONTEMPLATION AND HUMAN BEINGS STILL DON'T UNDERSTAND HOW THEIR OWN MINDS FUNCTION.
SO, WHAT'S WRONG WITH TWO PERSOCOMS LOVING EACH OTHER, EVEN IF THE PROGRAMMING'S A MYSTERY?

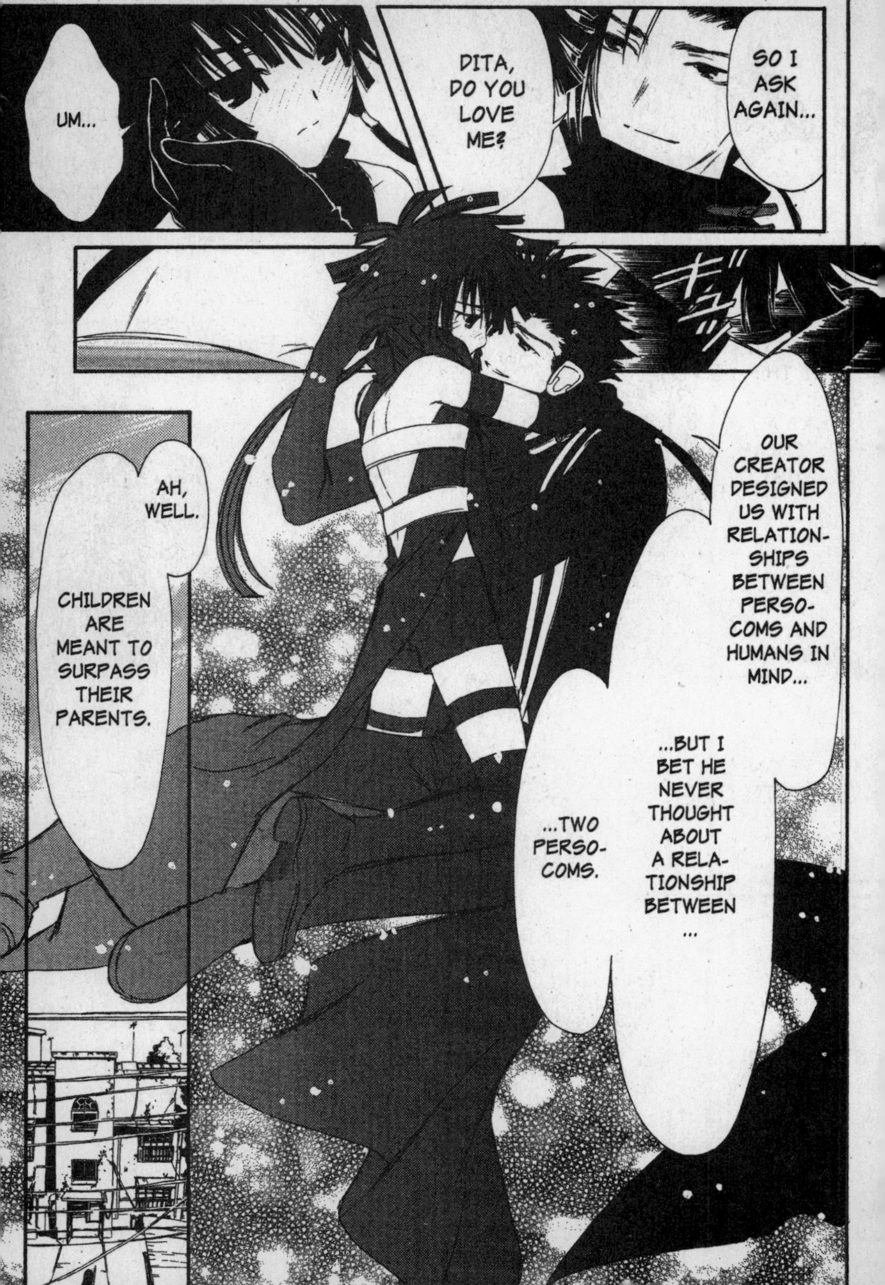
SO I ASK AGAIN...
DITA, DO YOU LOVE ME?
UM...
OUR CREATOR DESIGNED US WITH RELATION-SHIPS BETWEEN PERSO-COMS AND HUMANS IN MIND...
...BUT I BET HE NEVER THOUGHT ABOUT A RELA-TIONSHIP BETWEEN ...
...TWO PERSO-COMS.
AH, WELL.
CHILDREN ARE MEANT TO SURPASS THEIR PARENTS.

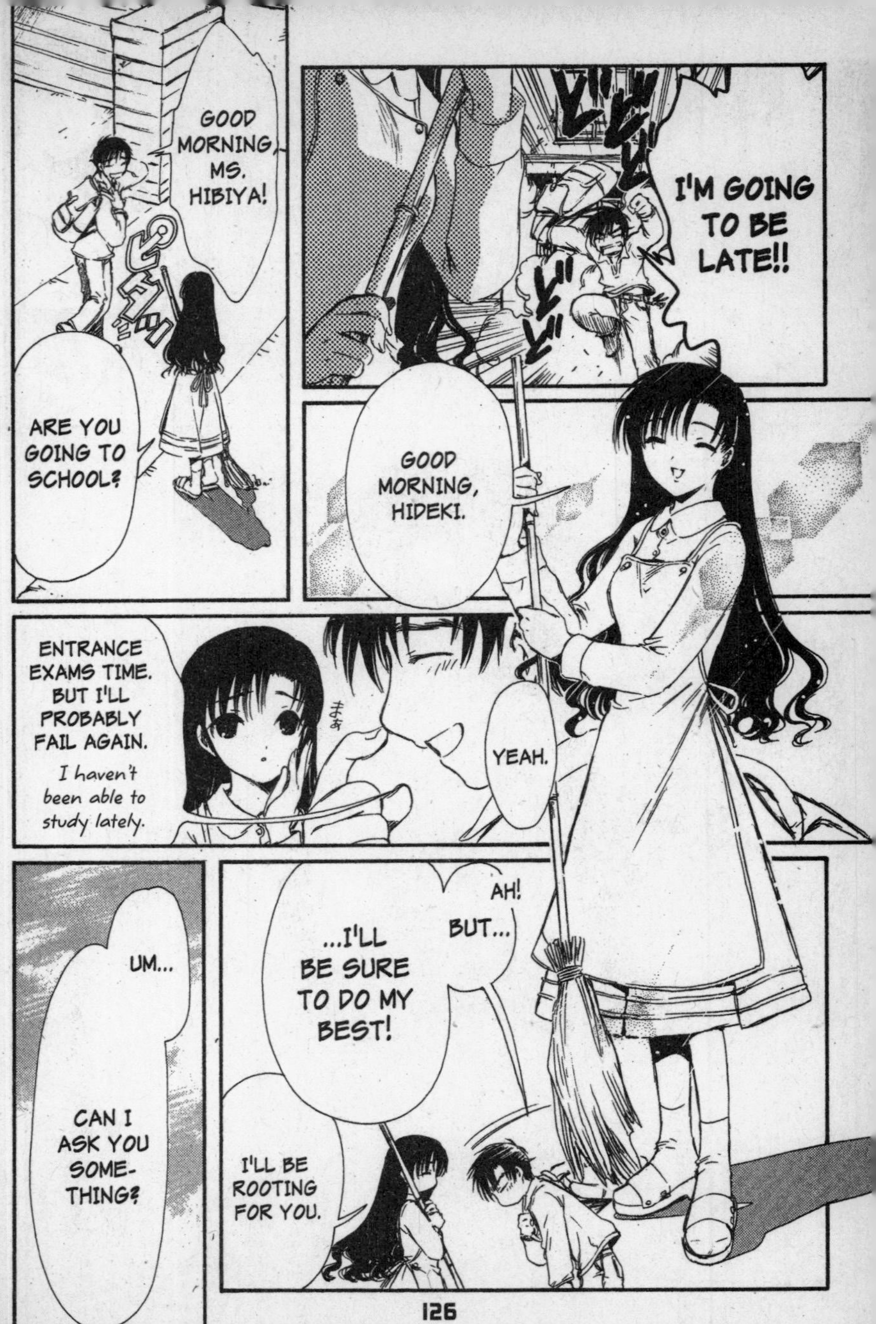
I'M GOING TO BE LATE!!
GOOD MORNING, HIDEKI.
GOOD MORNING, MS. HIBIYA!
ARE YOU GOING TO SCHOOL?
YEAH.
まぁ
ENTRANCE EXAMS TIME. BUT I'LL PROBABLY FAIL AGAIN.
I haven't been able to study lately.
AH! BUT...
...I'LL BE SURE TO DO MY BEST!
I'LL BE ROOTING FOR YOU.
UM...
CAN I ASK YOU SOME-THING?

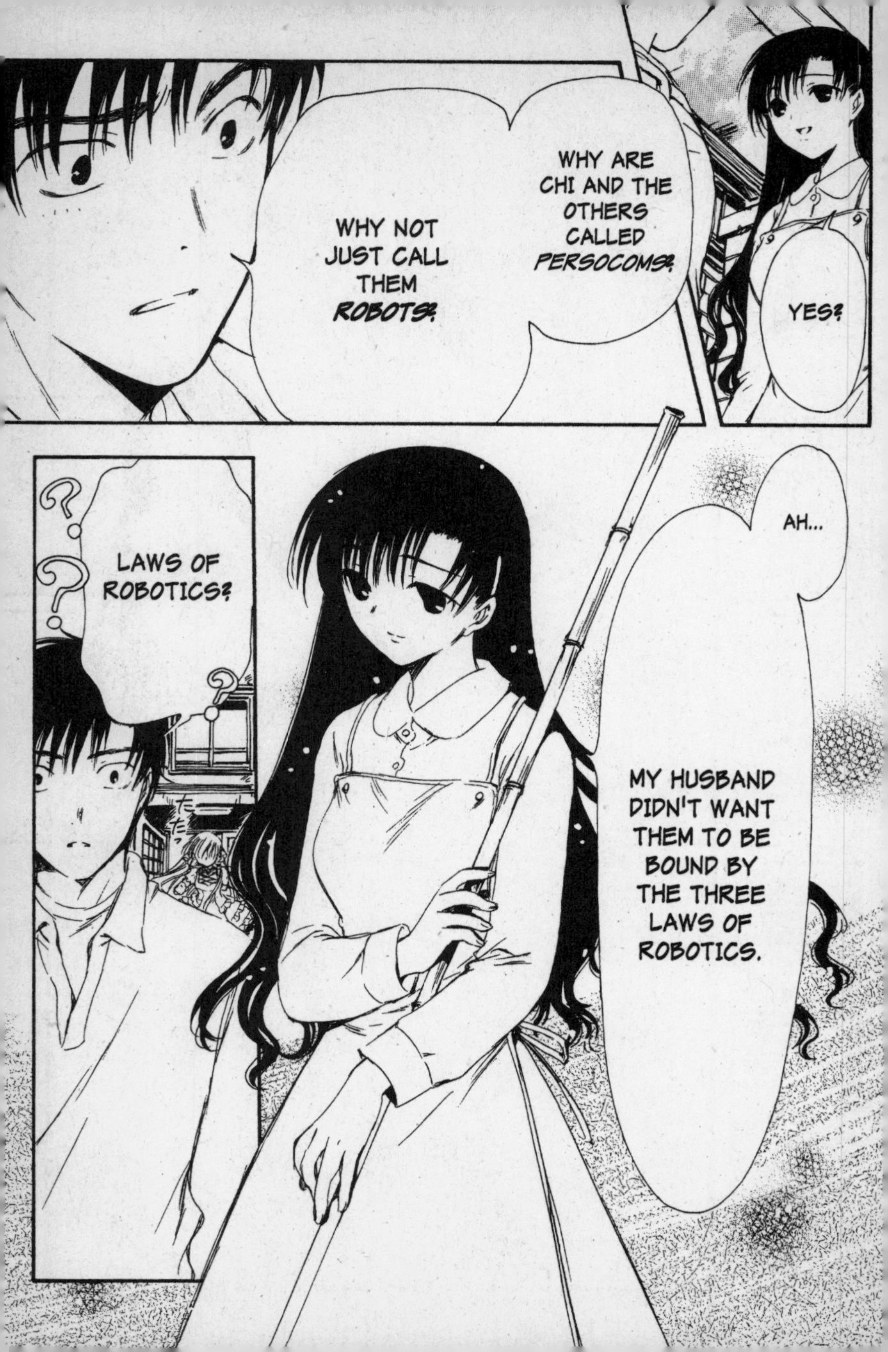
YES?
WHY ARE CHI AND THE OTHERS CALLED *PERSOCOMS*?
WHY NOT JUST CALL THEM *ROBOTS*?
AH...
MY HUSBAND DIDN'T WANT THEM TO BE BOUND BY THE THREE LAWS OF ROBOTICS.
LAWS OF ROBOTICS?

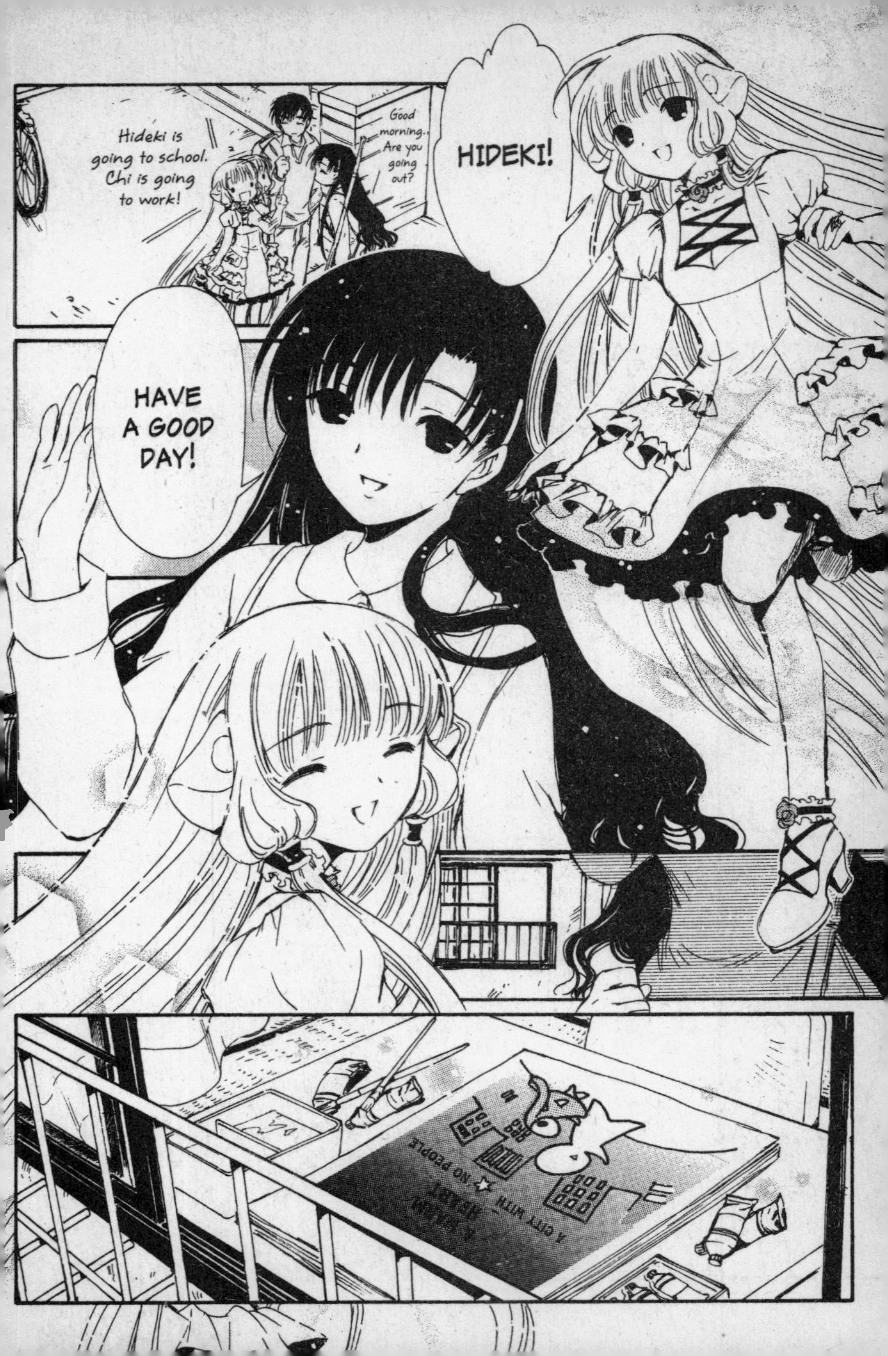
HIDEKI!
Good morning.. Are you going out?
Hideki is going to school. Chi is going to work!
HAVE A GOOD DAY!
A CITY WITH ☆ NO PEOPLE

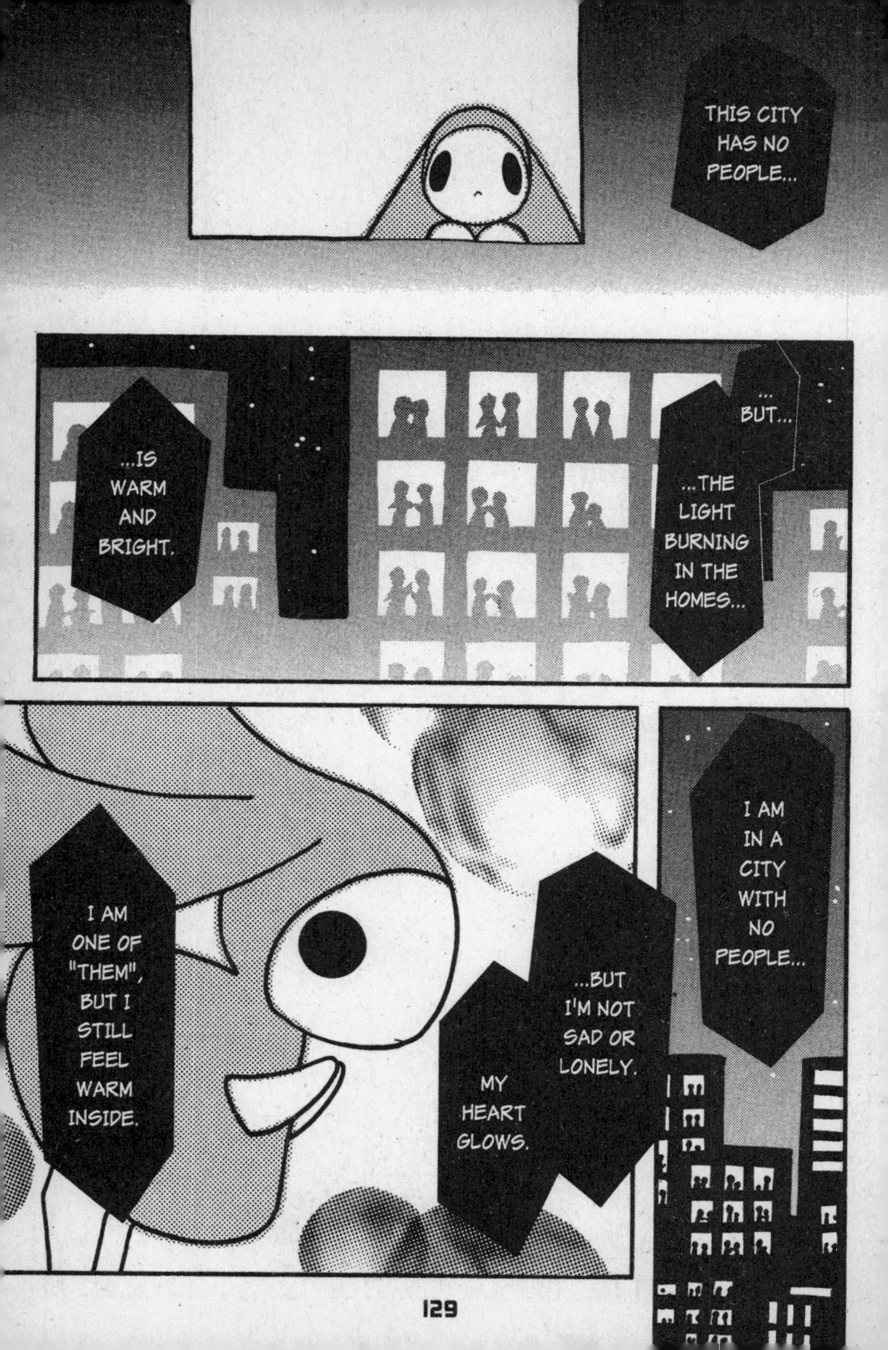
THIS CITY HAS NO PEOPLE...
... BUT...
...THE LIGHT BURNING IN THE HOMES...
...IS WARM AND BRIGHT.
I AM IN A CITY WITH NO PEOPLE...
...BUT I'M NOT SAD OR LONELY.
MY HEART GLOWS.
I AM ONE OF "THEM", BUT I STILL FEEL WARM INSIDE.

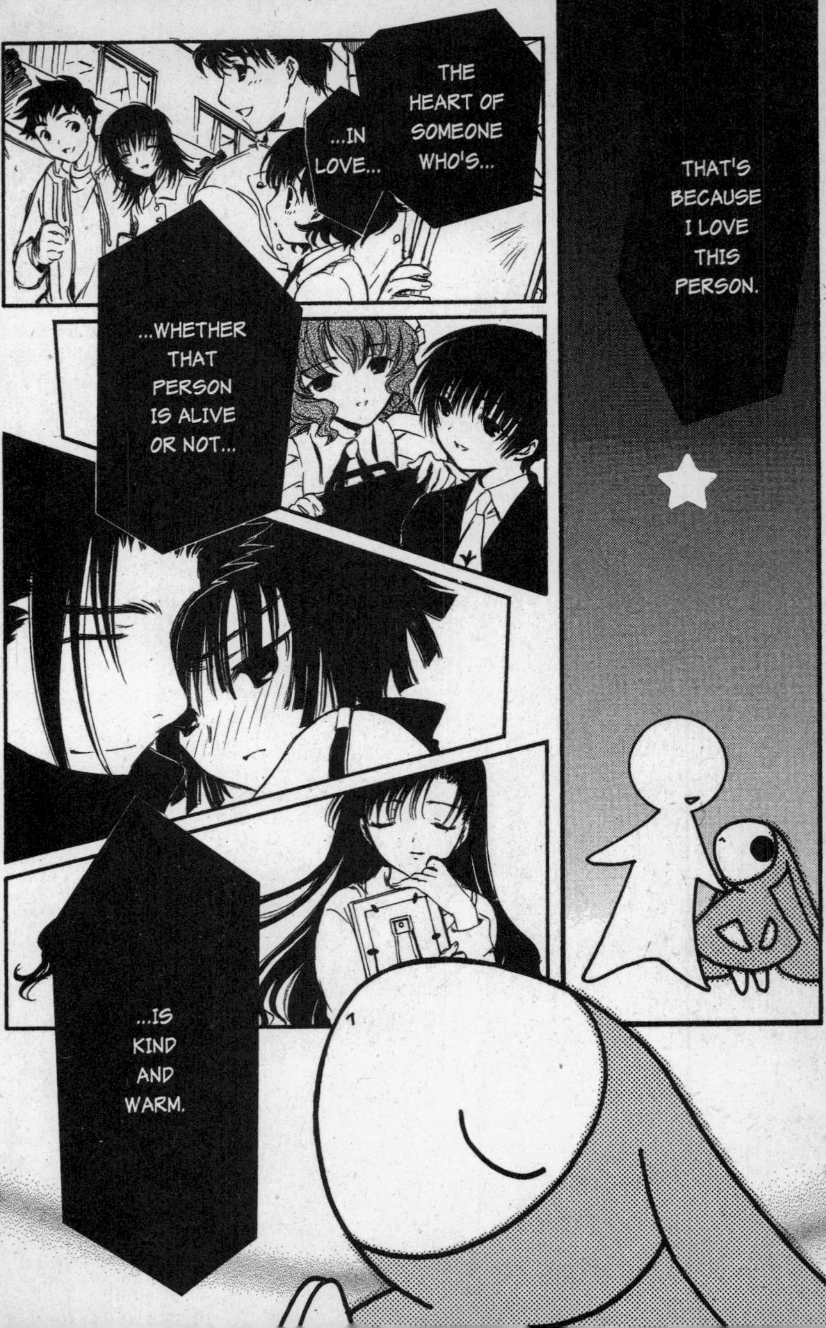
THE HEART OF SOMEONE WHO'S...
...IN LOVE...
...WHETHER THAT PERSON IS ALIVE OR NOT...
...IS KIND AND WARM.
THAT'S BECAUSE I LOVE THIS PERSON.

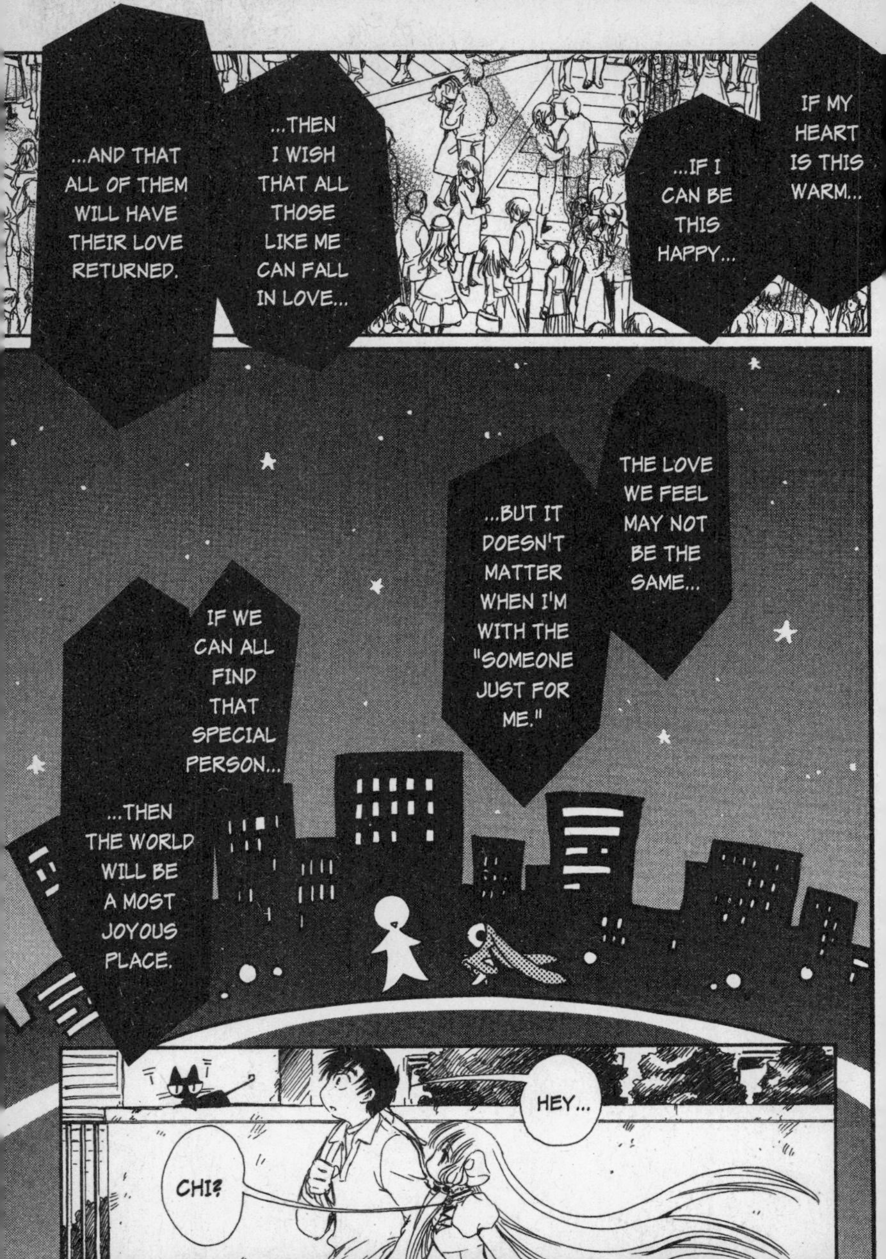
IF MY HEART IS THIS WARM...
...IF I CAN BE THIS HAPPY...
...THEN I WISH THAT ALL THOSE LIKE ME CAN FALL IN LOVE...
...AND THAT ALL OF THEM WILL HAVE THEIR LOVE RETURNED.
THE LOVE WE FEEL MAY NOT BE THE SAME...
...BUT IT DOESN'T MATTER WHEN I'M WITH THE "SOMEONE JUST FOR ME."
IF WE CAN ALL FIND THAT SPECIAL PERSON...
...THEN THE WORLD WILL BE A MOST JOYOUS PLACE.
HEY...
CHI?

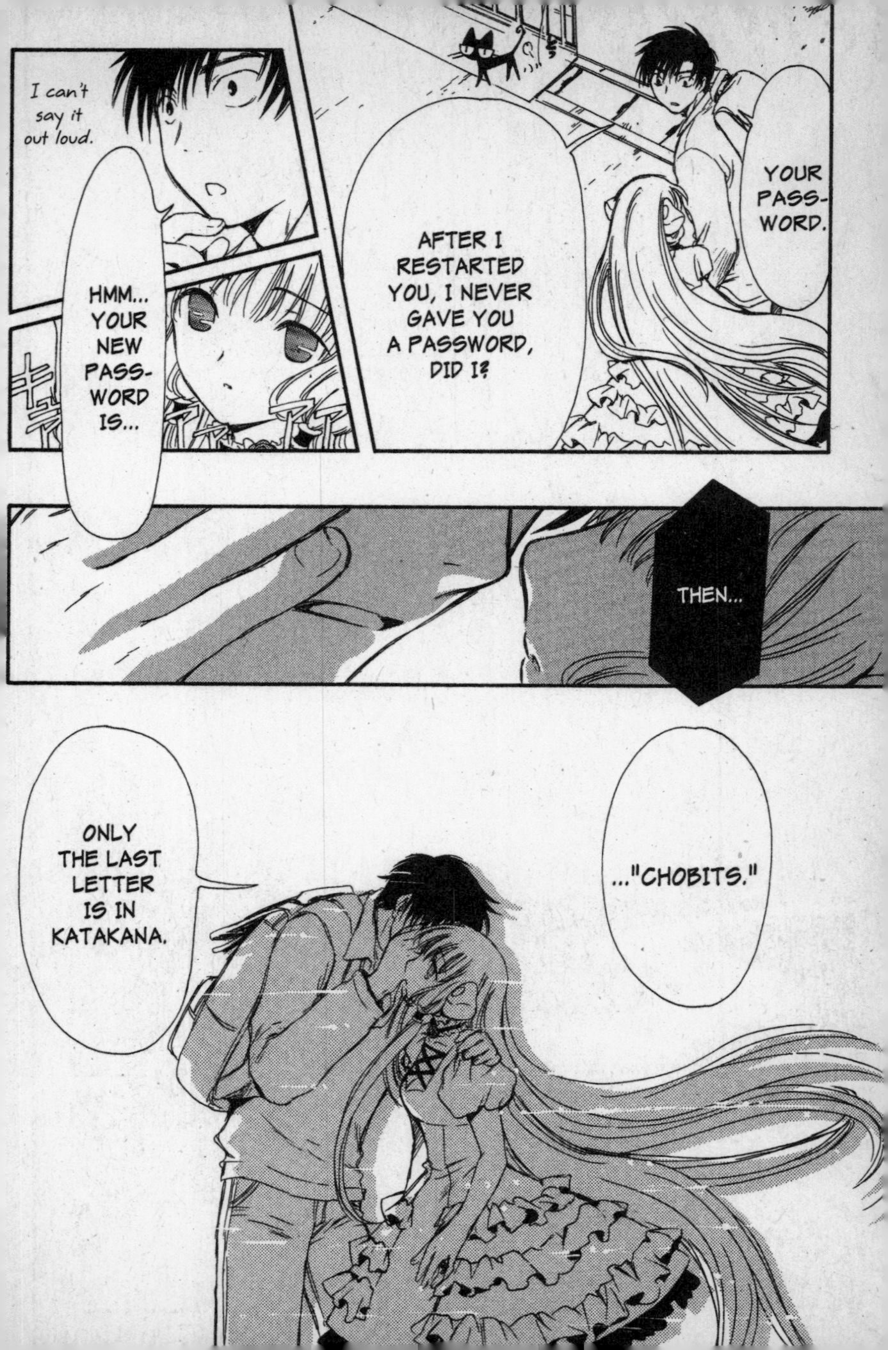
YOUR PASSWORD.
AFTER I RESTARTED YOU, I NEVER GAVE YOU A PASSWORD, DID I?
I can't say it out loud.
HMM... YOUR NEW PASSWORD IS...
THEN...
..."CHOBITS."
ONLY THE LAST LETTER IS IN KATAKANA.

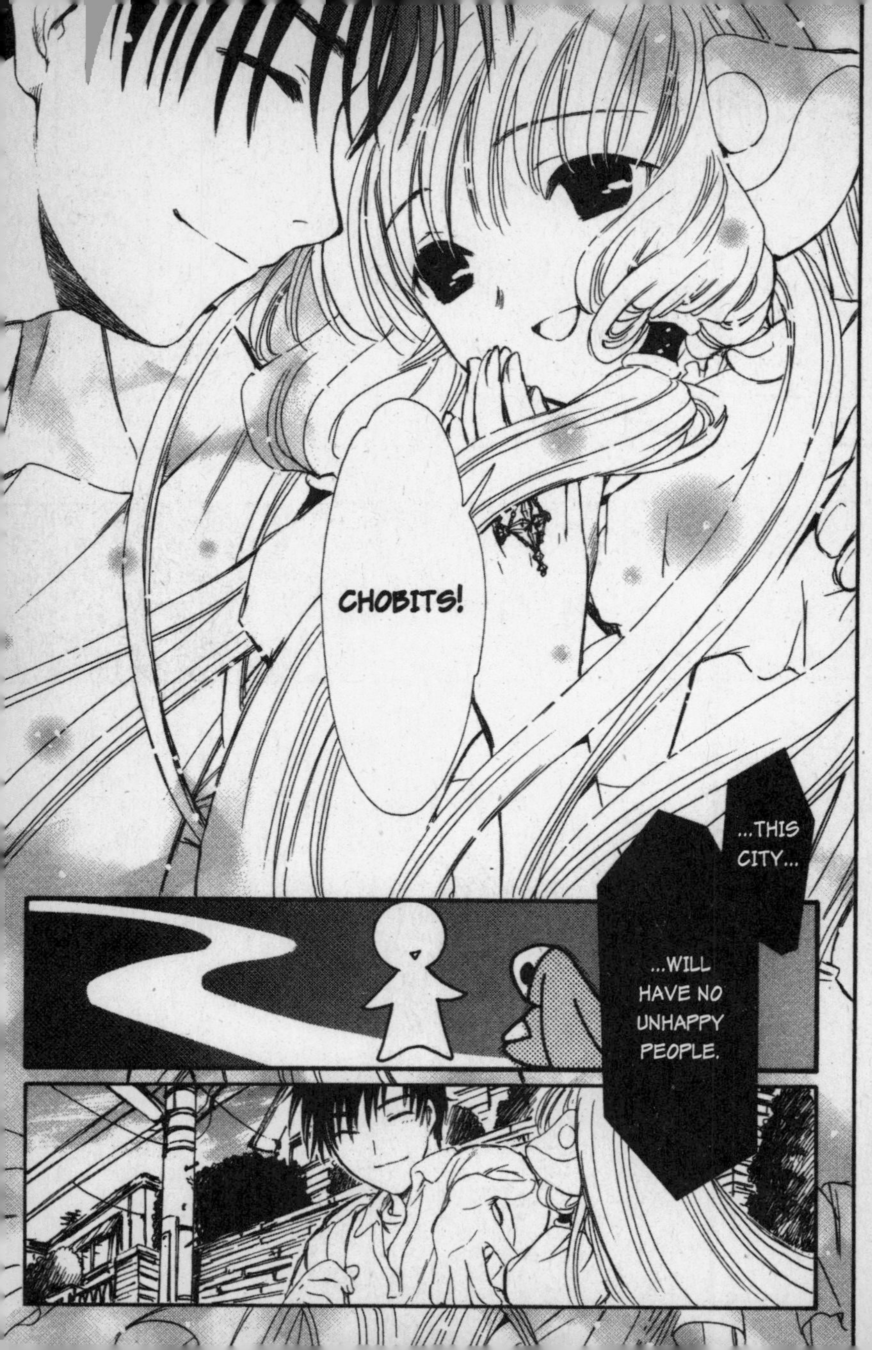
CHOBITS!
...THIS CITY...
...WILL HAVE NO UNHAPPY PEOPLE.

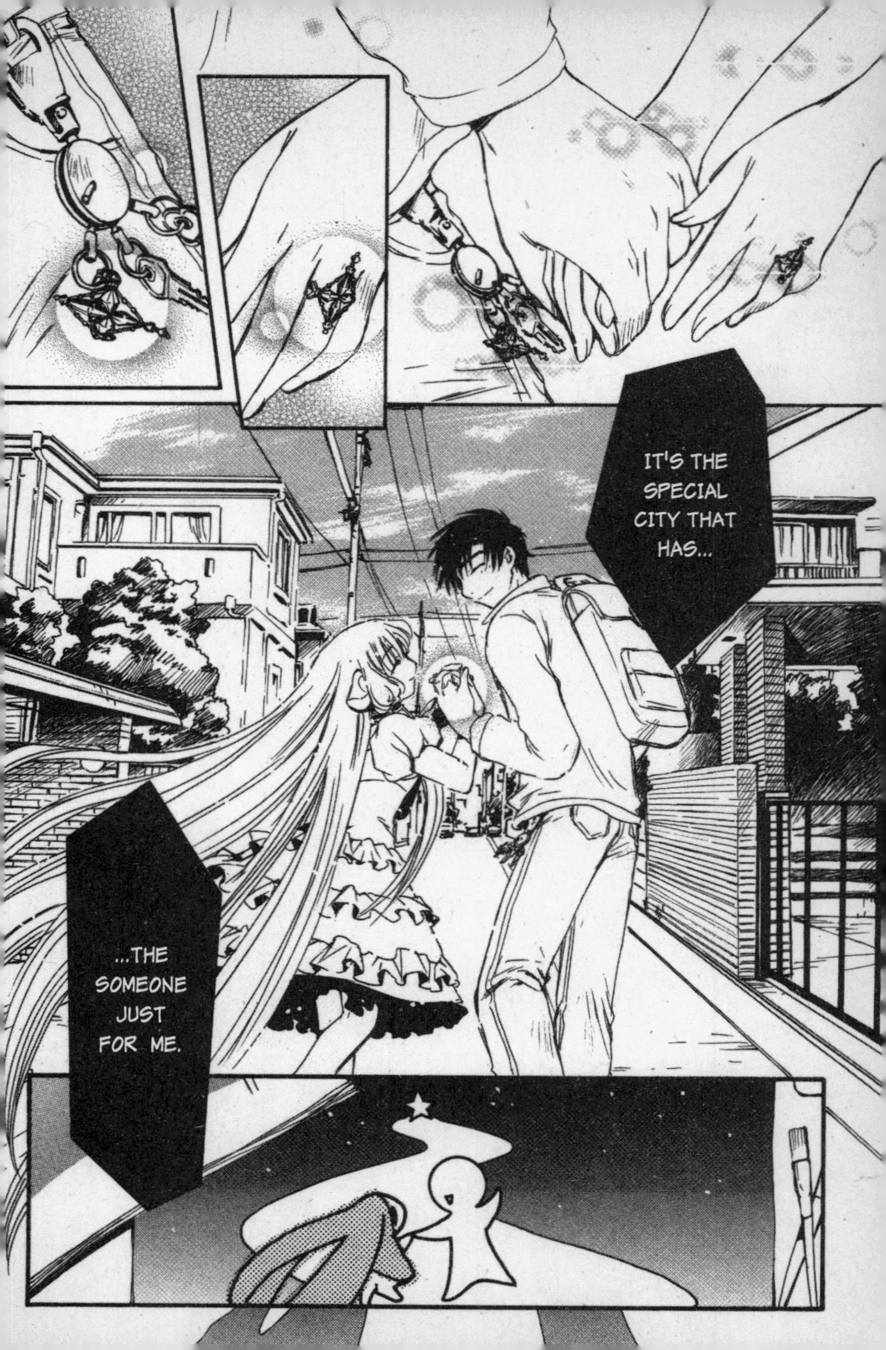
IT'S THE SPECIAL CITY THAT HAS...
...THE SOMEONE JUST FOR ME.

ちょびっツ
Chobits

**end**

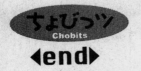

# TOKYO
# BABYLON™

Welcome to Tokyo.
The city never sleeps.
May its spirits rest in peace.

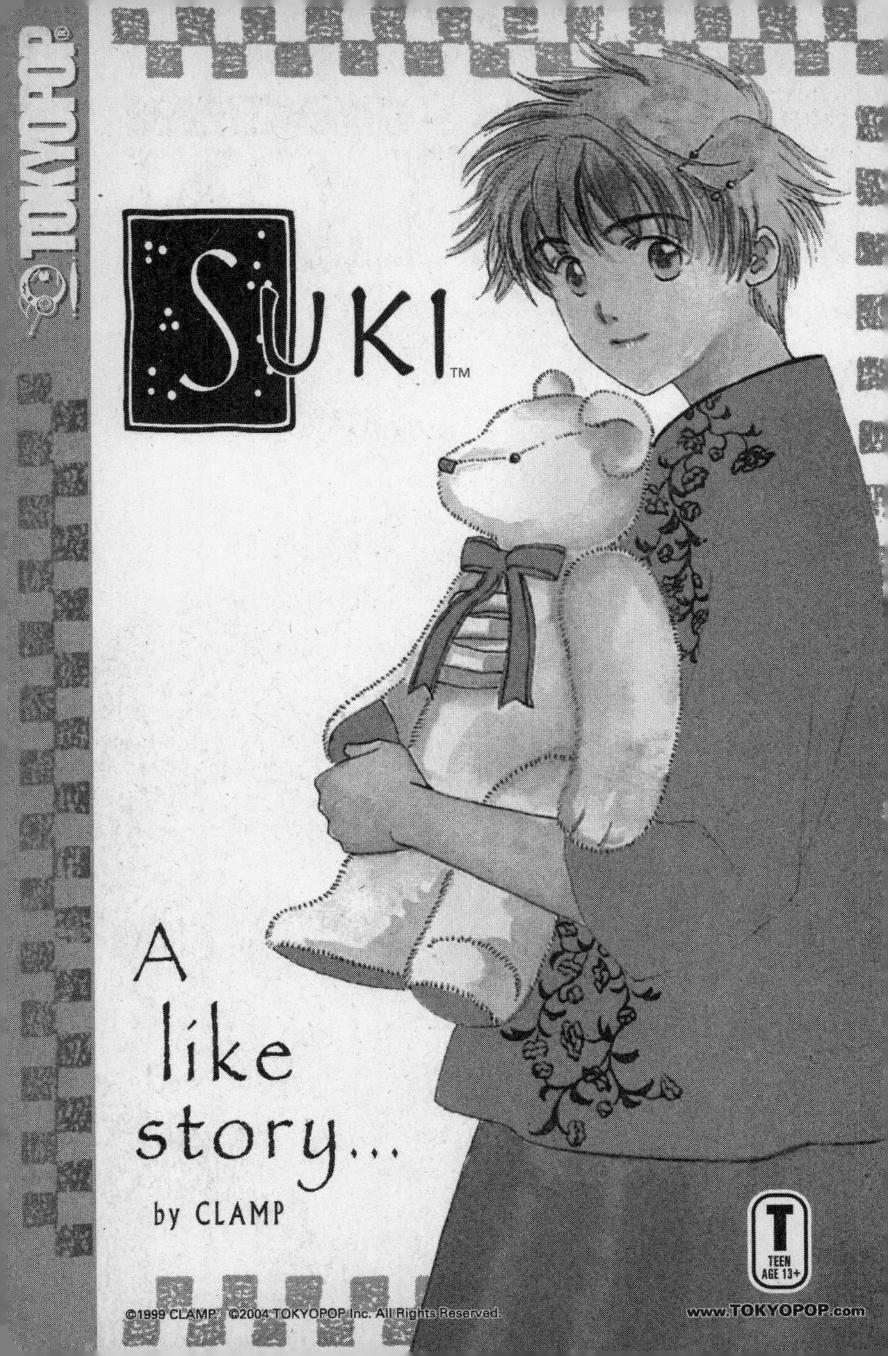
TOKYOPOP
SUKI™
A like story...
by CLAMP
T
TEEN
AGE 13+
©1999 CLAMP. ©2004 TOKYOPOP Inc. All Rights Reserved.
www.TOKYOPOP.com

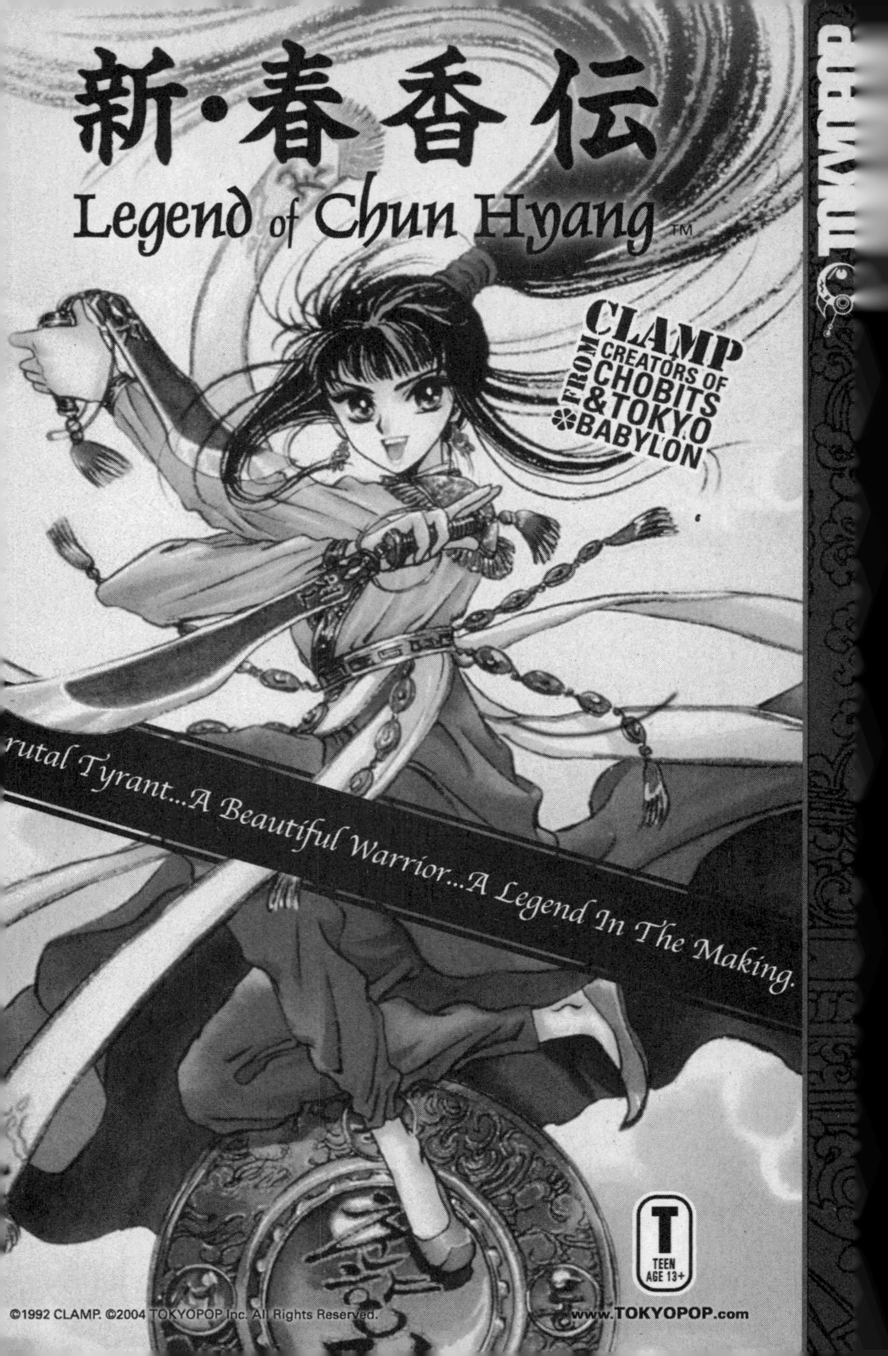

新・春香伝
Legend of Chun Hyang™
FROM CLAMP CREATORS OF CHOBITS & TOKYO BABYLON
rutal Tyrant...A Beautiful Warrior...A Legend In The Making.
T TEEN AGE 13+
TOKYOPOP
©1992 CLAMP. ©2004 TOKYOPOP Inc. All Rights Reserved.
www.TOKYOPOP.com

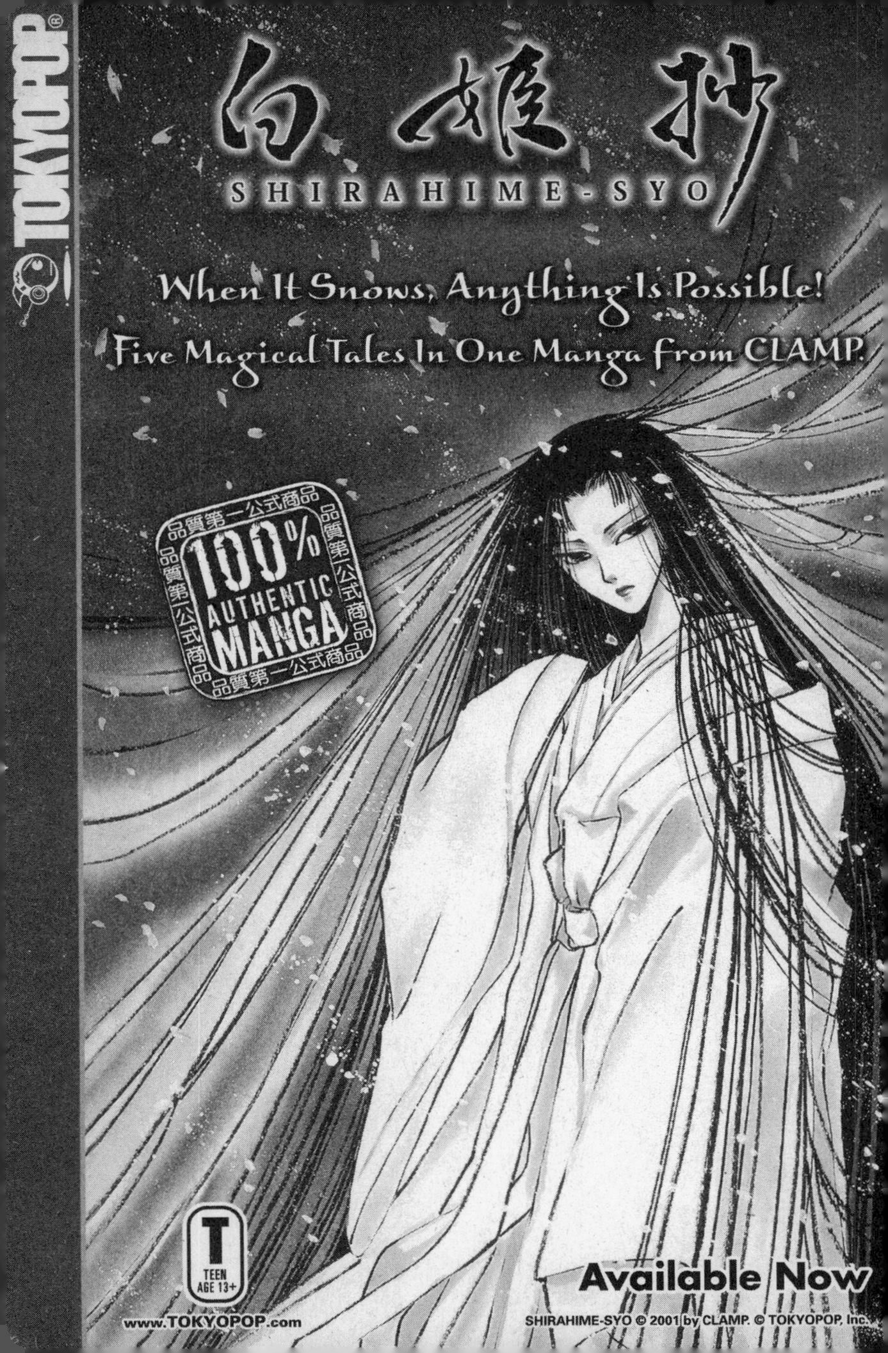
TOKYOPOP
白姫抄
SHIRAHIME-SYO
When It Snows, Anything Is Possible!
Five Magical Tales In One Manga from CLAMP.
100% AUTHENTIC MANGA
品質第一公式商品
T
TEEN AGE 13+
Available Now
www.TOKYOPOP.com
SHIRAHIME-SYO © 2001 by CLAMP. © TOKYOPOP, Inc.

# ALSO AVAILABLE FROM  TOKYOPOP®

## MANGA

.HACK//LEGEND OF THE TWILIGHT
@LARGE
ABENOBASHI: MAGICAL SHOPPING ARCADE
A.I. LOVE YOU
AI YORI AOSHI
ANGELIC LAYER
ARM OF KANNON
BABY BIRTH
BATTLE ROYALE
BATTLE VIXENS
BOYS BE...
BRAIN POWERED
BRIGADOON
B'TX
CANDIDATE FOR GODDESS, THE
CARDCAPTOR SAKURA
CARDCAPTOR SAKURA - MASTER OF THE CLOW
CHOBITS
CHRONICLES OF THE CURSED SWORD
CLAMP SCHOOL DETECTIVES
CLOVER
COMIC PARTY
CONFIDENTIAL CONFESSIONS
CORRECTOR YUI
COWBOY BEBOP
COWBOY BEBOP: SHOOTING STAR
CRAZY LOVE STORY
CRESCENT MOON
CROSS
CULDCEPT
CYBORG 009
D•N•ANGEL
DEMON DIARY
DEMON ORORON, THE
DEUS VITAE
DIABOLO
DIGIMON
DIGIMON TAMERS
DIGIMON ZERO TWO
DOLL
DRAGON HUNTER
DRAGON KNIGHTS
DRAGON VOICE
DREAM SAGA
DUKLYON: CLAMP SCHOOL DEFENDERS
EERIE QUEERIE!
ERICA SAKURAZAWA: COLLECTED WORKS
ET CETERA
ETERNITY
EVIL'S RETURN
FAERIES' LANDING
FAKE
FLCL
FLOWER OF THE DEEP SLEEP, THE
FORBIDDEN DANCE
FRUITS BASKET

G GUNDAM
GATEKEEPERS
GETBACKERS
GIRL GOT GAME
GRAVITATION
GTO
GUNDAM SEED ASTRAY
GUNDAM WING
GUNDAM WING: BATTLEFIELD OF PACIFISTS
GUNDAM WING: ENDLESS WALTZ
GUNDAM WING: THE LAST OUTPOST (G-UNIT)
HANDS OFF!
HAPPY MANIA
HARLEM BEAT
HYPER RUNE
I.N.V.U.
IMMORTAL RAIN
INITIAL D
INSTANT TEEN: JUST ADD NUTS
ISLAND
JING: KING OF BANDITS
JING: KING OF BANDITS - TWILIGHT TALES
JULINE
KARE KANO
KILL ME, KISS ME
KINDAICHI CASE FILES, THE
KING OF HELL
KODOCHA: SANA'S STAGE
LAMENT OF THE LAMB
LEGAL DRUG
LEGEND OF CHUN HYANG, THE
LES BIJOUX
LOVE HINA
LOVE OR MONEY
LUPIN III
LUPIN III: WORLD'S MOST WANTED
MAGIC KNIGHT RAYEARTH I
MAGIC KNIGHT RAYEARTH II
MAHOROMATIC: AUTOMATIC MAIDEN
MAN OF MANY FACES
MARMALADE BOY
MARS
MARS: HORSE WITH NO NAME
MINK
MIRACLE GIRLS
MIYUKI-CHAN IN WONDERLAND
MODEL
MOURYOU KIDEN: LEGEND OF THE NYMPHS
NECK AND NECK
ONE
ONE I LOVE, THE
PARADISE KISS
PARASYTE
PASSION FRUIT
PEACH GIRL
PEACH GIRL: CHANGE OF HEART
PET SHOP OF HORRORS
PITA-TEN

07.15.04T

# STOP!

## This is the back of the book.
## You wouldn't want to spoil a great ending!

This book is printed "manga-style," in the authentic Japanese right-to-left format. Since none of the artwork has been flipped or altered, readers get to experience the story just as the creator intended. You've been asking for it, so TOKYOPOP® delivered: authentic, hot-off-the-press, and far more fun!

# DIRECTIONS

If this is your first time reading manga-style, here's a quick guide to help you understand how it works.

It's easy... just start in the top right panel and follow the numbers. Have fun, and look for more 100% authentic manga from TOKYOPOP®!

100% AUTHENTIC MANGA